Collaborative Leadership: How to Succeed in an Interconnected World

Collaborative Leadership: How to Succeed in an Interconnected World

David Archer
Alex Cameron

AMSTERDAM • BOSTON • HEIDELBERG • LONDON
NEW YORK • OXFORD • PARIS • SAN DIEGO
SAN FRANCISCO • SINGAPORE • SYDNEY • TOKYO
Butterworth-Heinemann is an imprint of Elsevier

Butterworth-Heinemann is an imprint of Elsevier
Linacre House, Jordan Hill, Oxford OX2 8DP, UK
30 Corporate Drive, Suite 400, Burlington, MA 01803, USA

Notice
No responsibility is assumed by the publisher for any injury and/or damage to persons
or property as a matter of products liability, negligence or otherwise, or from any use
or operation of any methods, products, instructions or ideas contained in the material
herein. Because of rapid advances in the medical sciences, in particular, independent
verification of diagnoses and drug dosages should be made

British Library Cataloguing in Publication Data
A catalogue record for this book is available from the British Library

Library of Congress Cataloging-in-Publication Data
A catalog record for this book is available from the Library of Congress

ISBN: 978-0-7506-8705-8

For information on all Butterworth-Heinemann Publications
visit our website at books.elsevier.com

Typeset by Charon Tec Ltd., A Macmillan Company.
(www.macmillansolutions.com)

Printed and bound in Great Britain
09 10 11 10 9 8 7 6 5 4 3 2 1

Working together to grow
libraries in developing countries

www.elsevier.com | www.bookaid.org | www.sabre.org

ELSEVIER   BOOK AID
            International   Sabre Foundation

Contents

Acknowledgments

Writing this book has been a collaborative process in itself and we have many people to thank for the part they have played in its creation.

First and foremost we want to thank Sandra Greaves, who has worked with us tirelessly over 9 months helping us to research, write and edit large sections of this book. It wouldn't be what it is without her talent and input.

Thanks also to our families who have had to put up with all our moods as we've managed the ups and downs of creating this book. In particular, thanks to Joan Cameron who has looked after us so well during our Friday all-day writing marathons.

This book is partly a distillation of the experiences we've had in running our consultancy company, Socia. We want to thank everyone who has helped to make Socia such a successful collaborative venture: our chairman, Julie Baddeley, our advisory board (many of whom are quoted in the book), our non-executive director, Alison Grant, all of our associates and of course our clients.

And finally, we want to thank all of the collaborative leaders whose stories form the lifeblood of the book and who are quoted throughout. It's their success that we want to celebrate and their experience that we continue to learn from.

David Archer and **Alex Cameron** are founding Directors of Socia Ltd, a consultancy company which advises leaders of large organisations across the public and private sector on how to make partnerships work.

Before working as a management consultant David was a lecturer in Electrical & Electronic Systems at the University of Hertfordshire where he also led a British Library funded research program into the future of electronic publishing. Passionate about the ability of people to solve their own collaboration problems – he works to help groups create the right environment of governance, working practices and behaviours which will allow creative solutions to emerge.

Alex trained as a zoologist and taught in schools and in industry before progressing to a career in management consultancy and executive development. He coaches individual leaders and executive teams. He sees the possibility of avoiding the waste of effort and resources that can often occur in conflict situations – between individuals and organisations. He cares about the added value that can be achieved through the exploitation of difference.

Together they believe that collaboration can deliver business success in the twenty-first century and that it's the actions of leaders that will make this possible.

Foreword

TOWARD A NEW STYLE OF LEADERSHIP

The ideas behind this book were forged at the turn of the millennium in a time of rapid change. In 2001 we were both working as management consultants, advising a ballooning e-business at the height of the dot-com boom. Entranet was a start-up which briefly expanded to a company of more than 200 people, and then, just as rapidly, it imploded. It was led by a charismatic individual who espoused a heroic model of leadership. Such was the speed of the collapse that it made newspapers headlines when staff were told of its demise by text message.

At the same time, one of us was working at a far-flung outpost of Bernie Ebbers' Worldcom empire as its bubble expanded and burst. And like everyone else, we were watching open-mouthed at the scale of the spectacular rise and fall of Ken Lay and Enron. Something was happening to the received wisdom that defined successful leadership. The 'masters of the universe' were failing in spectacular style. Their approach to leadership simply didn't seem to fit the business conditions of the new millennium. A different model of leadership was required.

Things were also changing in the public sector. Over the same period we were coaching leaders at London Underground as they went through the very painful gestation and birth of the public–private partnership that would be tasked with maintaining and rebuilding the world's largest metro system. Many people had little confidence in the success of the new venture, governed as it was by an immensely complicated contract, but at the same time they knew it couldn't fail. Too much depended on it.

We knew there were leaders delivering success in complex multi-party collaborations but whose stories weren't making it to the press. Indeed we'd seen this for ourselves a few years before when we'd worked for Premier Oil. This small and nimble oil exploration company had succeeded by forming successful alliances and joint ventures with partners across many regions in Asia. Premier's leaders were a different breed, valuing different skills and attributes from the norm. We wanted to distill the leadership lessons from successful collaborations, wherever they were found, and create a model of collaborative leadership that could be applied to develop capability in many different partnership situations – public and private. So we founded a consultancy company, Socia, to take forward these ideas – with a declared mission to 'make partnerships work'.

OUR BACKGROUND

As two individuals with very different skills and education, we came at the problem of collaborative leadership from our own personal perspectives. We have each spent more than 20 years of our working lives as consultants, helping leaders to develop their own ability and confidence in this area. Neither of us started out with a career in management consultancy in mind – but then in all probability, few people do.

By professional background one of us is a zoologist, the other a systems engineer, and we have both spent some time teaching in the past. It's no coincidence that these three disciplines run throughout our work and through this book. We consider organisations as living things that interact with their environment and have to evolve to fit their changing circumstances. We use complex systems theory to make sense of partnership behaviour – viewing collaborations as non-linear systems where small changes in inputs can produce unexpected outputs, but also where surprising solutions can emerge as you balance risk and opportunity. And underlying all our work is a belief in the power of education and learning to transform individuals and the organisations they lead.

THE GROWTH OF PARTNERSHIPS

Back in 2001, 'partnerships' were appearing again and again in the news, especially in the context of rebuilding the national infrastructure of roads, railways, schools and hospitals in a series of public–private deals. But in a number of high-profile early cases, the reality fell way below expectations. Costs overran, projects were late and it was easy for the taxpayer to equate the word 'partnership' with 'black hole'.

In the years since then, we've seen a dramatic rise in the number and range of partnerships and other collaborative arrangements across government and the private sector. The ability of organisations from different backgrounds and cultures to work together has never been more important than it is today.

Across the western world we are betting the future of our public services on our ability to make public–private partnerships work. At the same time, many international corporations are betting their reputation on their ability to collaborate with a worldwide network of suppliers (some of whom they may never even meet face to face). Biggest of all, we are betting the future of the planet on the ability of nations to work together to tackle global problems such as terrorism, financial crises and climate change. So the stakes are high.

WHAT DOES THIS MEAN FOR LEADERS?

At its most basic, collaborative leadership is about delivering results across boundaries. The nature of that boundary is important, whether it's a formal contract or an informal agreement between two parties to work together for a common aim. And as a leader, you need to be clear about where the boundary lies and how to use the different capabilities on either side of it to build a positive and efficient relationship. As the poet Robert Frost once put it, 'Good fences make good neighbours'.

Getting value from difference is at the heart of the collaborative leader's task. But that is not without its challenges. As in many marriages, it's often difference – in skills, experience, resources or culture – that attracts organisations to work together in the first place. Then, as time goes by, people start to rail against that very difference and try to remove it wherever it causes frustration in the joint operation. An often-heard criticism is 'Why can't they be more like us'? But of course the truth is that if they were, you'd have lost the very reason that brought the two of you together.

So collaborative leaders have to pull off a tricky balancing act – on the one hand, respecting and valuing the differences of a partner, while on the other, smoothing out some of those differences in the interests of making the relationship work more efficiently. At the same time, leaders have to learn to share control, and to trust a partner to deliver, even though that partner may operate very differently from themselves. Collaborative leadership is a sophisticated art – but mastering this complexity lies at the heart of business success now and in the future.

THE AIM OF THIS BOOK

If you aspire to lead in a complex world of partnership agreements and joint targets, this book is for you. Surprisingly little has been written about the art of leading partnerships. Perhaps this is because each component of the task seems intellectually straightforward – you have to share control, handle conflict, build long-term relationships and so on – but from our own experience, and from that of all the leaders we've worked with, this represents a great personal challenge for most people.

This book is designed to help. It's written for leaders of all kinds of partnership – wherever you have to get things done through the actions of people you don't directly control.

The first part (from Chapters 2 to 6) explains the building blocks you need to set up partnerships properly and get them working effectively. It talks about the three foundations we believe underpin any long-lasting successful partnership: good governance, efficient operations and the right behaviours. The second part (from Chapters 7 to 10) is more personal, looking at the experience of individual leaders, analyzing what makes for success or failure in leading a partnership and examining the new skills you need to develop as a collaborative leader. It also looks at the role played by conflict in partnerships, and how collaborative leaders have a vital role in helping their people handle cross-organisational conflict in a healthy manner.

It's not a workbook, but at key points we've written some checklists and hints and tips that you can apply directly to your own situation. We've also used a mixture of interviews with real leaders, and case studies drawn from an amalgam of several public and private sector examples, to try to bring theory and practice to life.

WHY THIS MATTERS NOW

Finally, we believe that becoming a collaborative leader is a personal challenge that's well worth taking. To see groups of people and organisations succeed in achieving things together that they could not achieve on their own is one of the most satisfying leadership experiences in the world. Not surprisingly, getting it right is also good for your reputation and your career. More and more of the top leadership jobs in the private and the public sector demand candidates with a track record of delivering results in complex multi-agency environments. If you want to go far as a leader in the twenty-first century, you need to be able to work collaboratively.

As we face the ongoing impact of the global credit crunch and a highly challenging economic environment, the drive to gain value from business critical relationships of every kind can only become more urgent. Leaders not only need to find ways of making partnerships work, but also have to save money at the same time. It's easy to be generous to your partners when there is plenty to go around, but the truth is you need to rely on each other even more when times are tough. For leaders surrounded by stakeholders demanding attention for their own particular interest groups, it's quite a task.

So this book seems especially timely. We all need to get better at leading collaboratively. A lot is resting on it and a lot can be gained by getting it right. And we know plenty of people are doing just that. Throughout this book we want to celebrate the work of leaders who are doing a great job of helping organisations deliver together, working quietly behind the scenes. We've tried to bring their experience to life in lots of named and un-named examples. They are the unsung heroes of collaborative leadership.

In a letter from a Birmingham jail in 1963, Martin Luther King wrote: 'We are caught in an inescapable network of mutuality, tied in a single garment of destiny. Whatever affects one directly, affects all indirectly'. In business today perhaps we too need to listen to these words. As leaders, employees or citizens, we all live in an interconnected world. Those connections are getting wider and the speed of impact of one organisation's actions on another is growing year on year. This interconnected world demands the development of a new form of leadership – a collaborative form of leadership. We hope this book will help to show you how that can be done.

David Archer and Alex Cameron
November 2008, London

HOW THIS BOOK WORKS

Chapter 1: The Rise of Collaborative Working

Over the last two decades, we've seen a huge increase in partnerships of all kinds. Yet a high proportion of partnerships are doomed to failure. We examine what makes them so difficult, and what is fueling the continuing rise.

Chapter 2: To Collaborate or Not To Collaborate?

Partnerships are neither close-knit teams nor transactions. So just how much do you need to collaborate? This chapter explains why collaboration matters most at the points of interdependence between two or more parties, and sets out a tool, the collaboration spectrum, for assessing what kind of collaborative relationship you require.

Chapter 3: The Partnership Roadmap

This chapter is a roadmap for those who are new to leading partnerships (if you're relatively experienced, you might want to skim it and move on to the next). It sets out the four stages of a partnership – selection, transition, maintenance and ending – and the indicators at each stage that tell you if you're on the right track or going off the road.

Chapter 4: The Three-Legged Stool

Every partnership needs a solid framework. We describe a simple model – as sturdy as a three-legged stool – to help leaders work out where they need to focus their efforts. Get each leg right, and you have the essential structure to set up and run any kind of collaborative venture.

Chapter 5: The Octagonal Tape Measure

Many organisations only use traditional measures of performance. But in a partnership, you need eight different types of measure to understand how the different parties are working together and how the partnership is likely to operate in the future. This chapter explains how and what to measure.

Chapter 6: The Grit in the Oyster

Clashes of culture are one of the biggest challenges in partnerships. But partners shouldn't be clones of each other – they need to use the differences between them to create value that none could achieve on their own. This chapter shows how to make potentially damaging difference work to your advantage.

Chapter 7: The Secrets of Successful Leaders

In this chapter, four successful leaders from very different fields discuss what it takes to lead effective collaborations and what they've learned over the years in sharing control.

Chapter 8: Why Some Collaborative Leaders Fail

While partnerships fail for many reasons, it's often down to the leadership. In this chapter we tell the stories of four leaders – the expert loner, the idealist, the incrementalist and the selfish fast-streamer – who didn't understand the nature of collaborative working, with disastrous results for the partnerships they headed.

Chapter 9: Risk and Opportunity

Collaborative ventures are fraught with risk, and it's up to leaders to navigate a path through the dangers. But at the same time they need to make the partnership work – and that means exploiting the opportunities that joint working offers, innovating and creating new value together. In this chapter, we explore how leaders can manage both risk and opportunity.

Chapter 10: Conflict and the Collaborative Leader

Conflict is inevitable in partnerships. But it's not all bad. In fact conflict has a central role in collaboration, as different parties learn to engage with each other productively to produce something new. This chapter outlines how leaders can learn to deal with conflict in a healthy way.

Chapter 11: The Future of Collaboration

Collaborative working has taken firm root over the past decades. Is it now here to stay? In the final chapter we look at why partnership may prove even more necessary in the future, not only in business but in tackling some of the biggest issues that face our planet, and the unavoidable challenges this presents for collaborative leaders.

Chapter 1

The Rise of Collaborative Working

BEYOND COMMAND AND CONTROL

In March 2008, a San Francisco-based finance company raised $17.9 billion by listing on the New York Stock Exchange. It was the world's biggest IPO – and it happened right in the middle of the credit crunch that had toppled Bear Stearns and Northern Rock.

That company was Visa, an entirely collaborative venture founded a quarter of a century earlier by visionary CEO Dee Hock. It has been called 'a corporation whose product is coordination', a highly decentralized, largely self-organizing group of member companies that both cooperate and compete under the Visa banner. All members issue their own credit cards and are free to price and market them in whatever way they wish. At the same time there's a high degree of cooperation – each member has to agree to accept any Visa card, regardless of issuer, and everyone participates in a central clearing house that handles transactions and customer billing. It's a formula that has proved remarkably successful. Visa is the world's largest credit card network and its products are used in more than 170 countries.

An article in *Fast Company* describes Dee Hock's motivations in setting up the radical Visa structure back in 1970, a time when credit card companies were locked in desperate competition, sending out pre-approved cards to any customers they could lay their hands on. 'Command-and-control organisations were not only archaic and increasingly irrelevant', says Hock. 'They were becoming a public menace, antithetical to the human spirit and destructive of the biosphere. I was convinced we were on the brink of an epidemic of institutional failure'.[1]

Instead, Hock decided that 'the organisation had to be based on biological concepts to evolve, in effect, to invent and organize itself'. With those principles well established, he tested the concept of self-organisation by resigning from Visa in 1984 to follow his own pursuits (and to develop his theory of

---

[1] 'The Trillion-Dollar Vision of Dee Hock', M. Mitchell Waldrop, *Fast Company*, Issue 05, October 1996.

'chaordic' organisations – a synthesis of chaos and order). According to *Fast Company*, 'Visa never missed a beat'.

EVERYTHING IS MUTUAL

Two months before Visa's record-breaking IPO, leaders in government, business and NGOs from all round the globe converged on the Swiss ski resort of Davos for the annual meeting of the World Economic Forum. Their theme was 'collaborative innovation', and over the 5 days of the forum, they examined how organisations and governments could work together on issues ranging from sustainable agriculture to conflict and terrorism in order to make the world a better place.

'Globalization is forcing changes in how people collaborate in a fundamental way', said former Prime Minister Tony Blair, one of the co-chairs of the forum. 'If we are interconnected and the world is interconnected, the only way for the world to work is to have a set of common values. We have no option but to work together'.

It's not just rhetoric. Collaboration is on the rise everywhere. Over the last century we began to collaborate on the big things – fighting world wars and trying to keep global peace. And ever more frequently we're collaborating on a global scale to tackle major global issues – epidemics, poverty and climate change. In 2003, at the behest of the World Health Organisation, a team of 11 research labs around the world collaborated to isolate the virus that caused the deadly SARS outbreak in just 1 month. The Kyoto Protocol entered into force in 2005 and has been ratified by more than 180 governments. And in the same year, Make Poverty History brought together NGOs and voluntary organisations all round the world.

When the issues that touch us have global impacts, our response is increasingly one of global collaboration. In a 2001 speech in New York, Gordon Brown recalled President John F. Kennedy's words of 40 years earlier: 'As the worldwide effort for independence, inspired by the American declaration of independence, now approaches a successful close, a great new effort – for interdependence – is transforming the world about us'. Today few people would disagree. We're all in it together. And we need to work together to sort it out.

THE ULTIMATE PARTNER

Collaboration is an evolutionary adaptation – and we're not just talking ants, bees and termites. At its most basic, collaboration is displayed throughout the animal kingdom in pair bonding. Many organisms also form wider social groups that offer greater protection and allow roles such as food gathering or looking after young to be shared.

But the life form that really excites us from the collaborative point of view is pretty unprepossessing – it's slime mold, the nasty reddish jelly-like stuff you sometimes find under half-rotted bark. Slime mold has fascinated scientists for decades. We have a special affection for it (after all, one of us originally trained as a zoologist), because it's the ultimate model of partnership.

Slime mold has been hard to classify, as it's not a mold at all. Cellular slime mold is a single-celled, amoeba-like organism that spends most of its time minding its own business. But when resources are scarce, individual slime mold cells start to cooperate to form a more complex organism that behaves as one. What's more, when slime mold cells get together, they can display surprising levels of apparent 'intelligence' – like solving the puzzle of a maze by stretching between two food sources at either end. Then when the crisis is over, they split up and go back to existing as single cellular organisms once more.

Steven Johnson tells the story of slime mold brilliantly in *Emergence: The Connected Lives of Ants, Brains, Cities and Software*.[2] His point is that slime mold displays emergent behaviour – the 'intelligence' it demonstrates comes about from aggregating a mass of relatively simple elements. No one element is directing the show; rather, this complex behaviour emerges from the level of individual cells.

The reason we like slime mold so much is rather different. It's because it has clearly got the hang of how to be a good partner. Slime mold knows when to be independent and when to collaborate. It doesn't spend all its time as a team – each single cell manages perfectly well on its own for large stretches of time. But when slime mold cells get together, they can do amazing things.

We realize that aspiring to the condition of slime mold may not be for everyone. But for us, it's seriously clever stuff. And if the world's collaborative efforts to stave off the direst predictions of climate change don't succeed, we'd put our money on slime mold making it through.

THE EXPLOSION IN BUSINESS PARTNERSHIPS

This brings us to the focus of this book – collaborating within and between organisations. Visa, Davos and our favorite slime mold may be leading the way. But over the last two decades, the whole of the business world has woken up to the possibilities collaborative working offers – things like efficiency, risk-sharing, opening up new markets, launching new products, tackling massive problems and innovating in all sorts of ways.

Over that time we've seen an explosion in partnerships of all kinds. Take outsourcing, for example. Everybody is doing it. Even though all ipods bear the message 'Designed by Apple in California' etched on their back, Apple is silent about where its products are now manufactured – in East Asia. Aerospace company Boeing estimates that 'just about 70% of the value-added in most

---

[2] *Emergence: The Connected Lives of Ants, Brains, Cities and Software*, Steven Johnson, Penguin, 2002 [first published in the USA by Scribner 2001 and in the UK by Allen Lane The Penguin Press 2001].

products that bear the Boeing name was put there by suppliers'.[3] In fact it no longer sees itself as an aircraft manufacturer, but a 'systems integrator'. Other companies go further still. Electronics company Philips and consumer goods giant Procter & Gamble outsource not just manufacturing but innovation, looking to the outside world to generate a high percentage of their product ideas.

At the same time, high-profile joint ventures in the private sector have become brands in their own right, reading like a list of pop duos: Sony and Ericsson, PepsiCo and Starbucks, Disney and Pixar (now fully merged), and, of course, the long-established Exxon Mobil.

Meanwhile, public–private partnerships are reaching a new stage of maturity, no longer aiming solely to cut costs but looking for ways to innovate and improve public services. Within Whitehall the concept of joined-up government has been slowly taking root for some 10 years now. The first Public Service Agreement (PSA) targets were set in 1997, and although they claimed to be about joining up delivery to the public, they started off as a large collection of about 600 individual targets, each relevant to a separate department.

But 10 years later, the PSAs set as part of the Spending Review 2007 have been radically reduced in number to just 30. Each one is a broad outcome relevant to the public, and cuts across a large number of departments and agencies, which have to work together to deliver it.

And for third sector organisations, collaboration is pretty much a way of life. Charities, voluntary organisations and NGOs often rely for their existence on joint funding, and use joint working as a means of raising the profile of issues – think only of the Disasters Emergency Committee, the group of major charities that forget competition in the face of major disasters and join together to raise funds.

And finally, there's a whole new area of collaborative working – the virtual mass collaboration beloved of the Web 2.0 generation, who take it for granted that sharing knowledge, ideas and problems with millions of others makes total sense.

Everyone has to collaborate at some point in their working life. Whether it's across functions, organisations or borders, face-to-face or virtual, working in partnership has become unavoidable. And we believe it will continue to rise, transforming the face of organisations in the future.

The trouble is that, by and large, people aren't very good at it. When it comes to successful collaboration, slime mold knocks the spots off us.

THE PROBLEM WITH PARTNERSHIP

It's hard to get convincing figures on the number of partnerships in the UK, let alone worldwide. But what is certain is that very large numbers of them

---

[3] 'Outsourcing: The Real Issue', a speech by Boeing president Harry C. Stonecipher given to the Orange County Business Council, California, on 2 June 2004 [on Boeing website – boeing.com].

come to grief. Around half of all alliances collapse, inflicting financial damage on both partners – just about the same failure rate as that found in mergers and acquisitions. In fact, research by the authors of a 2004 *Harvard Business Review* article found that 48% of alliances between American firms ended in failure in less than 2 years.[4]

In public–private partnerships, too, there's also plenty of high-profile evidence of failure. In 2007, Metronet, the organisation responsible for maintaining and upgrading two-thirds of the London Underground network under a complex public–private partnership contract, went into administration. While the final cost to the taxpayer is still to be calculated, interim payments of £1.7 billion have already been budgeted to keep trains running until a solution is found.

Partnerships fail because collaboration is downright difficult. It's hard to handle on a personal level because it necessitates unlearning traditional management skills – they simply don't work in collaborative situations. You can't incentivize, motivate, build, shape and discipline your team in the same way because it's not your team any more. You can't control all the resources. You may not even share the same goals.

So why is the whole process so hard? There are many reasons, but three stand out. The first two are personal: you have to let go and trust your partners, and you have to get beyond the comfort of your own tribe. But the third is even more problematic: partnerships create complex systems, and complex systems can get way out of control.

You Have to Let Go and Trust Your Partners

For most managers, the hardest part of leading a collaboration is feeling stripped of power and authority. To succeed, you need to abandon the comforting delusion that you control the levers of power, and accept the uncertainty of delivering through the actions of others.

Managing well is no longer enough – you have to start trusting your way out of problems. It may sound flaky, especially to people trained in a machine view of management, but it takes real and sophisticated skills to pull off. Worrying about the lack of control and trying to tie down every future eventuality in a contract simply makes lawyers rich and gives you ulcers. Instead, you need to build a high level of trust with each partner, and then leave them to fulfill their part of the bargain. You no longer have control of your destiny; it's now a shared outcome.

---

[4] 'When to Ally and When to Acquire', by Jeffrey H. Dyer, Prashant Kale and Harbir Singh, *Harvard Business Review*, July–August 2004. The authors studied 1592 alliances that US companies formed between 1993 and 1997.

Trust lies at the heart of most successful collaborative relationships. However, we're not talking about blind or unconditional trust; it should be well-bounded and built on sound foundations:

- knowing that your partners have the capability and the capacity to do the job
- understanding what drives and motivates them
- having the right joint decision-making and escalation frameworks in place to govern the relationship
- having access to timely information
- knowing each leader in the partnership as an individual and being able to look them in the eye and ask for help

One of the big problems is that trust is hardest to give (or ask for) at the time you need it most. But in partnerships, you need to be able to do exactly that. And by building a healthy, trusting relationship with your partners, you can use your combined skills and experience to anticipate future shocks and respond to them better than any one of you could on your own.

You Need to go Beyond Your Own Tribe

Collaboration is also hard to handle on a much deeper, visceral level. In reality, we don't much like collaborating, at least until we get good at it. It doesn't come naturally, and that's because deep down, people are tribal. We feel most comfortable within our own tribe – our family, our extended family, our friends and people like us. Strangers from other tribes – a different football club, a different culture, a different race – provoke suspicion and mistrust.

The world of work often operates on similar tribal lines. People are comfortable within their own functional teams or cultures – designers are wary of accountants, while policy people don't usually mix with IT experts. Just as different tribes might engage in trading, or even come to a temporary alliance, interaction between the different work functions tends to happen at the edges.

When you don't perceive others as being like you, collaboration doesn't come easily. The more the people on a team who don't know anyone else, the less likely team members are to share knowledge. But in collaborative partnerships, diversity is part of the deal. There are at least two tribes, and often more – and all have to learn to get along without hostilities breaking out.

Overcoming the initial distrust and appreciating difference is a sophisticated skill. It requires greater attention, effort and fluency than dealing with your own tribe, and often it needs to be reinforced by stronger policing. A new partnership can't expect to get beyond tribal issues straightaway. After all, it's taken a very long time for human civilization to progress from warring tribes to the beginnings of global community. And while some people find that collaboration comes naturally to them, most do not. They have to learn it, and at times of stress, the tribal instinct may well kick in again.

Yet few collaborative ventures acknowledge the importance of tribalism at the start of a partnership or treat it seriously when it raises its head. That omission dooms many partnerships to failure.

You Can't Control Complex Systems

The third difficulty is even harder to deal with: partnerships of all kinds can have a life of their own. You can't try to manage them like cogs in a machine because the act of combining forces creates a complex system, and while complex systems tend to be well attuned to their environment and good at responding to new circumstances, they're also highly unpredictable.

All living things are complex systems. So too are the organisation of an ant colony (and the aggregating behaviour of slime mold), the ecology of a rainforest, the stock market and the earth's climate. In mathematical terms, a complex system is one where performance cannot be described by simple linear equations linking input to output, and because they're non-linear, small changes in input can produce large and unexpected changes in output.

A strong tradition of management theory looks at single organisations as relatively simple systems that can be controlled by increasing wages or resources, setting targets, scaling up successful areas of the business or managing by objectives. But partnerships, alliances, joint ventures and the like are more complex than that. Formed from an amalgam of different organisations and cultures, they behave much more like living systems, evolving and adapting over time, but often proving surprisingly resistant to simple levers of control. They require a different form of leadership altogether, and for leaders schooled in more traditional management techniques, this can be a tough going.

THE VIEW FROM THE TOP: PARTNERSHIP IS ESSENTIAL

To get beyond downsides like these, you need a very strong reason for going into partnership. Yet collaborative working is high on most leaders' agendas.

Back in 1994, Rosabeth Moss Kanter pointed out that 'being a good partner has become a key corporate asset'.[5] Today it's seen as more of a necessity.

In 2007 we commissioned a survey by Ipsos Mori into UK senior executives' experience of collaborative partnerships, both in the public and in the private sector.[6] Over half the organisations we spoke to are involved in up to

[5] 'Collaborative Advantage: The Art of Alliances', Rosabeth Moss Kanter, *Harvard Business Review*, Vol. 72, No. 4, July–August 1994, pp. 96–108.

[6] *Making Partnerships Work: A Survey of UK Senior Executives*, Ipsos Mori and Socia, February 2007. The survey was carried out with 92 director-level UK executives who are or have been personally involved in establishing or managing long-term collaborative business partnerships. It covered 51 public and 41 private sector companies, and participants came from a range of industry sectors and a range of functions.

15 partnerships at the same time, and one-third in more than 20. Most of these are long-term partnerships, lasting an average of 6 years, longer than the typical management appointment.

These senior executives see collaborative partnerships either as very important or as essential to the success of their organisations, and they expect them to be even more important in the future. But the vast majority of executives find it far easier to lead from the front and control all the resources to get the job done than to relinquish control of some operational functions. It seemed that letting go of some of that control raises deep-seated concerns about accountability and trust.

At the same time, leaders are convinced that the benefits of partnerships easily outweigh the costs. Only one in five saw partnerships as 'a necessary evil', and nine out of ten agreed that collaboration will be the foundation for long-term economic success.

WHY PARTNERSHIPS HAVE TAKEN OFF

What lies behind the worldwide explosion in collaborative ventures? There are three key drivers. The first is the atomization of organisations in the pursuit of efficiency. The second driver is technology, and in particular the massive increase in connectivity created by the World Wide Web. And the third is scale and complexity – some projects are so huge, complicated and costly that they can only be undertaken by collaborative ventures.

The First Driver: Organisations are Atomizing

Once it was possible for organisations to do almost everything. Think only of the East India Company, which held sway for over 350 years, until well into the nineteenth century, running the Asian trade in silk, spices, tea and opium. A military as well as a commercial power, the Company ruled its empire with an iron hand, setting up governance structures which became the prototype of the Indian Civil Service.

But with physical power no longer a serious option in running a business, the tide swayed in the last century from controlling everything to owning as little as possible. From the early part of the century, companies began to break their activities down into smaller and smaller units. First came time and motion studies, then production lines and increasing specialization. Bit by bit, companies divided up their supply chains, outsourced operations and began concentrating on what they did best.

Until relatively recently, for example, all the staff at a local railway station worked for the same company, no matter whether they were in charge of the signal box or the station café. Now if you go to catch a train, the station may be owned and operated by one company, the train by a second, and the track on which it runs a third. The person in the high-visibility jacket mending a fault in the signaling system may be employed by a different company to the one next to him who is checking that the track is safe to run on. You present a ticket bought from one company's online website to a ticket inspector who works for another. Cleanliness of the station will be the responsibility of yet another company, which will outsource the actual work to many subcontractors around the country. As for the cup of coffee you buy for the journey, that could come from any one of a dozen different suppliers.

In recent years, we've taken this idea further still, outsourcing everything from senior management to innovation. The business world has fragmented. And that means collaboration is no longer an option but a necessity.

In the private sector, the stock market is behind the drive toward atomization. Market analysts want to see costs stripped out of conglomerates to realize the savings in mergers. Meanwhile individual companies are under pressure to cut out overhead costs and pass them on to a specialist company.

In the public sector, cost is just as much of an issue. With increasing demand for public services and limited acceptance of tax, Western democracies don't want their public sector borrowing rate to get too high. Governments have found ingenious ways of keeping costs off the balance sheet, often by using private or third sector companies to take over some of the liability. Over the last 20 years we've seen an explosion of Private Finance Initiative (PFI) deals to fund capital growth. They haven't had a good press, at least initially, but they're here to stay and they demand advanced levels of collaborative skills to make them work.

Another push toward atomization is the inexorable rise of brands. Strong brands are acutely specialized, concentrating on a core idea and making every part of the brand's behaviour build that idea in the minds of the public. Hiving off non-core operations to other suppliers can however rebound badly on businesses. When something goes wrong, it's not the supplier that gets blamed; it's the originating brand. And sometimes, even an apparently minor partner can wreak havoc on the brand that owns the relationship with the customers. When BA's in-flight catering firm, Gate Gourmet, sacked nearly 700 staff over an unofficial strike in 2005, BA baggage handlers, loaders and bus drivers downed tools in sympathy. The resulting chaos affected tens of thousands of passengers, and those passengers blamed BA, not Gate Gourmet.

The consequences of outsourcing operations can be even more catastrophic. When senior officials at HM Revenue and Customs (HMRC) requested data to be sent to the National Audit Office in October 2007, they didn't expect to unleash a scandal that threatened government ministers. A junior official at HMRC copied sensitive information – dates of birth, National Insurance numbers, addresses and bank details where relevant – for every person claiming child benefit in the UK onto two discs, and then had them couriered by TNT. They never turned up at their destination, a failure that compromised the data security of half the population. It has been suggested that the reason the data was not desensitized first was because this would incur an extra payment to the data management supplier, EDS.

The dilemma for collaborative leaders is evident. Farming out parts of a business may cut costs but it also means losing control, and that can have totally unexpected consequences.

The Second Driver: Technology has Flattened the World

The second big driver for collaboration is technology. Now that we can digitize all kinds of data and send it remotely to someone else, it has become possible to collaborate with people and organisations anywhere in the world. The new connectivity has radically altered the economics of collaborative working, from outsourcing and 'homesourcing' to mass participation. And it's happening everywhere, even at school parents' evenings. A school we know in East London has to cater for no fewer than 73 languages, so it has come up with an ingeniously simple solution – using a Skype link (allowing free telephone calls over the internet) to relay multiple simultaneous translations from all around the world.

The list of virtual collaborations gets more exotic by the day. As Thomas L. Friedman describes in *The World is Flat*,[7] students now work with e-tutors living thousands of miles away; understaffed radiology departments are sending CAT scans to be diagnosed by doctors at the other side of the world; US accountants increasingly outsource the preparation of tax returns to India; and authors can hire remote executive assistants to research their books, making use of different time zones to get things done overnight and on their desk the next morning.

It's a brave new world, but it engenders undreamed-of collaborations and partnerships, and a host of new leadership and management challenges. The ability to connect with any part of the world, however remote, certainly increases the potential for collaborative working, but it doesn't confer an automatic ability to collaborate well. Individuals and organisations are suddenly making connections with people from entirely different cultures and backgrounds, and with organisations that differ from their own in shape, size, outlook, way of working and quite possibly in hemisphere. And while that offers plenty of creative possibilities, it also makes things a whole lot more complicated.

The Third Driver: Scale and Complexity Place Power in the Hands of the Few

The third driver behind the growth of partnerships is the concentration of power in some industries in the hands of a small number of players. Some contracts, like oil exploration, government IT projects, or major construction

---

[7] *The World is Flat: The Globalized World in the Twenty-First Century*, by Thomas L. Friedman, Penguin Books, 2006.

efforts, are so huge or so complex that they tend to be dominated by a handful of firms with the capacity to deal with them.

It follows that a handful of large firms keep on coming across each other in major contracts. Partnerships are essential. And while the big IT companies don't appear yet to have worked out the best way to handle their partnerships, oil companies have been searching for black gold for a long time and leaders in the oil industry know a great deal about fruitful collaboration. It's in the DNA of their business because each block of land earmarked for oil exploration is bought into by several parties, often including governments, and no one party has overall ownership. Acceptance of joint venture goes with the territory.

While collaborations among such giants clearly bring benefits of scale and capability, the dangers of such near monopolies are obvious. Potential abuse of monopoly power, collusion and price fixing are all specters that haunt these industries. Where collaboration works, however, it's sophisticated and highly evolved. The oil industry in particular holds useful lessons for collaborative leaders everywhere, and we'll be looking at the views of one of its leaders in detail in Chapter 7.

The three drivers behind the explosion in collaborative partnerships – atomization, technology, and scale and complexity – remain potent forces. And while they continue, partnerships look set to rise and rise. As a leader, you can no longer get to the top without learning to collaborate. And in the rest of this book, we'll show you how.

FIVE TYPES OF ORGANISATIONAL COLLABORATION

Before ending this chapter, however, we'll take a lightning tour of the five different types of organisational collaboration and the challenges faced in each:

- private sector alliances and joint ventures
- public sector joint working
- public–private partnerships
- third sector coalitions
- self-organizing collaborations

Private Sector Partnerships

The private sector has been distinctly creative in its approach to partnership, spawning many different structures for joint working. First there are more transactionally based partnerships – from outsourcing a particular service to managing a supply chain across many different cultures and different countries. Then there are alliances of various kinds, from the informal to the contractual. In consortia (like the European consortium of aviation firms that originally formed Airbus Industrie in order to compete with American companies) each partner retains legal independence but agrees to share the profits of joint activities, whereas equity-sharing joint ventures create a separate legal entity for the duration of the partnership.

A *Harvard Business Review* article of 2004 estimates that more than 5000 joint ventures were launched worldwide in the previous 5 years, with the largest 100 JVs representing $350 billion in combined annual revenues.[8] Meanwhile, 5789 alliance agreements were announced by American companies alone in 2003 (and a massive 57000 in the period from 1996 through 2001).[4]

As we've seen, however, around half of private sector partnerships end in failure and financial loss, 48% within the first 2 years, according to the research by Jeffrey H. Dyer, Prashant Kale and Harbir Singh.[4] A recent Accenture study produces even gloomier figures: of every 100 alliance negotiations studied across all industries, 90 fail to reach agreements and only 2 survive more than 2 years.[9]

'Mistakes made during the launch phase often erode up to half the potential value creation of a venture', say McKinsey consultants James Bamford, David Ernst and David G. Fubini. 'Launching a world-class joint venture is complex and demanding. Research shows that it can, in fact, be more resource intensive than post-merger integration or internal business start-ups'.[8]

Yet few businesses treat their partnerships with the same healthy respect as a merger or startup. According to a Dataquest study, the most cited reason for alliance failure was being 'overly optimistic'.[9]

Public Sector Partnerships

One of the other growth areas for partnership in the last decade has been the explosion of agreements between public sector bodies to join up and work together to deliver more effective services. As we saw earlier in this chapter, Whitehall has been trying to break down silos and embrace joined-up government for the last decade. PSAs, first introduced in 1997, were intended to reduce fragmentation and break down artificial barriers in policy-making. They've now been simplified down into just 30 agreements, which at the time of writing include 'Promote better health and wellbeing for all', 'Improve children and young people's safety' and 'Lead the global effort to avoid dangerous climate change'.

At the local level, partnerships are often focused on bringing the resources of a number of agencies to bear in a locality in order to renew neighborhoods and aid regeneration. They exist in various different forms, such as local area agreements (LAAs) and local strategic partnerships (LSPs), and the scale of

---

[8] 'Launching a World-Class Joint Venture', by James Bamford, David Ernst and David G. Fubini, *Harvard Business Review*, February 2004.

[9] 'Grasping the Capability: Successful Alliance Creation and Governance Through the "Connected Corporation"', *The Point*, Vol. 2, Issue 2, 2002, Accenture.

these is enormous. In 2005 there were over 360 LSPs in England, with nearly every local authority in the country involved.

It's the same in the health sector. An organisation of Community Health Partnerships (formerly called Partnership for Health) brings together various parts of the local and national public health sector to manage the building and reconstruction of doctors' surgeries, clinics and other local purpose-built premises for healthcare. So far it has developed partnerships covering two-thirds of England's population and has delivered over £1500 million of investment in more than 210 buildings that are either open or under construction.[10]

But getting these sorts of organisations to work together is not easy. A major research report undertaken by the Universities of Warwick, Liverpool John Moores, West of England, Bristol and the Office for Public Management found that 'LSPs face a number of tensions in developing activity and action across a broad front. These include the compatibility (or lack of it) of government and local agendas, the question of the level at which to act – strategic or delivery focused and the extent to which the LSP is able to engage both agencies and communities. A further key issue is what action and activity is (and is best) undertaken by "the LSP", by sub-partnerships, or by partners with the collaboration or consent of the LSP'.[11]

Even in the heavily structured world of the public sector, being a leader means navigating a complex web of interdependent relationships and partnerships.

Public–Private Partnerships

Public–private partnerships are a relatively new phenomenon. Back in the late 1970s, the UK government was in charge of a vast range of public services, from utilities, coal and steel to buses and railways, while local authorities were almost solely responsible for schools, social services, refuse collection, and council housing. Two decades on, the picture had changed radically, with private and voluntary sector organisations taking on significant responsibility for delivering a range of public services.

In the early years, public–private partnerships focused mainly on reducing the public sector borrowing requirement, finding ways to keep major capital costs off balance sheet. In 1992, the Conservative government introduced PFI, a structured program to encourage private investment in public sector projects. Under this program, private developers fund the construction of schools, hospitals, prisons and so on, and then charge fees to the public sector for the use of the facilities. Embraced just as enthusiastically by the new Labor government,

---

[10] http://www.communityhealthpartnerships.co.uk/index.php?ob=1&id=5.
[11] *National Evaluation of Local Strategic Partnerships: Formative Evaluation and Action Research Programme 2002–2005*, Office of the Deputy Prime Minister, 2006.

the scheme has grown wholesale: since its inception, over 700 projects have been signed, delivering investment of over £49 billion.[12]

For a long time, public–private partnerships were greeted with skepticism on both the right and the left. The final report of the Commission on Public–Private Partnerships describes the two camps: on one side the 'privatizers' opposed the continuing role of government in public services, while on the other, the 'monopolists' viewed public–private partnerships as privatization by stealth. Despite some high-profile failures, however, those concerns have gradually died down as it has become clear that public–private partnerships are here to stay, both in the UK and around the world.

In recent years, the focus of public–private partnerships has shifted from reducing public borrowing and government capital spending to achieving increased efficiency and value for money in the delivery of public services. In this form, a public–private partnership aims to use the expertise of the private sector to transform the operations of public sector organisations through a transfer of knowledge across the partnership.

Not-For-Profit Collaborations

Third sector organisations have a long history of working in partnership. They're frequently involved in partnerships with central and local governments. The Citizens Advice service, for example, is part of a partnership examining how to tackle poverty in retirement led by the Department for Work and Pensions. And many local authorities rely on charities to deliver large parts of their social care provision. This is big business – in 2003/2004, councils were responsible for £3.2 billion of local third sector funding.

The difficulty with collaboration between the charity sector and the government is often one of scalability, particularly with smaller, less centralized charities. At a local level, collaborative relationships can be built up on the ground between committed voluntary sector workers and local public sector officials. But as we shall see in Chapter 4, you can't build a lasting partnership on personal relationships alone. When the same approach is scaled to a national level, the dozens of individual relationships that held together local partnerships can stand in the way of strategic decision-making and long-term planning.

Collaborations between third sector organisations are also common and becoming more so. In fact joint working is being strongly encouraged throughout the sector. In an attempt to drive efficiency and reduce duplication, the Charity Commission advised in 2003 that 'all charities should consider seriously and imaginatively whether there are ways in which they could do more and better for their users by working together'.

---

[12] PPP Forum PFI/PPP Factsheet, 25 July 2006.

Efficiency apart, voluntary organisations are becoming increasingly good at joining forces to campaign on particular issues. Coalitions like Make Poverty History, which mobilized individuals and voluntary groups all over the world, or Stop Climate Chaos, which campaigns to cut CO_2 emissions in the UK, allow many organisations with similar aims to raise the profile of issues, increase their credibility and multiply the impact they have individually. It's not always easy for voluntary organisations to work together like this – passion for individual causes and detailed questions of policy may get in the way – but where charities can achieve common purpose, it's a powerful way to make things happen.

Much in the same way, companies and institutions that normally compete fiercely with each other collaborate through non-profit associations in order to protect their joint interests. The Food and Drink Federation brings together rivals such as Unilever and Cadbury Schweppes to represent the common interests of the industry to government, regulators and the media. The Portman Group is an association of drinks manufacturers that aims to promote responsible drinking. The Scotch Whisky Association unites rival distillers in promoting their industry around the world. And the Russell Group, an association of 20 major UK universities, achieves massive lobbying clout on issues like tuition fees.

At the heart of such collaborations is clear self-interest. Not only do participating organisations achieve a louder voice through uniting, they also share and dilute the reputational risk of any negative messages associated with their industry. There is often safety in numbers.

Self-Organizing Collaborations

At the beginning of this chapter we looked at the self-organizing collaboration that made Visa the success it is today. And recently even more radical forms of self-organisation have emerged: mass collaborations enabled by the new computing power of the Web. They're the focus of many recent publications, among them *Wikinomics*, the 2007 bestseller by Don Tapscott and Anthony D. Williams, who argue convincingly that mass collaboration is the future.[13]

Self-organizing collaborations have been made possible by the new power of the Web, often called Web 2.0, which changes the way people use the Internet from passive surfing to active participation. Instead of 'publish and browse', it is becoming 'a giant computer that everyone can program[me], providing a global infrastructure for creativity, participation, sharing and self-organisation'.[13] The best-known example is Wikipedia, the online collective

---

[13] *Wikinomics: How Mass Collaboration Changes Everything*, Don Tapscott and Anthony D. Williams, Atlantic Books, 2006, 2008 [first published in the United States of America in 2006 by Portfolio, a member of Penguin Group (USA) Inc.; first published in Great Britain in 2007 by Atlantic Books, an imprint of Grove/Atlantic Inc.].

encyclopedia that began in January 2001 and now has over million articles in its English version alone, relying entirely on contributions from self-motivated members of the public. Anyone can amend an entry, and policing comes from vigilance by other interested individuals. Although Wikipedia has many flaws, most notably its unevenness – the classic example is that *The Simpsons* get more space than Homer – factual errors tend to get ironed out fairly quickly. In fact, a 2005 study in *Nature* found Wikipedia was just about as reliable as the *Encyclopedia Britannica*.[14]

Less democratic (but more accurate) is the open source movement for computer programming spearheaded by Linux. Linux code is designed by a community of voluntary 'hackers' (in its meaning of elite programmer rather than illegal system-breaker), who contribute to and amend each other's work online. They're highly skilled, highly motivated and highly efficient. Without any of the structure or rules of a traditional organisation, the Linux community is a serious rival to Microsoft.

What makes Linux work so well is a common purpose and a common work ethic. As Philip Evans and Bob Wolf have noted in the *Harvard Business Review*,[15] Linux hackers are obsessive about the pursuit of 'elegance' – minimal code shaved of all excess. They've also made simplicity a key part of their operations. Everyone uses the same, very basic, open technology – email and electronic mailing list software. And everybody can see everyone else's real work, unfiltered and unsummarized, just as it was written.

Trust is at the heart of the Linux community and the open source movement generally. Open source programmers gain more from sharing information than from withholding it, and trust the collaboration to produce something far better than any individual could have come up with. It's an effective substitute for any number of tightly worded contracts. At the same time, praise and acknowledgment is given freely and generously throughout the community. Reputation matters to the hackers. And many of them view their open source activities as more valuable and creative than anything else in their professional lives.[16]

Wikipedia has a rather harder job to do. It's relatively easy for an expert to spot a flaw in a small piece of code, but much harder to separate fact from fiction in an obscure encyclopedia entry. There's also more room for ego, self-promotion, partisanship and interest group power to take over, with entries skewed as a result. Gradually Wikipedia has moved away from a free-for-all model towards greater editorial control, more deliberate balancing throughout and stronger policing.

---

[14] 'Internet Encyclopaedias go Head to Head', *Nature* 438, 900–901, 15 December 2005.

[15] 'Collaboration Rules', Philip Evans and Bob Wolf, *Harvard Business Review*, July–August 2005. The authors examine Linux and Toyota as collaborations that break through organisational barriers.

[16] A survey by Bob Wolf and MIT's Karim Lakhani of more than 800 user-developers, cited in 'Collaboration Rules' (above).

However, there's no doubting Wikipedia's importance. It has revolution-ized the way we look things up, and for many current news events, it's the key source of comprehensive, reliable information. Against all the odds, Wikipedia is a collaboration that works. It's a fascinating lesson for would-be collabora-tive leaders. Giving away control can indeed pay extraordinary dividends.

TAKE THE FIRST STEP

As the wider world gets to grips with global collaboration, the business world is increasingly embracing partnership. Nine out of ten business leaders in our Ipsos Mori poll saw collaborative working as the foundation for long-term economic success. If this view holds good, it seems the rise in partnerships is to continue.

Yet the high failure rates tell a different story. Partnerships are costly, tricky, unpredictable and downright unsettling, and most managers simply aren't prepared for the difficulties that joint working entails.

Get collaboration right, however, and the rewards can be way beyond what you can achieve on your own. Far-sighted organisations are already reaping the benefits of ever-wider collaboration, from outsourcing to joint ventures. Dee Hock's radically collaborative model for Visa resulted in the biggest IPO in history, and the advent of mass collaboration is transforming the way people do business.

We believe collaboration is the future. Unfortunately, most people don't have the natural collaborative skills demonstrated by the fantastically adaptive slime mold we saw earlier in this chapter. With human beings, collaboration needs to be learned. Traditional management techniques simple can't cope with the very different demands partnerships bring. We need a new kind of leadership.

In this book, we show how leaders can avoid the many pitfalls of joint working and harness the rewards offered by collaboration. We help you choose the right level of collaboration for the venture in hand, chart the stages in part-nerships and deal with such issues as measurement, cultural difference, risk and conflict. We also take a close look at the stories of successful leaders, as well as some cautionary tales of leaders who got things very wrong indeed.

One of the most important things we have to learn as collaborative leaders is how to build trust. We need to be able to trust our partners to fulfill their part of the bargain because we can't achieve collaboration on our own. It's a bit like the scene in *Indiana Jones and the Last Crusade* where Indiana has to take a leap of faith and launch himself off the edge of a canyon. Only then does a bridge appear under his feet. Collaboration can unleash amazing opportunities, but only if you take the first step.

Chapter 2

To Collaborate or Not to Collaborate?

THE LIMITS OF TOGETHERNESS

Entering any kind of partnership means you're going to need to collaborate. But just how much collaboration do you need, and when? People may be attracted to the idea of working in close collaboration with their partners, but as we'll see in this chapter, if you try to manage a partnership as you would a directly employed team, you'll quickly run into problems. However, if you treat a partnership purely as a transactional relationship, where you're the customer and your partners are the suppliers, that's exactly what it will become – and you'll miss out on the potential value that could have been created in the space between the two organisations.

As we've seen in Chapter 1, partnerships are complex beasts. They are created in many forms to tackle many different sorts of problems – from the rebuilding of our railways and hospitals to the issues of homelessness and rough sleeping. And while they can all loosely be classed as partnerships, their fundamentally different character raises some quite different leadership challenges. A key foundation for a successful partnership is assessing just how much collaboration is required to make the relationship work. This chapter examines how to get a partnership off to a good start by choosing the right model of collaborative working to suit your particular circumstances. So we'll begin by clarifying our terms.

TRANSACTIONAL, SYMBIOTIC OR MUTUAL?

Partnerships are suffering from a terminology problem. These days, virtually any instance of working across functional, organisational or geographic boundaries gets labeled partnership. A lot of suppliers now call themselves partners. And just to add to the confusion, many partnerships say their vision is to work as 'one team'.

To put some order into this mess, we make a distinction between three different kinds of relationship: *transactional*, *symbiotic* and *mutual*. Of these three, we define only mutual relationships as true partnerships – the heart of this book.

As we'll see, partnerships usually contain elements of both transactional and symbiotic relationships. However, it's worth keeping the terms distinct in order to understand how the different types of relationships operate and what you as a leader need to do in order to deliver success across different organisational boundaries.

Transactional Relationships

Purely transactional relationships are relatively straightforward and clearly defined, boiling down to a simple transaction: I buy, you sell. A typical customer/supplier relationship, for example, is transactional – the client specifies exactly what's needed and the supplier delivers it, or a set of suppliers each set out their stalls in the market and the customer chooses which one they want to buy from.

As well as being tightly specified, these relationships are characterized by a low degree of interdependence between each party. Whether the purchase is a piece of furniture or a network of office PCs, buyer and seller don't need to spend much time together because all that matters is the transaction.

Things get a bit more complicated in situations when a customer has entered into a long-term deal with a single supplier. Here the amount of choice is reduced and the dependence on that supplier begins to grow.

But basically, a transactional customer–supplier relationship is still about getting a straightforward deal – perfect in all sorts of circumstances, but not a true partnership in our sense.

Symbiotic Teams

At the other end of the scale are what we call symbiotic teams, where each member is heavily dependent on the others. These are usually permanent (or at least feel that way to participants), and, when performing well, they can be highly collaborative. Team members are very close, they depend on each other, their objectives are the same or at least closely aligned, and they tend to spend a lot of time together both inside and outside work. These teams frequently generate strong loyalty.

However, because of the close and highly dependent nature, teams are not partnerships (and partnerships should not try to behave like teams, a point we'll come back to later).

It's worth mentioning that executive teams and boards are a bit different – these senior leadership teams are less tight-knit, but still need to operate highly collaboratively in order to run their organisations effectively. For that reason, we still include them in the symbiotic category.

Mutual Partnerships

Mutual partnerships – the relationships we're concerned with in this book – fall somewhere between these two extremes. They require a degree of collaboration between the parties, but not total loyalty to the combined unit. In fact, too much collaboration can create too much of a burden on mutual partnerships – many depend for their success on partners working in a more independent manner for much of their day-to-day activity. Otherwise, the degree of interference in each other's business would get in the way of efficient operations.

These periods of separation are enhanced by clear points when the parties need to come together, work collaboratively, perhaps decide something collectively and then move apart again. Sometimes the relationship will require a close degree of collaboration in order to resolve a particular problem. For the most part, however, separate parties can get on with delivering their own part of the whole, with very little contact with their opposite numbers.

Individuals in mutual partnerships have to divide their loyalties between their own organisation and the whole partnership – or as management guru Charles Handy puts it, they must manage the dilemma of dual nationalities or 'twin citizenship'.[1] It's something we should perhaps be good at in the UK. Someone born in England may support England against Wales in the Rugby World Cup, but root for Great Britain in the Olympics, and even support the European Ryder Cup team. It's much the same for people working in a collaborative partnership – you must balance loyalty to your own employer with the good of the whole partnership.

Sometimes this can create tensions and real conflicts of interest. However, the difficulties are balanced by the potential prize: partnerships allow you to achieve joint successes that would be hard or impossible to deliver on your own.

True partnerships, then, are neither transactional relationships nor closely bonded teams, but something in between, occasionally borrowing from each. Within different partnerships, the degree of collaboration required can vary widely – sometimes they will veer more toward team relationships, and sometimes more toward transactions. It's a dynamic process. But everyone in the partnership needs to be clear about what is needed and when.

One way to determine this is to understand the degree of interdependence between the parties and to map out the key points where responsibilities intersect.

POINTS OF INTERDEPENDENCE: LOOK OUT FOR THE EDGE OF THE PLATFORM

As a rule, the more points of interdependence in a relationship, the more collaborative you need to be. It's not always easy to see where the points of interdependence lie between organisations, or between different parts of the same organisation. But one clear example of interdependence is illustrated by a

---

[1] *The Age of Paradox*, Charles Handy, Harvard Business School Press, September 1995.

FIGURE 2.1   Green Park Station – a point of interdependence.
Tube map used with permission of Transport for London.

picture that will be familiar to many people across the world – the London Underground Tube map (Fig. 2.1).

The management of London Underground is organized around its different lines. People who work on Piccadilly Line trains or stations are managed by a different organisation to those who work on, say, the Jubilee or Victoria Line. And at one level that works just fine. For most of the time on most of the network, the two lines are quite distinct and staff don't need to bother themselves much with what is happening on another line.

But at an interchange station – Green Park, for example – what happens on one line has clear implications for staff working on the other. Staff at Green Park need to know how the Jubilee, Victoria and the Piccadilly lines are running and to be kept up to date with information on all three. The points of interdependence between the London Underground line organisations leap out from the Tube map – and these have to be managed accordingly.

The notion of points of interdependence goes deeper still. Within each line, some staff are employed by a part of the organisation that runs stations, and others by a part that runs trains and signaling. Again, for most of their working day the two parts of the operation can get along quite independently. But if a breakdown happens somewhere on the line, and trains and stations start to get very crowded, a vitally important point of interdependence comes into play – the platform edge.

The platform edge is one of the points of greatest risk in the system. If a train crammed with commuters pulls into a station where platforms are already full to overflowing and opens its doors, people could be seriously injured in the crush. In those conditions, the trains and stations organisation have to work very tightly together, with all the relevant people given access to enough information and paying minute-by-minute attention to managing the boundary between their two domains.

Defining and managing points of interdependence is a sophisticated operation. Too much sharing is as bad as too little. At London Underground, train managers don't want or need to know the congestion state of all the stations all the time. The sophistication lies in working out when to share information appropriately, and in being a tight-knit team only where it matters.

Leaders have to pay a lot of attention to points of interdependence because these are the areas they simply can't control on their own. Instead they must share responsibility and trust in the skills of their partner. Flagging up these points, making them explicit and working out ways to deal with them together cuts down on headaches – and minimizes potential disasters.

In any partnership, then, you have to pinpoint your 'Green Parks' and look out for your platform edges. It helps you decide where to focus management time and effort – and, just as importantly, where to leave individual partners to do their own thing. As a partnership becomes more collaborative, it doesn't do it uniformly; rather the number and significance of these points of interdependence increase across the relationship. And the more points where you have to share control, the better you need to get at collaboration.

WORK OUT WHERE YOU STAND

We've developed a simple tool called the *collaboration spectrum* to help leaders categorize the kind of relationship they need at key points in a partnership. This might be at the outset of a partnership, when the relationship is forming and both sides are trying to decide how close they want to get to each other. Or it might be when a partnership is struggling, and one side or the other feels that their partner isn't living up to their expectations. With the help of the collaboration spectrum, you can plot the characteristics of each relationship at a moment in time, examine how those characteristics are likely to change in the future and explore where the relationship needs to be in order to deliver its business goals.

Working out your position on the spectrum together can help resolve initial differences in perspective and approach. Often, though, it's the debate generated from this process that is of the most value. We've found it useful in stimulating conversations between parties that begin to answer some critical questions, such as:

- How much does each party want to collaborate? Do they want to operate as independently as possible or to interact closely?
- Where do parties disagree about the ways of working?

- Are there potential areas of conflict that are easy to predict?
- Are the answers to the first three questions driven by an understanding of the needs of the joint enterprise or by the preferences of each of the partners?

The Collaboration Spectrum

The collaboration spectrum, shown below, is a simple depiction of how the degree of collaboration changes in different kinds of relationship (Fig. 2.2).

Amount of Collaboration

High	Medium	Low

| Permanent team | Partnership | Customer supplier |

FIGURE 2.2   The collaboration spectrum.

At one extreme of the collaboration spectrum are simple transactional, customer/supplier relationships. At the other end are the symbiotic relationships found in a closely bonded permanent team. Both these outer ends of the spectrum are well understood, and there are large bodies of knowledge on what makes for effective performance in each case.

Far less well understood is the large area at the center – the mutual partnerships that are the focus of this book. Within partnerships, it's possible for different parties to have separate objectives and different ways of working – so long as they are together to create long-term value which no one party could create on their own.

At the right-hand side of the spectrum, you are working with straightforward transactions with low interdependence and a minimal need for collaboration. These may be quite short-lived relationships where each side takes what they need and moves on. As you move along the spectrum, from right to left, interdependence and the demand for collaboration increase. Each step along the way represents greater involvement and commitment. By the time you reach the left-hand side of the spectrum, you've moved a long way from dating – you're well and truly married. And while this commitment can pay huge dividends, at the same time the amount of choice you have in the relationship decreases. The consequences of changing your partner are far greater, more disruptive and costly. Divorces are rarely anything but messy.

FIND YOUR PLACE ON THE SPECTRUM

Where do your relationships fit onto the spectrum? Partnerships vary widely: some are more transactional, some more collaborative. It's important to analyze your own situation dispassionately and honestly – the data is only helpful if it reflects the reality of your situation rather than the way that you would like things to be. It's also worth remembering that high levels of collaboration aren't always desirable – in fact highly collaborative relationships come at a considerable cost in time and leadership effort.

The two most important issues to consider are whether there is a dominant player, and what are the measures of success.

Is There a Dominant Player in the Relationship?

If one party has all the power and is perceived to dominate the relationship and control the output of the partnership, it's easy to assume that there are low levels of interdependence, and therefore a lower requirement for the parties to collaborate. In such situations the contract often dominates the relationship.

However, take care when identifying the dominant party, as it may not be the obvious candidate. One partner may be larger and financially stronger, with more resource to bring to the partnership. Their way of working may also reflect their perceived power. But if you look hard at the critical skills in the partnership, you could be surprised at where the power really lies.

The creation of a national computer network for the NHS is one of the largest IT projects in Europe. It has been managed as an interconnected set of contracts between the public and private sector – and on the private sector side many of the organisations involved are themselves consortia with numbers of powerful players coming together to provide the capacity and range of skills required. But over the last few years, a small software house, iSoft, emerged as the most significant player in the whole network – because they supplied a key component on which the whole edifice was built. When iSoft hit financial difficulties, all the financial clout and perceived political power of the big players could do nothing to stabilize the situation, and a lot of time and money was lost as result.

It pays to understand where all your partners lie on the spectrum. Just because one player is small, you can't always afford to treat them as an anonymous and easily replaceable commodity supplier. In fact the smaller player may be the real dominant power in the relationship. But until the larger partner truly sees the need to collaborate actively, the effective functioning of the partnership is at risk.

What Are the Measures of Success?

The other key to finding your place on the spectrum is to examine your measures of success. Do those measures drive greater levels of collaboration, or do they ensure that the parties involved can deliver their part of the bargain independently from each other?

If you have a large number of output measures and a stringent auditing process to police them, this will drive the nature of your relationship toward the transactional. If, on, the other hand, the measures you adopt address the wider objectives rather than the detail – how the relationship will be sustained through the life of the partnership, how added value is shared and so on – this will tend to move you toward a more collaborative style, and you'll need to find effective ways of incentivising collaboration. What gets measured gets done – but *the way* things are measured also affects the way things are done. Measure a lot of outputs in a very transactional way and you're likely to get a transactional relationship whether you wanted it or not. We'll look at measuring success in partnerships in far more detail in Chapter 5.

Using the collaboration spectrum can help you to understand what kind of partnership you're getting yourself into. But first, a word of warning.

DON'T FIGHT SHY OF COMPLEXITY

Neither individuals nor organisations like complex relationships if they can be avoided. This means that leaders will often plump for one or other extreme of the collaboration spectrum shown below – either a close-knit team approach or a straightforwardly transactional customer/supplier relationship – and try to drive that approach through in the relationship. It may look simpler, but unfortunately it ignores crucial aspects of the relationship that are likely to come back and bite the partners later (Fig. 2.3).

Amount of Collaboration

High	Medium	Low

Symbiotic	Mutual	Transactional

Close		Distant
Same Objectives		Seperate Objectives
Loyal to the Group		Loyal to My Employer
Lots of Time Together		Little Time Together
They're Really One of Us		**They Give Us a Good Deal**

FIGURE 2.3   Finding your place on the collaboration spectrum.

The First Mistake: 'One Team' Rhetoric

Imposing a 'one team' ethos on a complex partnership can seem appealing on the surface. With many of their models adopted from sporting or military environments, teams can have heroic, do-or-die overtones. For these teams performance depends on each of the team members working in highly integrated way. People rely on each other and often can't play their own role without the support of the rest of the team.

The vision of becoming a 'high-performance team' is often talked about within organisations, and many groups aspire to this vision in their cross-organisational relationships as well. But the truth is that a partnership is not 'one team' – individuals must respond to the needs and pressures of their own 'home organisation' as well as the partnership. Pretending to be a team can be misleading at best, and at worst dangerous and damaging to morale.

Using 'one team' rhetoric when in fact you have separate reasons for entering into the partnership may also mask important differences in culture and approach. In particular, it can prevent people from airing problems early and store up conflict for later on. Partnerships shouldn't be about ironing out difference or simply pretending it isn't there – the last thing you want is to be clones of each other. In fact the most fruitful partnerships will tap into their different skills and approaches to create something that goes beyond the individual players' capabilities – an area we'll explore in more detail in Chapter 6.

Consider the case of a public–private partnership where staff are transferred (or TUPEd) over to work for a private sector organisation. A mix of public and private sector managers now leads the partnership. But if this group tries to take a traditional 'one team' approach, it risks losing much of the value civil servants were trying to gain by bringing in a different management style in the first place.

The Second Mistake: Transaction-Like Control

Seeking simplicity by trying to drive a partnership to work at the transactional end of the spectrum isn't a recipe for success either. Much has been written about supplier relationship management, but these techniques don't really apply to many partnership situations. As a powerful customer, treating your partners as a string of independent suppliers may seem attractive, but can result in each party simply doing what they are told, nothing more and nothing less.

Equally, specifying the processes and procedures of a partnership too tightly can choke a relationship if in fact there are multiple points of inter-dependence. The trend toward service level agreements for just about every-thing certainly hasn't made partnerships run more smoothly. And although the urge to control is understandable, it can cause frustration and resentment, and may even encourage subversive game-playing behaviour. In the end it's likely to lead to a blame culture, with each party pointing the finger at the other for poor performance.

The same risk of seeking to apply too much control is true in mergers. When a small company is taken over by a large multinational, for example, the temptation is to absorb the small business into the culture and corporate processes of the larger player. All too often the value of the smaller business is lost as morale dips, creativity declines and key players leave. In the end, the value of the merger is lost.

In both cases, opting for a simple operational model at either end of the collaboration spectrum can destroy the potential value of the partnership. There's no simple rule of thumb – you have to embrace complexity. Most partnerships contain elements from both extremes of the spectrum, but actually sit somewhere between them. And within the broad expanse of mutual partnership, different relationships require different degrees of collaboration. As a collaborative leader, you shouldn't rush toward straightforward models of team working or transactions. You need to get comfortable with shades of gray.

GET PICKY ABOUT WHO YOU COLLABORATE WITH AND WHY

The collaboration spectrum can also help prioritize how you work across different partnerships. When you're working with many different partnerships at one time – as we know is the case for many leaders – you can't afford to collaborate closely with everyone. It's expensive and often it's downright counterproductive. So you need to get picky.

Take, for example, the case of a government department charged with encouraging people to save for their retirement. The department can't do it alone – it needs partners from both the private sector and the third sector. It will also have to work closely with other departments – not least the Treasury. Finding the external partners is not difficult, but sustaining the right relationships over time definitely is, because suddenly everyone wants to talk to the department.

Keen to develop close relationships, departmental officials are concerned to find that all their time is swallowed up in endless partnership or stakeholder meetings. They don't have a map of what all these relationships are really for or how to get best value from them all. It's high maintenance and it requires a high level of communication – often to no purpose. Meanwhile the private and third sector partners are becoming more and more dissatisfied because they don't feel their views are being heard. Quickly, it becomes clear that the 'one team' approach is unsustainable.

Finally, the department realises that 'one size fits all' won't work in managing a complex set of partnerships like this. Each relationship needs a different amount of collaboration and a different approach – for example, more junior officials can attend the meetings with the smaller third sector organisations. The collaboration spectrum helps them negotiate the right approach with each partner – and in turn manages those partners' expectations of airtime with the department.

As a collaborative leader, then, you need to exercise discretion. Each partner won't necessarily require the same level of investment of time and effort – and shouldn't be given it. You need to select where it will be most beneficial, and put your effort into building collaboration only where you get the best return.

The Picky Collaborator's Checklist

As we've seen, indiscriminate collaboration doesn't help a partnership. You need to choose where to focus your efforts on collaborating, and where to back off.

The following questions can help you determine just how much effort to give each partner:

- **How certain can you be of the outcome?** Can you define the product or service you require clearly? And are you confident that your potential partners are fully capable of delivering it with little help from you? If so, then high levels of collaboration are a waste of effort, and you'll often be better advised to go for a productive customer/supplier relationship driven by a clear contract. In a long-term situation where the product being delivered is dependent on contributions from many parties, the investment in higher levels of collaboration may be justified. Do you and the other parties have similar assessments of the needs of the situation?

- **Where does your partner think you are on the collaboration spectrum?** Do the other parties involved assume that you will operate either in a highly interdependent or highly contractual manner? What are the signals that you and your organisation are sending to your partners about the type of the relationship that you want? Are the assumptions made by your partners explicitly stated or are they implied? What evidence do you have for your assessment? And are the demands of others realistic given the objective of the relationship and the other pressures on you?

- **What is the direction of travel?** How are the demands on the relationships in the partnership changing, and how might you need to change to meet the future needs of the situation? Instead of aiming for a close relationship at the outset, it can be better to start with lower levels of collaboration, until all parties prove they can deliver. Demonstrating that partners keep their promises helps to build high levels of trust, which, in turn, help enable the parties to collaborate more closely.

- **What will help you get there?** What processes, organisational structures and ways of working will inhibit your relationship from developing? What will enable it? If you want an effective contract-driven supplier relationship, then this demands a particular skill set and is likely to be distracted by a series of 'team building' meetings! Building relationships requires skill and the right attitudes along with the right structures and processes. What needs to be developed to help create the relationships that are required? And is this realistic?

- **What have you learned from past relationships?** Have you worked with this partner before? Does this situation require the same or a different level of collaboration, from past experience? What about your own style when it comes to cross-organisational working – do you tend to work more effectively in close highly interdependent relationships or in looser more distant relationships? What is most challenging for you in working with others? And when do you need to challenge yourself more in order to get the most from a relationship?

TELL IT LIKE IT IS

All this work to define your terms may seem a burden, but it cuts out much bigger problems down the line. Entering a relationship with a clear idea of what you're getting into prevents your wasting time on the wrong approach – and saves everyone time and money in the end. It's no use setting up expectations of high levels of collaboration if this isn't going to benefit all parties – after all, collaborative partnerships are a big investment, and have to be worth the effort for everyone involved. And realistically, no leader can expect to influence a dozen or more highly collaborative partnerships at the same time – yet half the directors questioned in our Ipsos Mori survey said they are running up to 15 concurrently, and a third said they were running more than 20.[2]

Working out where a partnership sits on the spectrum helps all parties focus on what they need to achieve their objectives. Just because one party wants a close relationship doesn't mean it should be granted: there has to be a mutual recognition of the need and the potential value in working closely together.

The spectrum also helps define where you as a leader should direct the greatest attention – not to the groups that make the most noise, but where it adds value to the partnership. By reflecting on the objectives you're trying to achieve, and on what you need from each party in order to deliver it, you may be surprised at the critical relationships that have been overlooked.

Finally, understanding the type of relationship you need makes it clear what kind of language you should be using. 'Team' talk instead of 'customer/supplier' language and vice versa can be deeply frustrating for the people involved who know the reality all too well. Categorizing your partnership properly lets you tell it like it is – and that's a whole lot healthier for everyone.

QUANTIFYING COLLABORATION: THE TEN-STEP GUIDE

We'll end this chapter with ten lessons to help you to invest your time in the right place to create the most value – and at the same time reduce frustration with partners who just don't see the relationship in the same way as you do.

---

[2] *Making Partnerships Work: A Survey of UK Senior Executives'*, Ipsos Mori and Socia, February 2007.

The Ten-Step Guide to Quantifying Collaboration

1. Understand your terminology – be clear what you mean by words like partnership and team, and check what others understand by these terms too.

2. Assess the collaboration needs of your situation. How much collaboration is needed in the relationship in order for it to deliver its objectives? Use the collaboration spectrum as a tool to help your partners visualize what is required. Don't assume that just because a relationship is called a partnership it needs a lot of collaboration to make it work.

3. Expect your partners to have different objectives and different ways of working. Don't try to turn them into clones of your own organisation.

4. Be clear about the 'points of interdependence' in the relationship. Work out where and when are you dependent on each other – these are the points where you should focus your time. Don't expect to eliminate the interdependencies – you can't control everything.

5. Relationships will change over time. Don't set things in stone – and put in regular review processes to assess how your role needs to change in response to changing needs.

6. Don't make assumptions about who is the most influential partner – size doesn't always indicate significance.

7. Be clear about where the long-term added value is created in the relationship – the value no one party could create on their own. Invest time in discussing this with your partners. It's a much better use of your leadership effort than doing endless post-mortems on past targets.

8. Look at the measures of success you have defined for the partnership – do they support the type and style of relationship that you are trying to develop?

9. If a relationship isn't working, go back to the collaboration spectrum to assess where you think the relationship needs to be, and then open up a discussion with your partners about their views.

10. Finally, avoid appearing strongly collaborative just because you feel it's a good idea or because others want you to be. Collaborative leadership is not a popularity contest.

Chapter 3

The Partnership Roadmap

KNOW WHERE YOU ARE

A partnership is not a static relationship, but a journey, made up of distinct stages covering different terrains. The beginning of a new business relationship is often difficult, with lots of deep dips, hazards and hairpin bends, and many ventures run into serious trouble. Get through these obstacles, however, and with some careful navigation, you can end up getting to your destination in good shape.

As the landscape changes, the behaviour of people within a partnership changes with it. In fact you can predict with reasonable accuracy how people are likely to behave at different stages of any partnership lifecycle. This means that leaders in charge of many partnerships at one time can't afford to standardize their approach – they have to be sensitive to the stage each individual partnership has reached. Driving flat out when you are in the mountains and the rain is starting to fall is courting disaster.

This chapter is a roadmap for any partnership (see Fig. 3.1). If you've been through plenty of joint ventures, public–private partnerships or alliances already, the four stages we describe – selection, transition, maintenance and

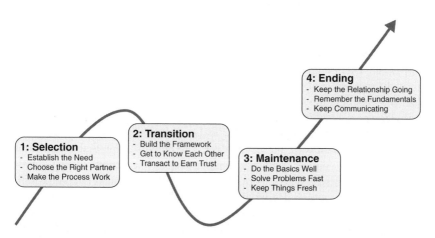

FIGURE 3.1 The partnership roadmap.

ending – should be familiar to you, and you'll probably want to skim through and only look in depth at the stages you habitually find hard. If you're starting out in leading a partnership, however, we recommend you read through this chapter in full. It shows you how to plan and deploy your resources, and which activities to prioritize at each stage – some need considerably more of your leadership time than others.

At each stage we give you two sets of road signs – first the indicators that you're on the right track, and second the danger signs that you're straying off the road. Pay attention to these and you should have a considerably easier ride.

STAGE 1: SELECTION – FIT FOR THE FUTURE

Selecting a partner and cementing the relationship can seem like an end in itself. Adrenaline-fueled teams work around the clock to seal the deal, hordes of advisers descend to fight it out, the contract is scrutinized in minute detail, and the whole process accelerates faster and faster up to the moment of signing.

But a partnership is considerably more than the deal. The early selection process should look not just at current fit but whether the relationship can go the distance. After the champagne and balloons comes the hard reality of getting on with the job. And while partnerships aren't for life, they tend to last many years, and sometimes decades.

Establish the Mutual Need

The first step in selection is to understand the exact nature of the mutual need. All parties should know what they stand to gain from a partnership and what each party can contribute toward it. Even more importantly, they need to understand what the real value is in the relationship and how it is created in ways that no one party could achieve on their own.

From there they can decide on the right model, which may not be a partnership at all. There might be a case for another kind of relationship altogether – a purely transactional one or even a merger or acquisition. A 2004 study in *Harvard Business Review* suggests that many acquisitions should be alliances and vice versa, resulting in high levels of failure for both. All too often, firms adopt the wrong strategy for their particular circumstances, destroy the value and watch the talent walk out of the door. The authors argue that acquisitions work best when you are combining hard resources like manufacturing plants, or when you generate synergies by sharing knowledge iteratively and customizing resources to a high degree, that is, by working more as a team. However if you're combining human resources rather than buildings or machinery, if you aim to generate synergies by one company completing a task and passing it on to the next, or if the outcome is very uncertain, you are best off choosing an alliance.[1]

Once you're set on a partnership route, it's important to unpick the meanings of terms like 'alliance' or 'partnership' and make sure all parties are using them in the same way. The collaboration spectrum discussed in Chapter 2 can help would-be partners work out the most appropriate model of joint working to deliver their business case. Mapping out each party's resource contributions and drafting joint success criteria will also help clarify the model.

Far more difficult is working out whether a potential partner has the right capability for your needs – not only now, but later on in the relationship's lifecycle. John Yard, leader of the Inland Revenue's massive IT outsourcing project in the 1990s, believes it is crucial to see beyond short-term suitability. 'I look for partners with the capability to give me what I asked for in the first year or two, then look for evidence of a capability to understand what my challenges might be in years three and four', he says. 'I want to have confidence they can deliver today, and that I'll be able to have profitable conversations about the future, when the time comes'.

However that assessment can be tricky. 'It's difficult to get people into the room before a contract is in place, to talk about what is really possible', says Julie Baddeley, adviser and board member on several major partnerships. 'It's hard because until the partnership is established, people don't want to enter into those conversations'. Without them, however, you have no idea of what you're letting yourself in for.

Choose a Partner You Can Work With

Even when partners can demonstrate both current and future capability, it may not be enough. It's not just what you do, but how you do it – as a conservative-minded building society from North of England found to its cost. Seeking to launch a new credit card, the building society eventually found a partner that seemed ideally suited to its needs. The credit card company was well known, respected and efficient. The problem was that its marketing methods were way too aggressive for the building society's taste.

While the credit card company tried to seek out new customers, the building society worried about its members getting into debt. The consequence for each side was profoundly unsatisfactory – the building society felt it was putting its relationship with members at risk, and the credit card company couldn't generate the volume it expected. The partnership soon foundered.

This doesn't mean that organisations should only seek out like-minded partners, as we'll see in Chapter 4, collaboration is not about cloning. Characters

---

[1] 'When to Ally and When to Acquire', Jeffrey H. Dyer, Prashant Kale and Harbir Singh, *Harvard Business Review*, July–August 2004.

and approaches can be radically different, yet still complementary. Difference matters – it's often the reason for the partnership in the first place.

However, you do need to know yourself thoroughly before being able to partner effectively. If you trade on your reputation as a local bank, you can't outsource to a call center on another continent, however attractive it might seem. If paternalism is paramount to your business, you shouldn't choose to collaborate with people who thrive on opportunism. And if you want to change the world, there's little point in entering a partnership with people who only want to change their bottom line.

Don't Let the Process Ruin the Relationship

Unfortunately the process of selecting a partner often seems designed to cause maximum damage to a fledgling partnership. At the point when you most need to get below the surface with potential partners, you're least likely to be able to do so. 'You end up with two principals surrounded by an entourage of advisers, all focusing on doing the deal within the timeframe and pulling the leaders away from each other', says Julie Baddeley. 'It makes it very difficult to focus on what's happening post-deal'.

In public–private partnerships in particular, the need to demonstrate fairness and value for money to a skeptical public has led to complicated, costly and highly formal tendering processes. Creating an enormous machine to run an apparently fair process puts heavy pressure on leaders to close the deal at all costs. Yet such tenders can become deeply adversarial: instead of assessing each other's cultures, would-be partners end up trying to extract the last pound of flesh from each other.

Defining the contract can be especially hostile, and this may well set the tone for the partnership in later stages. For some relationships it can prove a death knell. When London Underground's partnership with Metronet to refurbish the tube system ended with Metronet going into administration, Christian Wolmar wrote in the *New Statesman*: 'Flawed at the outset, the contracts proved to be unworkable. Their sheer detail and complexity ensured that. They were full of enormously complex formulae and ridiculous notions like rewarding contractors for moving toilets nearer the drivers' cabs at the end of the lines so they would take less time going to the loo between journeys'.[2]

While advisers insist on caution, it is leaders who have to deliver the partnership later down the line. 'It takes self-confidence to put your foot down', says John Yard. 'I'm straight with procurement – I say "you're advising me, but I will decide what to do, and I will decide the level of risk"'.

For some would-be partnerships, the burden of the selection process is simply too heavy. The £12.4 billion NHS National Programme for IT is a good

---

[2] 'The PPP is Gordon's fault', Christian Wolmar, *Evening Standard*, 17 July 2007.

case in point – in May 2003 potential bidders for what was to be the world's largest non-military IT project were given a 500-page 'output-based specifica- tion' document which was described as 'work in progress' and told they had to submit proposals in a little over a month. Little wonder that some of the most prominent bidders pulled out at the proposal stage. Contracts were awarded in October 2003, when only 190 days had elapsed between advertising the contract and awarding it. This was described as a 'ground-breaking schedule', but its enormous intensity had disturbing consequences. Not only did several potentially useful partners pull out in the selection phase, but Sir Christopher Bland, chairman of BT, which was one of the successful bidders, described the process as a 'slightly like a dog chasing a car. What do we do if we catch it? Well now we've caught it'.[3]

Learning from the lessons of failed partnerships, the government is now approaching selection with greater sophistication. Local authorities, for exam- ple, are being advised that price is not the be-all and end-all in choosing a partner. Potential partners need to be clear about their own goals, vision and values and those of their partner, the objectives of each, the different partner- ship models available and the economic case for each model. They must also pay attention to 'softer' issues, such as 'a clear understanding of each oth- ers' organisational imperatives, and how those imperatives are likely to feed through into day-to-day working arrangements'.[4] The Office of the Deputy Prime Minister publishes a useful assessment tool to help local authorities select a partner, which includes these types of considerations.[5] Meanwhile best practice advice from the Office of Government Commerce (OGC) now recom- mends that 'serious efforts [should be] made to align both the department's and the partner's culture and strategies',[6] and that 'the "soft" requirement for a productive, creative and trust-based relationship should be held in equal regard with the "hard" requirements for technical capability, workload capacity and track record'.[7]

There are encouraging signs of these less adversarial methods coming into use in the most high profile of projects. When the government was looking for a key partner to manage the construction of the 2012 Olympics site, it ran an assessment center for bidders to rate them on a wide range of criteria, not merely on price. The purpose of this approach, according to the ODA draft

---

[3] 'Health Officials say IT Scheme has Enough Scrutiny in Response to Technical Audit Call', Tony Collins, *Computer Weekly*, 18 April 2006.

[4] *Rethinking Service Delivery, Volume 3, Public Private Partnerships*, Office of the Deputy Prime Minister, 2004.

[5] *Assessing Strategic Partnership: The Partnership Assessment Tool*, Office of the Deputy Prime Minister, 2003.

[6] *Forming Partnering Relationships with the Private Sector in an Uncertain World*, Office of Government Commerce, 2002.

[7] *Effective Partnering – An Overview for Customers and Suppliers*, Office of Government Commerce, 2003.

Selection Road Signs

You know you're on the right track if:

- There is a business requirement for two or more organisations to form an alliance or partnership.
- All parties are involved in drawing up contractual arrangements.
- There is clear understanding of the risks involved, and of who is best able and best placed to manage them.
- Lessons from previous partnerships/contracts have been recognized and taken into account.
- The evaluation process includes mechanisms for learning from previous experiences of working with these potential partners.
- The selection process allows you to get to know your potential partners, you feel that you understand each other's strengths and weaknesses, and are confident that you will be able to work together.
- As a result of the selection process and the relationships formed through it, there is a good understanding of what needs to be done in the transition phase to get partners up to speed and to bridge cultural gaps.

You know you're going off track if:

- There is no clear understanding or agreement about the terms of the relationship needed to meet the business requirement.
- There is disagreement and conflict about where risks should be allocated between parties.
- Parties are talking about partnership and alliance but meaning different things by the terms.
- Key players (stakeholders) aren't engaged in planning discussions – conflict is being avoided.
- No allowance is made for relationship measures in the evaluation process.
- The mechanics of the selection process are throwing up a prime candidate that people feel will be difficult to work with in some way.
- Key business representatives who will implement the contract are not involved in the selection process.

procurement policy document, was to 'dispel the misconception that bids will be won on lowest price alone'.

STAGE 2: TRANSITION – SUSPEND JUDGMENT

In the transition stage – the vital first 100 days – partners have to learn to work together instead of merely building a contract together. It's easy to erode the value of an alliance for good here, and getting this stage wrong is a prime reason for the failure of many partnerships.

Nonetheless, you can't expect the partnership to work from day one – the transition phase is characterized by things going wrong. The key to managing here is not expecting perfection, but putting problems right fast. Leaders need to suspend judgment, and persuade key people throughout the partnership to do the same.

Build the Framework

Early actions have long-lasting impacts. So it's important to avoid rushing the bonding process on a partnership. Don't take a bunch of managers out whitewater rafting in the Lake District during the transition phase and think that the relationship job is done – it will be a disaster. This is absolutely not the moment for formal team building, and at this stage you don't know that taking a one-team approach will be the right answer anyway. Instead, get the structure right. Leaders should use this time to set up the relationship properly and jointly define governance processes, the measurement to be used throughout the partnership, escalation procedures, communication plans and so on.

In the next chapter we cover the framework of a partnership in detail. Remember, however, that the first 100 days are a special case and need to be treated separately. Set up dedicated and experienced transition governance and project management – research suggests that under-investment here can jeopardize the long-term health of the project.[8] In addition, our Ipsos Mori poll showed that 86% of respondents agreed that 'more planning at the set-up stage would have helped to avoid most operational problems later on'.[9]

So create a joint 100-day partnership plan. Identify champions within each business to support the partnership. Work out the ground rules for compensating each parent organisation for contributing specific services to the partnership. Go through the contract with a fine toothcomb and pick out the incentives and disincentives to what you're trying to achieve, and start ironing out the disincentives.

Above all, don't try to be too close. The first 100 days should stay relatively transactional. Each party needs to get on with their own side of the project, and keep out of each other's hair, that way they can begin to build trust by delivering what they've promised. You can use the collaboration spectrum (described in Chapter 2) to track how each party sees the level of collaboration within the relationship developing over time. Our advice would be to start by delivering

---

[8] 'Launching a World Class Joint Venture', James Bamford, David Ernst and David G. Fubini, *Harvard Business Review*, February 2004.
[9] *Making Partnerships Work: A Survey of UK Senior Executives*, Ipsos Mori and Socia, February 2007.

reliable transactions to each other and build up from there. In the early days, you shouldn't attempt to operate with the level of closeness you may aspire to once you know each other well. So be clear about the direction of travel, but don't be surprised if things slip back at times.

The need to track the progress of a relationship in the early days means that measurement also needs special consideration during transition. Over-expectation breeds failure, and a partnership can't start using the contractual productivity measures from day one. There is no point in hauling new suppliers over the coals in the first few weeks for missing their targets – that merely causes bad feeling and sets up a relationship to fail. By the same token, if you've changed a supplier, you shouldn't expect the new one to achieve the levels of your previous one straightaway. Instead, leaders need to set transitional measures with joint 100-day targets and include relationship measures as well as financial ones.

Get to Know Each Other

This is also the time for all parties to get to know each better. That doesn't mean pretending you're a team – you're not, and nor should you be. In fact we'd go as far as to say that if a newsletter emerges during transition proclaiming 'One team-one vision', you're asking for serious trouble.

In Chapter 10 (page 165), we talk about three stages of group formation to describe the psychological states that people go through when joining a newly formed group. Trying to short-circuit this process and leap straight to a state of assumed closeness will always appear false and simply doesn't work.

However, informal ways of learning about each other are very useful at this stage. Leaders should arrange a set of dinners for key people to meet each other out of their business context. Teams on one side should meet their opposite numbers (without having to perform tasks or play games). Inductions should be arranged for anyone joining the partnership who hasn't been involved earlier. And as far as possible down the hierarchy, individuals should get a chance to meet their counterparts within the partnership.

It's also worth incorporating more formal methods of understanding each other's culture. Transition is a useful opportunity to take a baseline reading of each party's organisational character in order to understand strengths and weaknesses on either side and to work out how best to collaborate in the future. This is covered in more detail in Chapter 6.

Show What Success Looks Like

After the adrenaline charge of making the deal, the transition stage can be an abrupt return to reality. You may find that staff are cynical about the partnership and that disagreements flourish. New people come on board who weren't part of the selection process and who want to make their reputation by doing things differently. And inevitably a whole lot of things will go wrong.

The first 100 days are testing times. Mistakes get blown out of all proportion. People revert to their original prejudices or happily embrace new ones. They may even start questioning whether they made the right decision in choosing a particular partner. The honeymoon is definitely over.

When this happens, it's time to go back to transacting. Each party has to earn trust and the best way to do that is to deliver. In addition, leaders need to demonstrate what success for all parties might look like. One way is to develop a partnership charter in which the leaders of each of the parties involved can set out some of the principles of how they will work together and what benefits they will generate as a result. For a charter to be valuable, it must be practical and help people at all levels to make decisions about how they deal with their partners.

For example, the partnership charter[10] between the London Borough of Kensington and Chelsea and their waste disposal and recycling partner states that 'to foster a successful working partnership at every level, the partners will ensure that:

- The contractor's staff will work immediately alongside the Council's staff, and not occupy separate rooms.
- Staff secondments between the partners will be encouraged.
- Joint training and induction of staff will be encouraged.
- The partners will share the same information and communication systems'.

Another useful activity in these early days is to find a number of pilot projects in non-critical areas where you can get teams working across boundaries to learn lessons in collaboration in a relatively low-risk environment. Pilot projects allow you to notch up some quick wins, not only in terms of delivering results, but also in understanding each other's processes and culture and in building interpersonal relationships that will be invaluable as you move into a steady state.

Finally, leaders should make sure everyone understands when transition is over. Transition is a countdown. It shouldn't drag on – people need a definite end point to work toward. They need to gear up to full-scale measures. And everyone has to understand that after this point, the real business of partnership begins.

---

[10]*Partnership Contract for Recycling, Waste Collection, Street Cleansing and Related Services*, Royal Borough of Kensington and Chelsea, available at http://rbkc.gov.uk/yourcouncil/foicontracts/wm_foi_partnershipcharter_main.pdf

100 Day Road Signs

You know you're on the right track if:

- All parties have put the necessary time and resource into the induction and set-up process.
- There is a single transition timetable and resource plan that all parties refer to on a regular basis.
- There are early opportunities to observe the capabilities and culture of all parties on pilot projects and other real-life tasks.
- Special transition governance arrangements are in place to facilitate rapid decision-making in this phase.
- Partnership project meetings focus on short-term joint problem-solving and risk management.
- There is evidence that partners are delivering on their short-term promises (in other words, transact before you can partner).
- There is a communication plan that has credibility with stakeholders, and consistent messages are being communicated across the partnership.
- A set of measures has been defined for the partnership, including a good balance of relationship measures as well as delivery measures.
- A clear end to the transition phase has been defined, which people are jointly working toward.

You know you're going off track if:

- Leaders are talking cynically about their new partners from day one, and the general feeling is 'I don't know why we chose this bunch'!
- Partnership project meetings are taken up with lengthy discussion about the contract.
- The main decision-making body (or steering group) isn't due to meet until the transition phase is nearly complete.
- Partners are working to their own plans, which are not shared.
- The first version of the partnership performance scorecard is mostly red because delivery of performance isn't up to the target specified in the contract, rather than specific targets for transition.
- Stakeholders complain that they don't know who to contact any more to get things done.
- New people have come in to manage the delivery (on all sides) and don't seem to know about the overall intention, let alone the details of the contract that was signed only a few months ago.
- One hundred days in, many people haven't met their opposite number in the partnership outside of a formal meeting.
- The phase seems to be dragging on and on, and no one knows when the partnership will enter a steady state.

STAGE 3: MAINTENANCE – KEEP THE MACHINE RUNNING

When you reach the third (and usually by far the longest) stage of a partnership, you take the brakes off and start motoring. This is where you drive out the real value of the relationship – fulfilling financial and productivity measures, rising to new challenges and taking advantage of the opportunities that come your way. But amid the rush to realize the objectives of your collaboration, you also need to remember to maintain and nurture the relationship.

Do the Basics Well

By now partners should have settled down into their roles, recognized each other's competencies (and deficiencies) and begun to get used to each other's different ways of working. Now you need to get the fundamentals absolutely right, honing governance, systems and behaviours to make them work as well as they possibly can. Look at things like the joint risk register – does it sit in a drawer for 3 months, or does it reflect the reality of the partnership and give early warning of the things that matter? Are the escalation procedures being used? And are partners sticking rigidly to their own information gathering or using one set of data?

It will gradually become clear how well individuals are able to collaborate when necessary and leaders need to support and coach subordinates in acquiring the requisite skills. Even more crucially, the partnership needs to keep developing talent so that staff don't see it as a dead end. Put in place joint programs to build leadership capability and develop skills that will be needed in the future.

You should also continue to monitor how cultural differences are affecting performance and how you can use differences to your best advantage. If you took a baseline reading in the transition phase, you should follow it up. If not, do it now, and keep on building your understanding of each other throughout the maintenance phase. Now is the time to invest in building joint teams in specific areas of the partnership that require close cooperation or integrated working. All the traditional tools of individual and team development – personality profiling, 360° feedback, away days and the like – can come into play here. The point is not to apply them uniformly, but to focus team building effort where it is most required, in areas of high interdependence between the partners.

As the relationship deepens, each party should get more comfortable about sharing more information and activities. Meanwhile, leaders need to continue to keep up the communication – involving people in both the short-term and long-term objectives, and highlighting both successes and failures, without resorting to propaganda. As things settle into a more established routine, it's easy to get blasé about these basics, but without good communication, a partnership will get bumpy surprisingly fast.

Tackle Problems Fast

Problems will of course continue throughout the maintenance stage and they may get considerably bigger. 'The start of a partnership is like a honeymoon – and then you go skiing', says John Yard. 'Round about year one or two you find you're going right down a slope, and you realise you can't go on like this. Either you crash or you start slogging back up the hill'.

The obvious issues are productivity failures – one or more parties may miss a milestone, raising the specter of penalties and all the resentments they can cause. Other problems may be less overt but more invidious. You might see poor decision-making, mismatches in how you measure progress or define success, a general lack of trust or faith in the future or even a relationship breakdown between individuals. All of these need to be addressed and it takes confidence, tact and firmness to deal with them effectively.

It's the job of leaders to spot the risks, prepare for them and tackle problems before they spiral out of control. No one can iron them out completely – problems are part of the process. But when they happen, leaders should go back to the fundamental framework of the partnership and check that it is all sound. Is the governance sufficiently robust? Are escalation procedures well defined and used when necessary? Have all parties aligned their systems and processes? Are measurement processes well defined, understood by all, and forward looking as well as retrospective? (For a detailed look at measurement, see Chapter 5.) And is behaviour – either individual or organisational – getting in the way of your goals?

It's important to read the warning signals early and to act swiftly when things go wrong. A classic example is the story of Nokia and Ericsson's different reactions to a failure in supply.[11] In March 2000, a fire in a Philips semiconductor plant in New Mexico destroyed or contaminated millions of mobile phone chips. Nokia and Ericsson accounted for 40% of the supplier's business and were duly prioritized by Philips. However, the difference of speed in the way each firm reacted had a radical effect on the outcome.

Three days after the fire, Nokia realized orders were not coming through as expected, so phoned the supplier and were told deliveries would be disrupted for about a week. They sent engineers to New Mexico to investigate, but when this was discouraged, they started daily checks on incoming supplies. As the depth of the problem emerged, Nokia exerted pressure to ensure all other Philips plants would deploy spare capacity to meet the order, and worked with other suppliers to escalate their production. At the same time it reconfigured its products to accept slightly different chips from other sources.

Meanwhile Ericsson accepted the suppliers' assurance that the problem was a small one. By the time Ericsson finally acted, Nokia had secured all sources

[11]*Creating Resilient Supply Chains: A Practical Guide*, Cranfield School of Management, 2003.

of supply. Ericsson lost an estimated $400 million in new product sales and Nokia consolidated its pole position in the market.

Sometimes the problem is closer to home and you need to grasp the nettle within your own organisation. John Yard tells a story of a personality clash between two otherwise extremely able managers that was causing problems in a partnership. Realizing the problem was continuing, Yard gave the managers a deadline – either they dealt with their relationship within a month or one of them would have to go. A month later he had to follow through with his threat. 'It wasn't about their capability, and I helped the guy who left to find another job – it was just one of those things that you can't have in a partnership', he says. 'But dealing with the problem definitely raised my credibility within the partnership'.

Finally if things are seriously breaking down, the best thing to do is to step back from collaborating and go back to transacting. When each party is delivering their side of the bargain effectively, you can start rebuilding trust in the relationship.

Keep Things Fresh

The maintenance stage is very different from the heady early days of a partnership. It's about getting on with the job, and some people will inevitably feel that the job has already been done. As things settle down, people become complacent, and you see leadership delegated down the hierarchy, deputies appearing at meetings and constant changes of face. The relationship risks going stale.

Leaders need to work hard throughout this stage to prevent this. Running regular health checks on the quality of the relationship – including detailed perception data – is essential. As the partnership matures, the potential problems are less obvious and you risk being taken by surprise, perhaps by something that didn't even feature on the risk register. Forward measurement (covered in Chapter 5) will help you predict the pitfalls, and scenario planning helps you prepare for them. Even more important is keeping your ear to the ground, and regularly asking your subordinates about what worries them.

You also need to respond to changing circumstances, and be alive to both risk and opportunity. Key people will change and new people need to be inducted into the partnership. Political, legal or regulatory changes may force a rethink of strategy. The business environment may alter dramatically. In every case the partnership needs to be prepared and poised to act. Whatever happens, it's important that the whole partnership understands the new climate and the possibilities it offers. Run one-off events to involve all parties in re-setting the strategy to take account of the changes, and make sure you communicate the new direction to all stakeholders.

When change happens, you need to rely on the relationships you've built. Close personal relationships, with your opposite numbers within the partnership and with other stakeholders, will come into their own and increase your flexibility in responding to change. For former Premier Oil CEO Charles Jamieson, they're the cornerstone of running a successful partnership – especially in an industry like oil where there are major highs and lows. 'You need to make friends with people', he says. 'And when something happens, you need to have a good enough relationship with your opposite number to ring them up and jump on a plane'.

Maintenance Road Signs

You know you're on the right track if:

- All partners are using the same set of data to view performance of the partnership.
- There is evidence of regular review of the quality of the relationship.
- There are practical and efficient escalation processes – used by all parties to identify and progress problems quickly.
- There are mechanisms in place to engage staff in the objectives and the progress of the partnership and to encourage them to feed in ideas to improve the way that the partnership functions.
- Joint programs exist to develop leadership capability across the partnership.
- There is a single joint risk register with agreed plans for mitigation for common risks.
- Senior leaders take personal responsibility to undertake the difficult conversations they need to solve partnership problems actively with their opposite numbers.
- The partnership looks ahead for significant changes, and picks them up and responds to them.

You know you're going off track if:

- Delays occur in addressing problems in the partnership – people are kept waiting for formal meetings, or communication is very poor.
- There is always a last-minute scramble to get the right skills in the right place, and therefore a sense of chaotic resourcing.
- There is an unwillingness to share resources, information or even space between parties.
- Leaders don't have a personal relationship with their opposite number.
- Deputies appear regularly at partnership meetings, or meetings are canceled.
- There is no clear communication of successes or of progress in the relationship to staff or stakeholders.
- Leaders are not bringing in ideas and best practice to the partnership from outside.

STAGE 4: ENDING - DON'T BURN YOUR BRIDGES

Breaking up is hard to do. Yet collaborative leaders need to get good at it, because partnerships rarely last for ever, and most have an inbuilt obsolescence. Skill in handling endings may often not be seen as being as crucial as getting the launch right, but it's nonetheless important. Sometimes a partnership drags on without a managed ending long after it's ceased to create value. Sometimes you need to re-tender to inject new life into the project or re-set its direction. And if a partnership truly isn't working, you have to walk away from it. Whatever the ending, remember that it's a small world, and you may end up working with the same partner again.

Re-Tendering a Contract: Keep the Relationship Going

When a contract approaches its end, but there's still the need for a partnership, it's time to re-evaluate existing relationships. Leaders need to assess what has worked in the partnership and what hasn't, and determine what they would like to change in the new contract and whether they intend to switch partners or not. This assessment should cover not just productivity and performance, but how the process worked, which skills were needed and which were in short supply, how leaders performed and how cultural difference and communication was managed between partners.

The problem of course is that this is a searing time for the incumbent. It's important for the lead side to maintain a strong relationship with their partner throughout this time – if the relationship is suspended because of procurement obligations, it will be hard to rebuild it later. Don't destroy the open communication you've developed over the course of the partnership by suddenly closing down and refusing to share information in deference to unwritten rules. Above all, don't bad-mouth your partner to other organisations tendering for the contract.

It's also important not to get distracted by the new contract. Create specific governance for the tender in parallel to the partnership governance, so that leaders remain focused – they need to be highly involved in concluding the old relationship, particularly during a handover period. Be clear about accountabilities, and don't leave it to chance that the outgoing partner and the new one will work collaboratively. You need to incentivize collaboration to make it happen – not only through financial incentives, but by building pride in a job well done.

You also need to communicate to everyone within the partnership exactly what will be happening and how. Whenever one of the construction companies we work with succeeds another contractor in a roads maintenance project, managers are aware of the risk that essential hand tools and road-digging equipment could disappear overnight in the changeover. So as part of their plan, they go around to the road workers in advance explaining that if there are any scrap or waste materials as part of the handover, they are welcome to keep them, but that all tools will be logged in an inventory and needed from that day on.

Job Done – Remember the Fundamentals

Many partnerships have very specific and time-limited deliverables and so come to a natural end. A new hospital gets completed under a PFI contract. An aircraft is finally built. An oil field runs out. Even if a new contract is to begin immediately afterwards, all alliances need well-managed conclusions. The last thing you want is for performance to fall away as people take their eye off the ball.

In the final months and weeks, everyone needs to understand exactly what needs to be delivered before the close of the project and what they are accountable for. The relationship should become more transactional again, with each side getting on with their list of deliverables.

Even though the end is visible, you can't afford to neglect the basics. You need fast decision-making, and specific, detailed communications throughout. You're likely to have to spend more time on governance, not less. And you should avoid disengaging from your partners too soon – keep the relationship open and direct.

Finally, as the end of the project approaches, you also need to build in time to identify the learning before everyone goes their separate ways. This should embrace not just technical issues, but what you've learned about behaviour in the partnership.

Forced Endings: Keep Communicating

Unfortunately some partnerships will end in tears. Disasters happen – businesses go into administration, stock markets crash, companies merge or get taken over – and all can have fatal consequences for partnerships. And sometimes the problem may be in the choice of partner: if there's no way of reconciling opposing objectives or conflicting values, you need to part company.

When disaster strikes, don't panic. This is the time for sober assessment before taking action; fast decisions are usually ill-advised. And the reality is that partnerships usually take a long time to disentangle. When Charles Jamieson was head of Premier Oil, he entered a partnership with Shell in Pakistan, where each side's strategies began to diverge so much that collaboration was proving impossible. Realizing the joint venture had become unworkable, Jamieson began the elaborate process of dismantling it. 'They were very sensitive about why we would want to do this', he says. 'I had to explain it was for corporate reasons and nothing to do with them personally. It took us 18 months to get into the partnership with Shell – and 18 months to get out of it'.

Charles Jamieson believes it's crucial for leaders to hammer out a preliminary solution before resorting to legal niceties. 'You need to go to your opposite number and get them to agree in principle before you let the lawyers work it out', says Jamieson. 'It's important to have agreed it at a high enough level before you throw it to the wolves'.

You're also likely to need changes of governance to address the demands of the new situation. Level-headedness is important; rather than rushing around to little purpose, exert control by re-setting the relationship, for example, by getting leaders from all sides together on a weekly basis with a new remit.

Finally, communicate more rather than less throughout the break-up. You need to get stakeholders on your side to support you through the difficulties, and if you've built up a network of strong relationships within and outside the partnership, this investment will pay off in a crisis.

Endings Road Signs

You know you're on the right track if:

- Leaders keep communicating with their opposite numbers, no matter how difficult the circumstances.
- Everyone is willing to learn and share the lessons from the partnership experience.
- Partners are willing to write references or testimonials for each other.
- Partners are jointly aware of the end point of the contract and are clear about their own accountabilities right up to that point.
- There are clear and agreed handover plans and a process to involve the successors in what happens next.

You know you're going off track if:

- Leaders are distracted by negotiating the next contract rather than paying attention to managing the current situation.
- Performance falls away over time, and this is not effectively addressed by the existing performance management/incentives process.
- Key people leave because they don't see future career opportunities in this contract.
- Vacancies are left unfilled without agreement.
- Leaders bad-mouth existing partners as they start the selection process for a new contract.
- Response times increase for any query or request for change.

THE PARTNERSHIP ROADMAP AND COLLABORATION

The roadmap we've outlined throughout this chapter is of course highly simplified. There are likely to be many peaks and troughs throughout the journey, as well as the odd detour. However, the stages remain highly distinct, and understanding their characteristics – and acting upon them – is an important leadership skill. Although some partnerships last decades – Shell and ExxonMobil in the North Sea, for example – this isn't the norm; usually there is an end in sight. That gives a clear shape to the journey, and you need to suit your pace – and your collaboration levels – to each terrain you cross.

One of the lessons of the roadmap is to show when close collaboration makes most sense. You can't rush trust, and pushing for a highly collaborative style in the early days is counterproductive. You should start out by transacting and go back to it at the closing stage, getting on with your own jobs with as little interference as possible. In the maintenance phase, however, collaboration comes into its own – you need to nurture and develop it, removing the barriers that make it difficult for each side. Only then can you start building the rewards that joint working was intended to bring.

Chapter 4

The Three-Legged Stool

BUILD A STABLE FRAMEWORK

Starting work in a collaborative leadership role can be a remarkably unsettling experience. Issues come at you from all directions, and the traditional mechanisms of exerting control may not work when you have to share your power with other parties.

Over the years we've developed a simple and robust framework to help leaders work out where to focus their time and effort to bring a new partnership into line, or to keep an existing partnership on track. We call it the three-legged stool, and not only is it a useful way to ground yourself at the outset, but it remains vital throughout the life of the partnership.

Over the course of this chapter we'll look in detail at the three-legged stool and how you can use it to build stability into your partnership. But before we do that, we'll start with a story that illustrates the dilemma of one leader faced with the difficult task of collaborating across several functions and organisations. It is based on a combination of the real experiences that leaders typically faced at the start of a new partnership or when taking over a collaborative leadership role.

Eleanor's story: IT isn't working

Eleanor has just been appointed chief information officer of an NHS Trust. It's a challenging post – the Trust wants to bring in new infrastructure, as well as trialing new ways of working, such as remote laptops for district nurses. With 40 IT staff, she's responsible for 10 000 IT users on three different sites. At the same time she's expected to bring in several new systems – without disrupting care services. All of this is complicated by the NHS setting up central contracts for new IT infrastructure as part of the national Connecting for Health program.

On her first day she's faced with a barrage of urgent tasks. Two IT suppliers who've just been awarded major new contracts are jostling for position. Both want to have the key relationship, and both want meetings straightaway. Meanwhile there are already signs of dissent among the hospital consultants who are due to get a new 'consultants portal' to give them all the data they need through one screen. The overall reliability of the systems isn't high, and is forecast to get worse in the short term as old infrastructure is ripped out and new cables are installed. To top it all, her own department is in permanent crisis mode, and its reputation is falling fast. As Eleanor walks through the corridors to her office, she sees that someone has put a big handwritten sign on one of the notice boards which simply says, 'IT isn't working'.

Sitting down at her desk to review the situation, Eleanor could adopt any one of three classic responses. She could decide that the supplier contracts are the most important thing, take a couple of days to understand them inside and out and then bring in the legal department to see what room she has for maneuver. She could concentrate on processes, hiring management consultants to map out every step from supplier to end user, benchmarking against best practice, and designing an ideal workflow. Or she could take a team building approach, starting with the problems in her own department and moving on to try to build a common IT vision throughout the trust. But the truth is that in a network of complex relationships like this, none of these classic responses taken on their own will get Eleanor very far.

Instead, the first thing she should do at this point is identify her critical issues and then map out her key relationships and work out how much attention they really require, which is discussed in Chapter 2. Understanding the interdependencies in each relationship and plotting them on the collaboration spectrum (see Chapter 2, page 23) will uncover which ones require high levels of collaboration and which can be tightly specified and then left to run with minimal involvement. For example, the provision of office and mobile PCs, including the ones being trialed by district nurses, is a fairly standard contract, with low dependence on other systems, and can be run in a transactional way. This means Eleanor can keep one of the demanding suppliers at arm's length, and put in place an account manager to handle the relationship.

The consultant portal, however, demands close attention. It gives consultants access to patient records and specialist information about their job – and it is both highly interdependent and highly significant. First of all, it is new technology, which means that even the supplier is anxious, while the consultants are downright jumpy. If they're unhappy with the delivery of service, Eleanor's staff – and quite possibly some patients – will suffer. And as a project, it is at the center of a Web of other significant IT systems and organisational relationships – its perceived success or failure will have knock-on effects in all sorts of places. Eleanor needs to focus on involving the consultants and making this system work.

Mapping out the significance and degree of interdependence of each project gives Eleanor a clear sense of what she personally needs to tackle first. The consultant portal scores highly on both – and it's an area she needs to prioritize.

Eleanor's next step should be to look closely at each relationship and check that all partnerships are built on solid ground. Over the rest of the chapter, we explore a simple but effective model for doing this. As we examine each part, we'll come back to Eleanor's story, and look at what she should do under each heading.

GOVERNANCE, OPERATIONS AND BEHAVIOURS – THE THREE-LEGGED STOOL

Any partnership needs a strong framework to see it through the bad times as well as the good. The model we use is based on our experience in working across scores of partnerships and collaborative ventures. It's simple, but highly effective, and it helps you plan where to focus your leadership time and effort in situations like the one Eleanor is facing in our example. It's called the three-legged stool.

There are three areas to focus on: governance, operations and behaviours – and each is important. As with a three-legged stool, miss out one leg and the partnership quickly becomes unstable (Fig. 4.1).

- By *governance* we mean the ways objectives are set, accountabilities are defined and decisions are made across the partnership.
- By *operations* we mean the process by which things get done, progress is measured and communicated and information and learning is shared.
- By *behaviours* we mean the way people act with each other to produce joint results.

In practice we've seen partnerships built on only one of these three legs, but they tend not to be resilient – something changes and they are vulnerable.

- *Governance*: A partnership built on strong contracts and formal govern-ance is often inflexible and slow to respond. People stick to the letter of the contract – there are often penalties in place if they don't and so they are unwilling to put themselves out to help their partners. That means that new opportunities can be missed – or the competition gets there first.
- *Operations*: A partnership built on slick processes and operations can be more adaptable – especially if the feedback and improvement processes are strong. A lot of the success of manufacturing and supply chain partnerships has come from a focus on efficient operations. But a pure focus on process

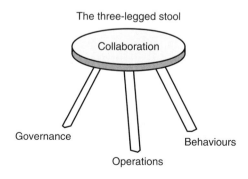

FIGURE 4.1 The three legged stool – essential elements of collaboration.

The focus of leadership
At different points on the collaboration spectrum

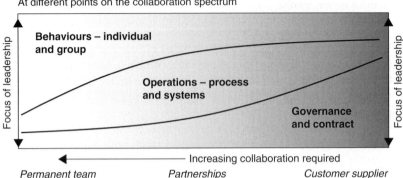

FIGURE 4.2   Governance, operations and behaviours.

can produce systems which aren't good at dealing with strategic change. They find it difficult when they need to shift direction and perhaps to throw away many of the old systems and start again. The governance isn't there to force a re-evaluation of the situation, and the right behaviours haven't been encouraged to make people feel able to raise the awkward questions that inspire change.

- *Behaviours*: A partnership that focuses on getting the behaviours right might look ideal at first glance – but it's only sustainable if the other two legs are in place as well. Truly collaborative leadership behaviours and great relationships between people at all levels can get you a long way. But although people may start off with the best intentions to work closely with their partners, contracts and incentives drive behaviours, and if these are wrong, the tensions will build up over time. And what happens when the key people move on or fall out with each other? Suddenly there can be nothing left to fall back on.

The results of our Ipsos Mori survey showed that the majority of directors questioned had put most of their efforts to date into operations – closely followed by governance. However, over half thought that the greatest additional value was to be gained by focusing more on behaviours.[1]

The diagram below (Fig. 4.2) illustrates where we believe the focus of leadership attention should be, and the relative amount of effort required in the three areas of governance, operations and behaviours.

Although all three areas matter, the emphasis on each will vary according to where a partnership sits on the collaboration spectrum (as discussed

---

[1] *Making Partnerships Work: A Survey of UK Senior Executives*, Ipsos Mori and Socia, February 2007. [For full details see footnote in Chapter 1.]

in Chapter 2). Transactional relationships at the right side of the spectrum demand a strong emphasis on governance and contracts, and this will be where leaders need to pay most attention. In a tight-knit permanent team at the other end of the scale, individual and group behaviours are by far the most important things to get right, although the attention to governance and operations doesn't go down to zero. Mutual partnerships, however, need leaders to focus equally on all three areas at once.

To make it easier to see just what to pay attention to, we've split each leg of the stool into three key areas which are listed in the table below. In Chapter 5, we will look at how you can measure progress of the partnership under each of these nine headings. Over the rest of this chapter we'll explore each leg in turn, and for each leg we'll come back to Eleanor's story.

Governance	Operations	Behaviours
Clarity of purpose	Aligned systems and processes	Role modeling
Quality of decision-making	Effective communications	Cross-cultural awareness
Clarity of accountabilities	Capability improvement	Joint problem-solving

THE FIRST LEG: GOVERNANCE

Governance

Clarity of purpose
Quality of decision-making
Clarity of accountabilities

By governance, we mean the formal and informal joint governing structures of the collaborative venture, from the contract through to management and steering groups, reporting lines, accountabilities and decision-making structures.

Governance is the skeleton of your partnership – the supporting frame that holds everything together. And it's important to get it right – and to be prepared to change it if it's not working. While some governance may be specified in the contract, it is not necessarily the best for managing the partnership over time. As the partnership progresses and matures, you may need to alter and simplify some of the structures. And in times of crisis, you may need to put in extra layers of governance.

Clarity of Purpose: Know What You're Both After

One of the most important success factors in any partnership, according to executives in our Ipsos Mori survey, is having a common purpose and shared objectives.[1] This has to go well beyond a bland statement like 'delivering value together' – you need to know what the value is, and exactly why it's worth working together. If you don't understand each other's objectives in detail, you won't know what success looks like to each other, and you're likely to get in the way of that success. Even more dangerously, you may find your motives are actually in competition with each other.

London Underground's public–private partnership with Metronet to modernize the Tube infrastructure is a case in point. One of London Underground's main objectives was to minimize the costs of renewing track, power cables and trains. However, Metronet, one of the two firms responsible for the upkeep and upgrading of the Tube, was largely owned by companies that were part of its own supply chain – the people that built the trains and supplied the power systems. It's a bit like expecting that if supermarkets were entirely owned by farmers they would keep down the cost of milk. This was a partnership that always had a conflict at its heart – the two organisations' objectives were incompatible. And in the end this was probably one of the causes of Metronet going into administration in 2008.

This is not to say that success has to look exactly the same for each party. It doesn't – in fact, it's pretty unlikely that everyone's motives will match. You don't need to find a clone of your own organisation – but it's important that individual partners are transparent about their motives for entering the partnership. That way, each can consider from the outset whether it's possible for them to contribute fully to their partner's success.

When Alan Braithwaite, a widely respected authority on supply chain partnerships, named his Seven Laws of Logistics, the sixth law was entitled 'the Law of Supply Chain Asymmetry'. It reads, 'The commercial interests and strategic priorities between partners in the supply chain are never symmetrical and working to share mutual interest is an unreal proposition – [therefore] defining trading or functional relationships to work to co-operative self-interest is the objective'.[2]

For example, a construction firm appointed to build a new hospital wants several things from the partnership: the project to be profitable; recognition of their abilities in the market; and their stakeholders to demonstrate their satisfaction publicly.

The hospital trust, meanwhile, has its own separate set of objectives. It wants the construction finished on time and on budget, stakeholders to see it

---

[2]'Laws of Logistics & Supply Chain Management', Chapter 4, Alan Braithwaite and Richard Wilding, In: *The Financial Times Handbook of Management* (Ed Crainer and Des Dearlove, eds.), 3rd edn, pp. 249–259, Pearson London, 2004.

as a good investment, staff to find the new building an attractive and efficient place to work, patients to be impressed and for the overall building to contribute to healthcare outcomes.

Interestingly, the joint objective – building a good hospital efficiently – doesn't tell you very much. It's only meaningful when you separate it out into individual components for each member of the partnership.

Knowing what you're both after is crucial. As a leader, you need to be honest about your motives from the start – otherwise, how can you expect your partner to help you achieve them? We advise prospective partners to take the time to map out three statements of purpose: I'm in it for x, you're in it for y and we're both in it for z. Make sure you understand them fully, and that they're not in conflict. Because without clarity of purpose, you're fumbling in the dark.

QUALITY OF DECISION-MAKING: GET THE RIGHT PEOPLE IN THE ROOM

Organisations legally structured as partnerships – law firms or accountancy firms, for example – are notoriously clumsy at decision-making. Key issues that require a full partnership vote are preceded by frenzied lobbying, tacit vote-counting and quite possibly promises of favors.

Cross-organisational partnerships are far more fragile edifices than law firms or accountancy firms. It stands to reason, then, that they need better decision-making structures if they're to survive. The contract alone is not enough. While it often specifies the vehicle for making joint decisions – for example through a steering group – what matters still more is their quality. And unfortunately that can't be tied down in a legal document.

The principles of good decision-making are straightforward: you need the right people to make decisions at the right time and to adhere to them. The reality is more complicated. If your steering committee only meets once a quarter, it can't act as the gatekeeper for every operational decision. There's no use waiting for an agreement on buying new gritting lorries if the meeting isn't until March and the snow has been and gone.

However, it's also important that sensitive decisions get made together. To take an extreme example of decision-making, but one that affects us all, one of the biggest decisions in recent history was going to war in Iraq. Two behind-the-scenes accounts of the White House have argued that President Bush's process for making foreign policy was both closed and deeply hierarchical, relying on a tiny inner circle and excluding other expert advisers.[3] The decision to go

---

[3] *Against All Enemies*, Richard Clarke, first published in Great Britain by The Free Press, an imprint of Simon & Schuster Ltd, 2004, and *Plan of Attack*, Bob Woodward, first published in Great Britain by Pocket Books, an imprint of Simon & Schuster UK Ltd, 2004.

to war was made without directly asking Secretary of State Colin Powell – the proponent of coalition – for his advice. Although Colin Powell later supported the decision, he was known to have wanted a far greater consideration of post-war management.

Criticizing decisions from hindsight is always easy. But some structures are a format for failure. Having a small number of like-minded people in the room may make it easier to come to a decision, but it increases the risk of that decision being severely flawed. Sometimes you need to allow the devil's advocates in there too, and put up with the friction they create, because it makes for a better decision in the end.

Thankfully, collaborative business ventures don't have to decide whether or not to go to war. Nonetheless, the decisions they make can still have major consequences for the public or for stakeholders. Leaders of partnerships need to make sure they get everyone in the room when decisions really matter. And even though the process is time-consuming, it helps considerably to know as much as possible about each partner's views on any important decision.

The complexity of partnerships makes decision-making much harder than in single organisations or structures. Leaders need to allow for that and not rush the process unduly. Sharing information – and concerns – is vital, because you may not realize until it's too late that some elements are interdependent and make a difference to the quality of the decision. Yes, it can be a drawn-out process. But good decisions consider all the consequences. In a partnership, that is time worth taking.

Clarity of Accountabilities: Stop the Turf Wars

Clarifying roles and accountabilities is another element of governance that requires close attention. In a typical television crew, for example, most of the people will be on freelance contracts, and some may meet for the first time on the day of filming. Yet each person is entirely clear about their role, right down to the runner whose job is to fetch and carry, and feed and water the rest of the crew at regular intervals.

Everyone turns up punctually on location (lateness is rarely tolerated because the cost of a single filming day is so high), they get on with their own specialist jobs independently, follow the director's instructions, waste no time and collaborate only when necessary. Most of the time, it's a well-oiled machine.

Yet this tight definition of roles also allows the crew to respond rapidly to changing circumstances. Things often go wrong during filming – the weather takes a turn for the worse, one of the subjects doesn't work out or a hoped-for event doesn't materialize. At this point, the crew goes into overdrive, rejigs the filming sequence and often pulls new content out of thin air. The goal for the crew is to come home with useable footage at the end of the day, and although they have a firm plan at the outset, they're highly flexible in how they achieve it – and quite prepared to throw that plan out of the window if necessary.

At first sight this tight-role, open-task approach doesn't appear to fit other types of partnership – it seems counterintuitive. Surely spelling out the approach to the task matters more than fixing the roles for each team member? Won't you ensure a greater interplay of ideas and contributions, and greater innovation, if you leave the roles loose?

The answer in collaborations is absolutely not. Research by Linda Gratton and Tamara J. Erickson[4] has shown that what matters in a collaborative team is for each team member to know exactly what their role is and be able to fulfill a large part of it independently. They call it 'role clarity and task ambiguity' – and it's essential in partnerships because it cuts down on distrust, time-wasting and turf wars. Leaving the definition of the task relatively open also leaves room for creativity in the collaboration.

Some partnerships fail to define roles sufficiently to their cost. One example is to be found in London Underground's public–private partnership. Under the terms of the partnership, the rail design company, Bombardier, became responsible for building and designing trains. Previously this had been the job of London Underground's own engineers. These engineers were left unhappy, not knowing what their new role was.

Were they still hands-on technical engineers? Should they try to design the trains for Bombardier? Should they audit what Bombardier had done and find fault if it was different from the way they used to do it? Should they inspect the finished trains? The same issues were also there for engineers at Bombardier – what were the boundaries of their role? The on-going confusion led to frustrations on all sides and contributed in part to the long-running dispute over the cost of the upgrading the whole underground network.

Partnerships are difficult enough without blurring the lines of accountability. Being crystal clear about people's roles cuts out overlap and waste, but it also makes people happier about their competence and sphere of influence. It lets them get on with their jobs. And that certainty of role makes it possible for them to get creative when it really matters.

Governance and Eleanor's story

So how does a consideration of governance apply to Eleanor's situation as a new CIO? First of all, she needs to deal with the question of aligning objectives. The hospital consultants, managers and ward staff all want different things from the new systems, and her own staff and the two suppliers clearly have different views about what the new contracts should provide. In terms of decision-making, she faces multiple layers of steering groups and user groups for each separate project,

---

[4] 'Eight Ways to Build Collaborative Teams', Lynda Gratton and Tamara J. Erickson, *Harvard Business Review*, November 2007.

all of whose decisions can apparently be overruled by the hospital trust's finance committee, which often gets bogged down in details of approval of changes to IT budgets at its monthly meetings.

Eleanor's response is to simplify the governance process, dramatically slimming down the number of steering groups, and creating clear terms of reference for each that specify which are discussion groups and which have real decision-making authority. She also sets up a single IT portfolio management board for the whole trust, with responsibility for setting priorities across the full range of projects and user groups – and presenting a single view to the finance committee if new funds are needed.

In addition, Eleanor runs a series of workshops for suppliers, customers and IT staff to reach agreement about 'what success looks like'. This isn't easy, but over time they begin to understand each other's viewpoint and accept that the IT portfolio management board has the authority to set priorities and targets for them all to work to.

THE SECOND LEG: OPERATIONS

Operations
___

Aligned systems and processes
Effective communications
Capability improvement

By operations, we mean the processes that have to work across the whole partnership, from communications and information sharing to joint learning and staff development, to ensure that the relationship thrives and grows. Operations within a partnership should be like jigsaw pieces – they have to fit together properly if the partnership is to run smoothly.

If good governance is like a skeleton supporting the structure of a living partnership, good operations are its blood supply, pumping information to all parts of the body. And like the bloodstream, operations are dynamic. What works one day may not be right for the next. So a healthy partnership is always reviewing and improving its operations and learning as a result.

The problem is that the single parties entering the partnership all need their own efficient systems and processes. So why can't they just combine operations or pick the best for use across the partnership? The answer is distinctly human: people are used to doing things the way they have always done them. In addition, sharing the intimate details of your own company's processes with a partner can feel uncomfortable. It may take months or years of inefficiency, frustration and crisis before fundamental processes are linked together. Get them right at the beginning, though, and your partnership is off to a solid start.

Aligned Systems and Processes: Make Sure the Plug Fits the Socket

It's the little things that get in the way: data that has to be re-keyed to fit your spreadsheet package; invoices that don't get paid because they're in the wrong format and timesheets that don't tally with the number of hours you're apparently supposed to be billing. They can drive you mad – and they erode faith in a partnership remarkably fast. As one partnership director put it, 'It's like trying to put a UK plug in a European socket – you can only push so hard and then someone is going to get a nasty shock'.

One of the basic questions that needs to be addressed at the outset of a collaboration is whether everyone is looking at the same data – a much bigger problem than it might seem. A single source of truth can be hard to find if each side of the partnership is sticking rigidly to their own systems.

Trust is the essence here. Misunderstandings often occur when partners don't have enough faith in each other enough to keep score without supervision. A roads department at a local authority, for example, is frustrated that none of the 27 complaints received by its call center have been dealt with. The private contractor insists that in fact it's doing a great job because it's been charged with 12 jobs and closed all of them. Who is right? The only way to sort out the confusion is to make sure the systems fit together properly – or, better still, to make everyone use the same system.

One warning sign that things are going wrong is the need to rekey data at every stage in a process: the customer service desk sends a written request to the council works department, which rekeys it to generate a works order, then prints it out for the people who mend the road, who in turn rekey it for jobs scheduling. At every point there's a huge opportunity for errors to creep in – and for greater frustration all round. We can't all be as efficient as the self-organizing Linux community discussed in Chapter 1, which uses the simplest of shared tools. But leaders need to strive for as much simplicity as they possibly can.

An obvious example of the need for process alignment is in HR, and particularly in performance management and incentive schemes. When these are badly out of kilter – for example when there are hugely differing payscales for the same job – it's a recipe for resentment. And if the rules are different across a partnership, people may see staff in their partner organisations 'getting away with' things they would never be allowed to do, or being rewarded in ways that seem unfair or disproportionate. There is no easy way around these issues – policies and practices that have been negotiated over years with staff can be thrown into sharp relief by a partner that does the opposite. In our experience, the most important thing is to get these issues out into the open and to not let them fester. We've seen partnership relationships soured for many months by something as seemingly trivial as the policy on what to do with air miles earned on company business trips.

The hard truth is that if systems and processes are to be aligned, then somewhere along the line, people are going to need to compromise. It's certainly a pain to fill in timesheets when you never had to before, but if it means everyone's working from the same set of figures, it's worth doing for the sake of the partnership. Bureaucracy has a bad name, but it isn't always a bad thing. A partnership with its systems and processes working well together has sorted out the petty stuff and can concentrate instead on the big picture.

Effective Communications: Cut the Propaganda

Communications within a partnership are like communications in any organisation: they have to be timely, targeted and effective. But above all, they need to be believable. Trust is far more of an issue in a partnership than in a single function or organisation, so a monthly newsletter stuffed with self-congratulatory articles just won't wash. People on the ground know the reality, and a lot of the time it tells a different story. Put out too much propaganda and people are likely to suspend their belief in the collaboration – and quite possibly to stop collaborating at all.

Although it's tempting to treat cross-partnership communications as a PR exercise, leaders have to resist the urge. Instead they need to take a deep breath and start sharing the downs as well as the ups, allowing the critical voices an airing, and holding their hands up when they get things wrong.

When the world's largest cement manufacturer, Lafarge, entered a sponsorship agreement in 2000 with global environmental charity WWF, it seemed an unlikely match. Yet both had much to gain from the partnership – not least by demonstrating that big business could work successfully with NGOs. Despite facing major challenges to their relationship (in particular over the proposed siting of a superquarry on the Scottish island of Harris), the partnership was 'open, straightforward and inclusive'.[5] Skeptical voices were invited to meetings, there was no attempt to hide major disagreements, and Lafarge even published both sides of the argument on the superquarry in its 2001 sustainability report.

This unusual level of frankness helped the partnership scale some steep obstacles. According to Michel Picard, vice president of environmental issues at Lafarge Group: 'the permanent dialogue with WWF challenges our beliefs, our strategies, and our practices, and produces tangible results. I am convinced that through this process Lafarge is gaining a competitive advantage for the future'.[6] For Picard, the partnership has become the company's 'environmental insurance', allowing it to address environmental issues before they become

---

[5] *'Tough Dialogue Pays Off': How Lafarge and WWF make their Partnership Work to Help Preserve the World's Ecological Balance*, Claudia Heimer, Roger Pudney, Jean-Paul Jeanrenaud, Luc Giraud-Guigues, and Michel Picard, Ashridge Practitioner Paper, 6 October 2006.
[6] Ibid., p. 3.

urgent, and way ahead of the competition. Meanwhile, for WWF, it's an effective way to deliver their mission by engaging with business from within – and a model for other NGOs.

When communicating externally, it's not always possible to be quite so frank. However, taking joint responsibility in all communications is vital – even when things go wrong. Having a single person in charge of communication for the partnership helps, so long as they take care not favor one party over another. But if partners end up presenting separately to stakeholders, or briefing journalists on their own, they need to honor the partnership and hold the party line. Without this discipline, it's all too easy to descend into back-stabbing and mutual recrimination.

The essence of good communication in partnerships, then, is to behave as one. You have to drop your guard and accept that you're in it together, for better or worse. This doesn't mean ignoring differences in culture, skills or contribution. Those still matter, and failure to acknowledge them can throw a relationship off course. What it does mean is sharing good news and bad across the whole partnership, being honest with each other, and standing together when it counts. A little solidarity goes a long, long way.

Capability Improvement: Build Together for the Future

Our Ipsos Mori research found that the length of the average partnership is around 6 years, outlasting most management appointments.[1] It's inevitable, then, that good people are going to leave before a partnership runs its course.

The implications for leaders are clear. You need to look at the capability needs over the whole length of the collaboration and to invest in skills and capacity long before you're likely to lose them. Succession planning is a necessity. Equally important is the need to develop staff all through the life of the partnership so that they stay motivated – you can't afford to let a partnership become a graveyard for ambition.

Some partnerships manage to do this in imaginative ways. One county council's partnership with its consulting engineers, for example was a model of far-sightedness. When the council realized its quantity surveyors were all going to reach retirement age at around the same time, it knew it needed to address the issue fast. It's not easy to recruit experienced quantity surveyors and the council didn't want to be at the mercy of the market. In an ideal world, they would take on new graduates immediately and train them up, but with a headcount freeze, this wasn't going to be possible. The solution was unexpected but inspired. Their partners agreed to step in and recruit the graduates, and set up a joint training program that saw people moving between public and private sector posts as their career developed so that when the time came they would have opportunities to work either for the council or the contractors.

Building capacity and capability together in this way is highly collaborative – a marriage rather than a cohabitation. It's not for the faint-hearted, but the mark of a mature and sophisticated partnership. When partners are prepared to put in time or money to help each other out of a dilemma that hasn't yet happened, it sends out a clear signal. They're in it for the long term, and investing for the future – together.

Operations and Eleanor's story

The biggest issue for Eleanor in the field of operations is getting everyone to work from a single version of the truth about IT performance. She is regularly berated by angry hospital consultants and managers about the poor performance of IT, with people demanding that she should extract penalty charges from the suppliers as compensation for their problems. Yet her own teams tell her that although they aren't satisfied with what is happening, the suppliers seem to be hitting the majority of performance targets.

The trouble is that there are dozens of ways to measure performance formally, and dozens more anecdotal measures. It's clear that users aren't happy, so no number of barcharts demonstrating on-target performance will make a difference. On the other hand, a high percentage of help desk complaints are actually caused by users who don't understand some of the new features of the system.

Eleanor puts her effort into two immediate short-term initiatives. The first is to use the newly formed IT portfolio management board to develop a simple performance scorecard that reflects the day-to-day reality of the system, and that contains measures of user satisfaction with the service. As everyone reviews and acts on the same data month on month, they gradually begin to see the real (and perceived) performance improve.

Her second initiative is to start a program of user communication and education to help people get the most out of their existing systems. By training her own staff to improve their communication skills, and then sending them all out for a day each week to train groups of users at their desks, she improves not only perceptions of IT, but also the relationships between IT staff and clinicians.

In a long-term initiative, Eleanor conducts a skills inventory to see what skills she has in-house and what skills are available through her suppliers. With this she is able to build a long-range development plan so that as the current contracts draw to a close, she has the right skills in place to tender for the next ones.

THE THIRD LEG: BEHAVIOURS

Behaviours

Role modeling
Cross-cultural awareness
Joint problem-solving

Many leaders of partnerships address at least some aspects of governance and operations, but forget all about behaviours. They spend all their time sorting out the contract, pinning down the processes and dreaming up penalties for if things go wrong. Yet if they don't concentrate on behaviours, there's every chance that things will go downhill rapidly – and no one will understand why.

It's rare to see managers trained in how to behave collaboratively. Some firms, however, have taken a lead on training their employees in relationship skills. May Gurney, a construction firm based in East Anglia that we'll hear more of in Chapter 7, runs an induction program for all new staff to explain the company's approach to partnering and collaboration. All its managers go through development programs to build their skills in coaching and holding difficult conversations, and when it starts a new partnership contract they hold joint leadership development workshops for their own staff and managers from the client organisation.

Similar capabilities are needed to run internal partnerships. When LloydsTSB was moving to a corporate shared services model, it needed to set up a network of internal business partners to cover functions such as HR, IT and Finance. In order to prepare the people appointed to these new business partner roles for the behavioural challenges of working in a shared service environment, it defined a development program to build the core capabilities of managing the customer relationship, developing strategy, delivering business results, influencing, leading others, using information effectively, making good decisions and making change work. The aim of this corporate program was to mitigate the risks of different parts of the shared service organisation not working together to meet the needs of their internal customers.

Role Modeling: Stand by Your Partner

Leaders need to model the kind of behaviour that's needed in a partnership by standing by their partners through thick and thin. The trouble is that when things go wrong, it's easy to find fault. And if you succumb to that temptation, so will everyone else. Backbiting is like an aggressive cancer – left unchecked it spreads rapidly throughout an organisation.

Leaders need not only to model good behaviours themselves, but to stamp out carping when they see it, and to challenge staff when they avoid personal responsibility. Even when you have true cause to complain of a partner, you need to hold back wherever possible, seeing it as an opportunity to address the issue constructively and to improve the partnership for the future.

When the world press broke the story that high street clothing chain Gap was using child labor in India to hand-embroider fashion tops[7], Gap didn't

---

[7]'Child Sweatshop Shame Threatens Gap's Ethical Image', Dan McDougall, *The Observer*, Sunday, 28 October, 2007.

immediately strike off the Indian supplier that had sub-contracted the work. Instead they took a financial hit by preventing these products ever being sold in stores, and convened a meeting of suppliers to reinforce their prohibition on child labor. Their aim was first and foremost to protect their own reputation – but also to try to tackle the causes in an attempt to stop the same thing happening again. It's not enough to stop working with an individual sub-contractor that is using unethical labor – Gap needed to ensure that its first-tier suppliers understood why they must monitor the ethical practices of their own sub-contractors and take responsibility for the way the work is carried out right down the supply chain.

Truly collaborative leaders look for contribution, not blame – in other words, they examine what both parties have contributed to make the problem arise in the first place. It's a technique that allows people to stop judging each other, and instead try to disentangle what happened between them so they can do better next time.

John Yard, a former CIO at the Inland Revenue, is a strong advocate of mapping contributions to a problem instead of dishing out blame. Early into a massive IT outsourcing contract with EDS, there was an issue with their underperformance. While the Inland Revenue board wanted to press for penalties, John Yard realized this could not be an effective solution for either party. Instead he argued the case for readjusting the deal to make it more commercially viable for EDS in return for improvements in service.

Cross-Cultural Awareness: Get Beyond First Appearances

Some partnerships are like love at first sight. 'Many executives use romantic analogies to describe the enthusiasm that accompanies their discovery of a new corporate partner', says Rosabeth Moss Kanter. 'The best intercompany relationships are frequently messy and emotional, involving feelings like chemistry and trust'.[8] In other words, some deals depend on a strong personal rapport between chief executives, and on similar cultures and philosophies in the partner organisations.

Similarity of outlook will take a partnership a long way. But we'd argue that it's not essential to the success of the collaboration. In fact, most partnerships – even cross-functional ones within organisations – are likely to bring together differing cultures. And part of the sophistication of leading a collaboration is getting under the skin of a partner who's different.

It's easy to say and much harder to do. All too often, differences in culture breed suspicion and mistrust. The first warning sign is hearing stereotypes being bandied around: a partner is overly bureaucratic, brash, slow, slick, corporate, American, French, whatever. The slogans are a smokescreen for a more basic misunderstanding: they're not like us.

---

[8]'Collaborative Advantage', Rosabeth Moss Kanter, *Harvard Business Review*, July–August 1994.

We'll cover the subject of understanding cultural difference in more detail in Chapter 6. Here, though, it's worth noting that to get beyond first appearances, partners need to start looking not just each other's output but at their approach. What motivates them? What gets them riled? What upsets them? What ways of behaving do they find easy or difficult?

If partners can work out what makes each other tick, they can start to figure out how to accommodate each other's preferred ways of working. Where there are strong cultural differences, they may need to invest in tools like the Organisational Partnering Indicator (described in Chapter 6) to analyze how best the relationship can function. Social events help break down barriers too although it's important to make sure content of the event isn't skewed heavily to fit one culture rather than the other.

So while some marriages may be made in heaven, others require a little more work. Taking time to understand what your partner is really like pays off. What's more, it can spark creative dialogues that simply wouldn't happen if everyone was just like you. If a partnership is to reach beyond the skills and capabilities of individual members and create something new, difference may be exactly what it needs.

Joint Problem-Solving: Let the Air in

Finally, the vexed question of how to deal with problems. Any partnership will have its fair share of them – but the way those problems are managed is a strong indicator of the health of the collaboration.

When a problem surfaces, do the different parties flag it up and get together to try and solve it? Or do they close ranks? Worse still, do they moan about their partners' apparent deficiencies rather then helping out? This can emerge at first in petty squabbles and stalemates – one party won't pay invoices, for example, because they're not presented properly, and rather than showing their partner what 'right' looks like, they fail them for getting it wrong. Although such behaviour looks harmless enough in isolation, it bodes badly for a time when the partnership faces more difficult challenges, and leaders should take care to nip it in the bud early.

When things go wrong in the healthiest partnerships, groups quickly come together to find innovative solutions. Of course this is more likely to happen – and easier to facilitate for a collaborative leader – in close relationships that are at the 'permanent team' end of the collaboration spectrum (see page 24 in Chapter 2). But even in transactional relationships, you can promote a culture of joint problem-solving by putting it in the contract and setting budget aside to cover the costs.

One example of innovative problem-solving can be seen in a partnership between London Underground and a construction project team involving Costain Taylor Woodrow, Ove Arup, the Department for Transport and English Heritage, to build new ticket halls for Kings Cross station. The difficulty they faced was in digging holes – an activity which in London is fraught with problems. At any point you may turn up something unexpected – from ancient ruins to unexploded bombs. To deal with this, the partnership contract stipulated that whenever workmen turned up something unknown, they had to fill in a method statement on how to solve the problem. This statement went to all the other parties involved, including English Heritage.

London Underground recognized that Costain Taylor Woodrow had a serious problem with the length of time allowed for parties to respond – they couldn't ask their workmen to lean on their shovels for 3 weeks until all the paperwork had been dealt with. So they brought all the parties together to hammer out a solution.

It soon emerged that English Heritage was the bottleneck – as a charity it was low on administrative resource, and on top of that, the method statements were far too complicated for their needs. But a creative solution was found. Costain Taylor Woodrow would send them only the documentation that was essential, and in addition, they agreed to supply them with an administrator for the course of the project.

Solving problems jointly takes creativity and courage. It means opening up. It means washing your dirty linen in public. It means asking for help when you need it, and offering it where you can. For most organisations, this doesn't come naturally – it's easier by far to resort to carping and insularity. However, finding a joint solution speeds things up, and usually saves money. What's more, joint solutions are often more creative, more ambitious and long-lasting than those made – or ignored – in the comfort of one's own boundaries.

Behaviours and Eleanor's story

Let's look for a last time at Eleanor's story and see what she pays attention to when it came to behaviours.

First and foremost, she acts as a role model. She invests time in making good relationships with key customers and suppliers and makes it obvious to all those around her that that is what she is doing. She also runs a series of workshops that look at the different cultures of her two suppliers and her various user groups. From these workshops the leadership group jointly defines a charter of behaviours to which they expect staff across the partnership to sign up. It lays some basic ground rules such as 'never knowingly let colleagues fail' and 'explain decisions openly and transparently'.

The leaders also agree to meet regularly to review progress, not just on the delivery aspects of the contract, but also on how people perceive the state of play. As part of this they plan to set up a 360° feedback process measuring perceptions of governance, operations and behaviours of people across the partnership on an annual basis.

Finally, Eleanor tackles the short-term problems early by bringing together the groups concerned, airing the issues and helping them to find solutions that benefit them all. These end-of-the-week lunchtime problem-solving sessions soon become part of the new culture. They even get their own name: 'fix-it Friday lunches'. And the skeptical consultants are also starting to come around and engage in constructive debate with the IT department. Several of them offer to collaborate on the design of the next update to the 'consultants portal' to make sure it meets their needs. Eleanor begins to feel that she has turned a corner and the chaos of her first few months is behind her.

THREE LEGS GOOD, ONE LEG BAD

When problems are flying at you from all sides – the typical experience of partnership – it's tempting to focus only on the areas you feel most comfortable with. If you see procedure as highly important, you're likely to spend most time on the governance of your partnership. If you're highly organized, you may well concentrate your attention on processes and systems. And if you're primarily a people person, you tend to hone in on behaviours.

But the point of the three-legged stool of governance, operations and behaviours is that you have to do all three. Eleanor's story demonstrates how the three areas work tightly together to create a strong framework. If you take away one leg, a partnership loses its stability – and it then won't take much to cause it to collapse.

As we've seen earlier in this book, partnerships can easily go off track, or even spiral out of control. But a solid and simple framework based on the three-legged stool is robust enough to deal with pretty much anything that comes your way. And in the next chapter, we go on to look at how you can measure progress in your partnership using the same three-legged stool as your guide.

Chapter 5

The Octagonal Tape Measure

YOU GET WHAT YOU MEASURE

Ever since Frederick Taylor published his 'Principles of Scientific Management' in 1911, measurement in business has proved its value. Taylor's time and motion studies focused on getting the most out of individual activities – 'the science of shoveling', for example, determined the optimal shovel load a worker could lift. The answer – 21 pounds – delivered a three- to fourfold increase in productivity.[1]

Today scientific management has morphed into the strongly held conviction that you get what you measure. Every organisation, from the police force to Tesco, employs scores of measures to run its business. We no longer just measure productivity, but also customer satisfaction, process improvement, people development and many more. And the pressure to deliver value, either to shareholders or to the public, has given rise to a slew of measurement techniques, from service level agreements to the balanced scorecard. All of these have duly made their way into partnership contracts.

Across partnerships, the adoption of formal measurement can vary widely. A 2002 study by Accenture[2] found that only half of business alliances were using formal performance measures. In the public–private world, however, the picture is very different. Intense public scrutiny means the output of every project is closely examined – not just by the organisations in question, but the National Audit Office, the Public Accounts Committee, the Treasury and probably the national press too. In particular, a massive industry of measurement has grown around PFIs, because politicians have needed to prove that outsourcing to the private sector can provide both good service and value for money.

The problem is that many of the measures employed for the purpose of political and public scrutiny don't actually evaluate how well a partnership is delivering the objectives of the deal. What's more, they rarely show leaders how to improve the way they run things over the life of the partnership. In the Accenture study, only 20% of executives thought that the performance measures they used were reliable predictors of success.[3]

---

[1] *The Principles of Scientific Management*, by Frederick Winslow Taylor, 1911.
[2] 'Grasping the Capability: Successful Alliance Creation and Governance Through the "Connected Corporation"', *The Point*, Vol. 2, Issue 1, 2002.
[3] Ibid.

THE REAR-VIEW MIRROR ONLY LOOKS ONE WAY

Traditional measurement is all about delivery. It relies on key performance indicators (KPIs) or other metrics to determine outputs and quantify improvement or decline – anything from 'average revenue per customer' to 'number of potholes mended per week'. These indicators are easy to read and easy to specify, so they're well loved by accountants and solicitors. Because of this, they get written into 'output-specified contracts', and used to incentivize and punish alike. Unfortunately, while they give an accurate picture of the past, they're not much help in predicting the future.

Delivery measures tend to come in droves. Often there are hundreds of KPIs in each contract. Gathering the data and checking it all becomes a huge task in itself – and individuals and organisations soon learn to play the game of manipulating and maximizing KPIs even at the expense of other important (but non-measured) things. Meanwhile, if the indicators get too complex, there's a danger that people lose sight of why something is being measured and end up working against the objectives that inspired the KPIs in the first place.

Sometimes the right measures aren't there at all. Although everyone has an impression of what they should be, no one has sat down and agreed them. It's particularly true of internal partnerships, but not unknown in more formal partnerships either. We've worked with a number of HR and IT business partner teams who say that although they have personal objectives and targets in their own job descriptions, they don't have a clear set of joint measures of success for the relationship they are meant to be managing with their internal clients. And without this, the whole relationship is built on shaky foundations.

But even when they exist, output-based targets and measures can only ever show half of the picture. Imagine building an extension using an architect and a construction firm, and relying only on output measures. Your indicators would probably include the extension's being built to budget and delivered on time, meeting building regulations and having heating, lighting and plumbing systems that worked properly. Each week you could check on progress against these measures. But with the best will in the world, they wouldn't in themselves prevent the usual litany of disasters: budget overruns, late delivery and quite possibly an extension that doesn't match what you had in mind at the outset. The measures are important, but they're not all that you need. At worst, all they do is give you the basis for a row with your builder. Ensuring the work gets done on time, budget and quality is about performance management not just performance measurement. And effective performance management depends on having the right foundations of governance, operations and behaviours that form the three legs of the stool we discussed in the previous chapter.

BULLDOZING WITH DETAIL

Contracts that tried to specify every detail of future performance were a feature of early public–private construction partnerships. The theory was that all the risk should be transferred to the private sector, but in actual fact, there was little trust in this happening. The consequence was that public sector officials (and lawyers) tried to control the risk by specifying in incredible detail exactly what had to be delivered. Of course, this approach didn't take into account the fact that needs would change over time, and that legally enforcing contractors to do exactly what they were told in the contract took away any incentive for them to find innovative lower cost solutions that might deliver a perfectly acceptable service.

Over-specification is still an unfortunate characteristic of many public–private partnerships. To take one example, the *NHS Healthcare Cleaning Manual* runs to 215 pages, including appendices. Written for hospital staff and managers, it covers important specialist tasks like decontaminating fluid spills. At the same time it sets out in detail how to dust, polish, mop and scrub floors ('when the mop is completely dirty, submerge into the second bucket (water) and wring'). You can see what's driving the minute attention to detail, and on one hand it's reassuring to know that every eventuality is covered. On the other hand, too much specification can be counterproductive, evening out the mundane and the extraordinary, and driving all intelligence and care out of the process. And no amount of detail is a substitute for pride, commitment or experience.

In the end, over-specification is simply dehumanizing. In Chapter 4 we saw how making roles crystal clear but leaving tasks relatively open fostered team working, fast responses and creativity. Clearly there are limits to how open ended you can make a task, especially where public health and safety are concerned. But by transactionalizing the relationship with contract cleaners, the NHS has ensured that pride in a job well done doesn't enter into the equation.

A MEASURING STICK TO BEAT YOU WITH

Measurement can also be used to bludgeon partners and suppliers into submission. A multinational drinks company, for example, wanted to reduce the number of global suppliers for its bottles and at the same time radically reduce the cost of this key component. They used their knowledge of the comparative costs of different suppliers and of the glass industry to measure what they believed the cheapest cost of a bottle should be, and then set this as a target price. Because of their size, they had enough power to force suppliers to accept this deal, and for a while everyone was happy. The drinks company reduced its costs, and a few global glass manufacturers had some large (if not very profitable) contracts. But as the market changed and the demand for new bottle shapes and sizes grew, the glass manufacturers couldn't afford the R&D and re-tooling costs to change their production lines. The tight measurement regime had all but bankrupted the supply base. All the drinks company's focus had been on a single goal – to secure the lowest cost of supply. They had taken their eye off the real purpose of their relationship with bottling suppliers – building the right capability to meet future needs.

In this case no one had foreseen the consequences of a tight measurement regime. But occasionally leaders have rather more Machiavellian aims. We once worked with a leader in a dysfunctional partnership who used measurement as a device to catch people out. On top of the measures already specified in the contract (and there were many of them), he invented a whole battery of his own, most involving an extra stage of approval – by him.

In this aggressive climate, someone would always be under-performing. The leader then used this evidence to beat up his suppliers. Not surprisingly, the other parties in the partnership quickly stopped raising problems or highlighting awkward performance data. Issues were covered up, performance deteriorated and finally it became impossible to address the situation collaboratively. The lawyers were called in.

MEASURING WITH A LIGHT TOUCH

Overloading the contract with detailed demands can wreck a partnership. So how do you measure effectively without them? The oil industry offers some interesting lessons.

We saw in Chapter 1 how leaders in the oil industry tend to have highly honed collaboration skills. Searching for oil is a joint venture because it's hugely expensive and involves many vested interests – governments, landowners and environmentalists to name but a few. In addition, it's highly uncertain. Only one in twelve wells will ever lead to commercial success. Failure is part of the process of discovery.

With all the players in the industry well used to working in partnership, contracts cover the basics in a fairly standard way. But given that oil exploration is inherently risky, there's no place for excessive caution (except on safety issues). So instead of over-specifying performance aspects, leaders of partnerships and JVs in oil exploration partnerships take care to emphasize what to do when things go well – or when things go wrong. For example, the contract will cover what to do if one partner wishes to sell their share, or if a partner doesn't like the proposal in a particular situation and wishes to drill a well elsewhere.

Rather than imposing penalties for minor failures in performance, then, these contracts emphasize the mechanisms to govern, and spell out how to deal with disputes. And when a partnership fails to find oil, it learns from that for the next time.

GO EASY ON THE PENALTIES

Traditional measurement in partnerships not only specifies multiple output measures, but attaches incentives and penalties to those measures in the contract. The problem is that the contract ossifies a particular moment. Yet circumstances change. If the contract doesn't allow for this, it can end up incentivizing or penalizing entirely the wrong things.

Penalizing a partner when they've missed a deadline has some attractions, but if it doesn't get to the cause of why the deadline was missed or how each partner contributed to the problem, it merely takes money out of the system.

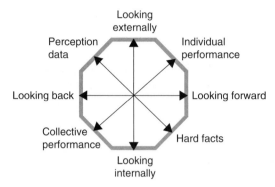

FIGURE 5.1   The octagonal tape measure.

And throwing penalties at your partners can also start a tit-for-tat round of claim and counterclaim where no one benefits.

There are other ways to run a partnership. For example, one local authority has set up a joint investment fund for its partnership with private contractors, so that whenever a target is missed the fund can be used to help finance performance improvement actions to get it right next time. And in the construction phase of Terminal 5, BAA set up around 20 multi-contractor project teams as 'virtual companies'. While BAA held overall responsibility for the risk of the construction program, each team had a small joint contingency fund that they could draw on. If it wasn't spent, it was then available to another team – which the same contractors would probably be involved in too.[4]

Punishing a partner for failing to deliver is not the best guarantee of future results. Instead, good measurement systems should draw clear boundaries of what is and what is not acceptable, and help all parties improve performance over time. Generosity has its own rewards.

AN OCTAGONAL MEASURING TAPE

Recognizing that traditional output measures are easy but flawed is the first step. The next is to understand why you want to measure in the first place. Are you doing it because you don't trust your partner? (If so, think carefully about why are you entering into partnership with them!) Are you trying to improve your partner's performance, or simply confirm a prejudice? Are you doing it because the contract or an external body tells you to?

Let's assume your reasons for measurement are good ones: you're trying to understand how the partnership performs and to predict future needs or problems. If so, for each aspect measured, you need to get both sides. And for that, we reckon you'll need an octagonal measuring tape (Fig. 5.1).

---

[4]'Project management at Heathrow Terminal 5', Christian Wolmar, *Public Finance*, April 22 2005.

The eight sides of measurement are:

- *Forward looking measures as well as backward looking ones*: Besides asking whether the partnership hit its performance targets and milestones for last month, you need to ask whether you have targets agreed for next year, budgets in place and people recruited. This could also be described as measuring contribution versus measuring results.
- *Measures for the partnership as well as for each partner*: Measures for each partner's performance are important, for example, how long it takes one partner to close a helpdesk query. But you also need to measure collective outputs such as the overall customer satisfaction level for the whole IT service.
- *Internal measures as well as external ones*: Partnerships need to look externally for benchmark measures, and in many cases will have them imposed upon them, for example, government-specified best value targets. However, the partnership should also jointly agree a few of its own internal KPIs – the things that the team are really motivated to achieve and will stand as symbols of success of their joint endeavor.
- *Perception data as well as hard fact*: Obviously you need numerical data on key areas in order to be able to analyze how well the partnership is going. But you should also collect opinion data on the state of the relationship at frequent and regular intervals (and it can often tell a different story).

A good measurement suite covers all eight of these components, with equal weight being given to each one. That way you have delivery measures *and* diagnostic measures, so you can assess how you've done so far and how you're likely to fare in the future.

Good measurement gives a partnership an early indication of problems to come. It tells all parties where to focus their attention for the future benefit of the partnership. It discourages self-interested behaviour and encourages collaboration. And it can be interpreted consistently by all parties – in other words, it's undeniable.

But in our experience, measures enshrined in the contract rarely meet all the good measurement criteria listed above. They're often drawn up without reference to the people responsible for implementing the partnership, and certainly before there's any experience of operating it.

Even when leaders use the eight sides of measurement, they're not always even-handed about it. Biases creep in because leaders have natural preferences – they're hard fact people, or benchmark enthusiasts, or sticklers for lagging KPIs. In addition, their previous experience will push them toward one type of measure or another. It's important to be aware of this possible bias and to do your utmost to give sufficient attention to each side of the octagon.

WHAT AND HOW TO MEASURE

The octagonal tape measure addresses the *type* of measurement needed in any partnership – forwards and backwards; the whole as well as the parts; external as well as internal; and perception as well as hard fact. But *what* are we actually measuring, and *how*?

First, the output measures. A 2005 KPMG study suggests that in business alliances, financial measures tend to dominate.[5] Though important in measuring short-term results, they are clearly far too narrow. There's a lot to be said for following the classic balanced scorecard model, using indicators of customer satisfaction, financial performance, process improvement and people development.

Remember, though, that output measures look backwards, and that you also need forward-looking indicators. These are harder to come by, and depend on perceptions as well as hard fact. Most of this data will need to be gathered through surveys. In fact successful partnerships are big wielders of surveys, regularly polling staff, customers and other stakeholders in order to drive their decision-making.

The secret of a good survey is to have a portion of standard data, agreed by all partners, which not only turns up incipient problems early but accumulates over time to reveal trends. The remainder of the survey then focuses on analyzing a set of risks specific to its time or place. It also helps if surveys are short, easy to interpret and contain both quantitative and qualitative data.

Surveys should not be treated as a soft option. There's no point in sending out 'happy sheets' asking questions like 'how good is communication across the partnership'? and offering tick boxes from A to E. To be useful, they need to be evidence-driven, and tightly focused on measuring the effectiveness of the partnership – asking questions like 'Is it clear where and when key decisions are taken and who is involved in the process'? They also provide a useful tool for measuring diverging perspectives in the partnership – if one side thinks things are fine and the other sees a host of problems, something is clearly going badly wrong with communication in the partnership.

MEASURE THE THREE LEGS OF THE STOOL – GOVERNANCE, OPERATIONS, BEHAVIOURS

To collect good perception data, we recommend surveying each leg of the three-legged stool described in Chapter 4 – governance, operations and behaviours. We've used this measuring system many times over the years on different types of partnership, and the greatest value comes in being able to track changes in perception over time as the partnership develops. The example below illustrates the sort of results you might get from measuring the quality of partnership between two organisations and comparing the results in two measurement periods (Fig. 5.2).

In the following sections, we examine the symptoms you'll see in each area if things are going wrong, and offer a sample of specific questions or evidence statements that can be used to create a questionnaire to survey each area. Each

---

[5]*Alliances and Joint Ventures: Fit, Focus, and Follow-Through*, KPMG International, 2005.

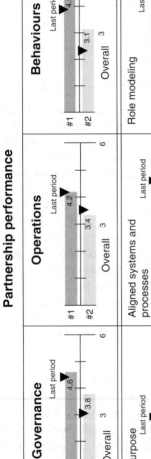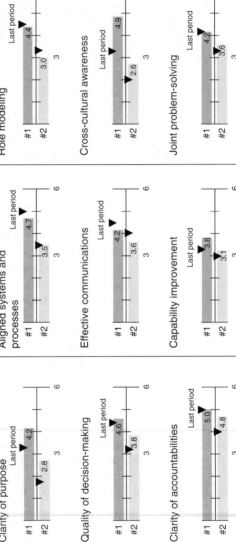

FIGURE 5.2   Measuring the legs of the stool.

of the areas can be expanded further, but it's valuable to keep the questions you chose constant over time so that you can determine trends. Regularly polling staff on each leg of the three-legged stool gives a mass of hard evidence on the health of the partnership and reliable indicators of future performance.

Governance: How Clear Is Your Purpose?

Measuring clarity of purpose starts with having an agreed document for the partnership that sets out individual and joint objectives. Everyone needs to know what success looks like – and if it changes for one party (the besetting sin of government contracts), all sides have to agree on the changes fast.

When clarity of purpose is lacking, competition heats up between the parties, especially over money or resources. If one side isn't sure what their partner is after, the natural reaction is to start protecting their own turf – with disastrous consequences for collaboration.

In addition, an unclear purpose means that decision-making is likely to be confused, and decisions may conflict. People lack confidence and start to dither over what to do next because priorities are not evident. If it gets too bad, it can pose a serious threat to the continuation of the partnership. Measuring clarity of purpose is especially important at the start of a new relationship when different parties may make different assumptions about what they are each working toward. It's also vital to track this measure when the purpose changes. We've noticed that in partnerships with central government departments, civil servants who work closely with government ministers tend to take changes in policy or direction in their stride, seeing it as part of the political cycle. But their partners are often shocked by these rapid changes in direction – particularly if they are from a third sector organisation with an unswerving sense of mission. Measuring these tensions is only a first step in what can be a long road to resolving them, but it's a vital one.

Clarity of purpose: sample statements for a survey

- The aim of the partnership is understood and agreed by all parties.
- My own organisation can achieve its objectives without bringing us into conflict with our partners.
- I believe that all the partners are heading in the same direction.
- Each partner understands how they contribute to the overall aim of the partnership.
- The collective and individual goals of partnership for the year are well documented and understood.
- There is a single set of agreed priorities for the partnership.
- The business benefits as defined in the contract are included in each partner's business plan.

Governance: How Good Is Decision-Making?

Measuring quality of decision-making covers all the decision-making processes, from the mundane (do meetings have agendas?) to the extraordinary (are the right escalation procedures in place to deal with sensitive problems?). Members of the partnership need to understand the points of interdependence in the relationship in order to know what decisions they can take separately and what needs to be agreed jointly. They also need to know when to take things upwards to the board.

If the processes aren't right, people don't feel empowered or engaged. There's likely to be frustration and confusion. And a particularly bad sign is when splinter groups or cabals begin to form.

Internal partnerships such as shared service IT or HR functions often have particularly low scores in this decision-making area. Before the shared service was set up, people across the business knew more or less how decisions were made and how to influence them – but with lots of new business partners and steering groups, no one is sure how and where key decisions are taken. Tracking scores in this area can often give useful early warning signs of an internal partnership that is heading for trouble.

Decision-making: sample statements for a survey

- I know how to influence decisions taken by my partner regarding the operation of the partnership.
- It is clear where and when key decisions are taken and who is involved in the process.
- Escalation processes are clearly defined when partners cannot come to agreement.
- The partnership has a governance process with clear terms of reference that enables effective decision-making.
- The partnership has effective mechanisms to address tactical, operational and strategic decision-making.
- Decisions are made in a timely fashion.
- Decisions appear never to be reversed and don't have to be revisited regularly.
- Decision-making meetings focus on the right things to meet the aims of the partnership.
- Decisions made by the partnership take into account the needs of all stakeholders.

Governance: How Clear Are Accountabilities?

Teams work more creatively as well as more efficiently if their roles are well defined. In partnerships, there's an extra layer of complication: all staff also need to understand where their personal responsibility ends and where joint accountability begins.

When accountabilities aren't clear, you see duplication of effort, role conflicts and tasks falling between gaps. All too often this can turn into turf wars. People lack confidence in each other's abilities, and inefficiencies develop within the relationship as people try to do each other's jobs.

Measurement in this area can be particularly useful in industries like construction, and in 'design, build and operate' partnerships, where the many handovers from initial design to final delivery make it easy for people to duplicate some of the role of the next person in line. Tracking this area of measurement helps to involve the right people at the right time in the design and construction process.

Accountabilities: sample statements for a survey

- There is little duplication of effort between the partners.
- Partnership accountabilities are incorporated into my role specifications.
- There are no arguments about who does what across the partnership.
- Joint accountabilities are specified and documented in the partnership.
- Accountabilities for financial management and operational delivery are clear and well integrated.
- I know who to go to when I need to get things done.
- Each partner is clear about what information needs to be reported to other parties and when.
- There is little or no confusion about authority levels across the partnerships.
- Individuals take responsibility for delivering their accountabilities for the benefit of the whole partnership.

Operations: Are Your Systems and Processes Aligned?

The measurement of how well a partnership's systems and processes fit together should cover not only the way data is entered but also business planning and aspects of HR such as rewards and incentives.

When there's no alignment of systems and processes, frustration builds over multiple bureaucratic tasks, and arguments develop over the accuracy of data, because people are looking at different sources and often having to re-key information. In the end people stop making the effort and start doing their own thing. Meanwhile, when HR processes are out of sync, there's scope for frustration and resentment over differing pay scales and benefits. And if staff from one firm are incentivized to do something for the partnership, yet their opposite numbers only incur costs for doing it, the partnership can rapidly reach stalemate.

Problems at the interfaces between systems are one of the most commonly cited causes of frustration in the first few months of a new partnership. Tracking how people see the alignment of systems and processes and whether or not this improves over time is one good measure of the success of the transition phase of a partnership.

Aligned systems and processes: sample statements for a survey

- There is one common set of measures used by all partners to measure performance of the partnership.
- A joint planning process ensures that the business plans of each partner fit together.
- The escalation process is clearly defined if conflict occurs between partners.
- All partners have access to the same set of data on the performance of the partnership.
- The rewards and incentives for delivery are transparent to all partners.
- Staff are co-located with their partners where this is possible and desirable.
- Common standards have been defined across the partnership where consistency of operation is desirable.
- There is no duplication or re-keying of data at the interface between organisations.

Operations: How Effectively Do You Communicate?

If communications aren't good enough within a partnership, you don't just waste time – you destroy trust. People feel they don't belong to the partnership and start thinking 'them' rather than 'us'. They invent conspiracy theories about what the other side is up to. And because of the lack of trust and openness, they make up their own stories about what's happening in the partnership as a whole.

In this climate, people don't want to help their partners out. If they know the other side is doing something wrong, they'll leave them to it and then complain after the fact. The consequences for the partnership are costly in both time and goodwill.

It's far better to over-communicate than under-communicate with your partners, but the tone matters too. We've seen far too many partnership newsletters with titles like 'Integrate' or 'Working Together', when the truth is anything but. That's why it's important to track people's perception of the honesty of communication as well as its timeliness.

Communications: sample statements for a survey

- The partners keep each other well informed about progress.
- The information that I receive about the performance of the partnership is believable and sufficient for my needs.
- The partnership has one communication management plan that delivers consistent messages to all parties.
- I am well informed about the many issues that face the partnership.
- I know who is responsible for what across the partnership.
- The right people are consulted and involved in decisions.
- Good and bad news is shared in a timely fashion across the partnership.
- Partnership performance meetings are effective and productive.
- I am informed about all decisions that affect me.
- Communication with the stakeholders of the partnership is proactive and effective.

Operations: How Well Are You Improving Capabilities?

Checking that a partnership has the necessary capacity and capability for the future is a complicated task. As we saw in Chapter 4, partnerships often last longer than the average management appointment, so joint succession planning and long-term thinking becomes a necessity.

When it isn't working properly, there's high turnover of staff. Because the partnership can't get the right skills in the right place internally, it ends up buying more external expertise or consultancy. The partnership doesn't grow or develop. And the same mistakes keep on happening again and again.

You know it's going badly wrong when you hear one side saying 'they don't know what's going to hit them in January'. When people stop thinking jointly, they forget that a lack of capacity or capability on one side will hurt the other. They don't concentrate on how to sort out the problem together, focusing instead on the penalties that will be incurred when one side fails to deliver. And in the long term, that helps no one.

Joint development programs and joint skills audits are a way of seeing where the capability gaps are and what can best be done to plug them. If partners are involved in programs like Investors In People, then some of the capability measurements they collect through that process can be very useful data in this area.

Capabilities: sample statements for a survey

- We have the right skills in place to manage our involvement in the partnership.
- Our partners have the right skills in place to manage their involvement in the partnership.
- There is an ongoing effort by all partners to improve skills by following through on improvement actions.
- I rarely (or never) observe individuals working beyond their ability and experience.
- I believe that the partnership has access to the capability it needs to deliver.
- There is a process in place to identify and invest in the skills required by the partnership.
- The partnership has one common knowledge base of skills and experience.
- Joint development programs exist across the partnership.
- A joint performance management process used by all across the partnership.
- There are regular reviews of partnership performance and processes.

Behaviours: How Good a Role Model Are You?

Leaders of partnerships need to be highly aware of how they're behaving toward their partners, because it's echoed throughout the partnership. If they have arguments with their opposite numbers, this swiftly permeates all levels, with silo behaviour being justified by the leaders' lack of collaboration. Self-interest grows rapidly, and people end up looking after their own patch. In the end, this denies the reality of the partnership.

Of course, the same applies the other way around for positive leadership role models. The UK rail industry is rarely held up as a good example of partnering behaviour – Network Rail, its private sector maintenance partners and the competing privatized train operating companies (TOCs) are often seen to be trading insults in the press. However, when Virgin Rail boss Richard Branson spoke up after the Grayrigg train derailment in which one passenger died, he was widely praised within the industry for not seeking to blame any one party, and for setting the tone for an investigation where everyone was to work together to learn the lessons from the incident.

Role modeling: sample statements for a survey

- The leaders in my organisation can share control and work for the benefit of the whole partnership.
- The leaders of the partnership speak with one voice.
- The leader of each party in the partnership encourages collaborative behaviour in their staff.
- The leaders challenge each other constructively to ensure that they come to the best outcomes for the partnership.
- The leaders balance the demands of their partnership role effectively with their internal role.
- The leaders are visible across the partnership.
- The leaders demonstrate empathy in their dealing with colleagues from other sides of the partnership.
- The leaders act as role models, meeting the behaviour standards that they set for their staff.
- The leaders put the needs of their own organisation first when times get tough.
- The leaders build commitment to the partnership in their own organisation.

Behaviours: How Aware Are You of Cross-Cultural Differences?

Cross-cultural awareness in a partnership is a complex area, and is covered more fully in Chapter 6. However, the symptoms are easy to spot: embarrassing misconceptions about what a partner thinks or wants, and a resulting bad atmosphere. If people don't know what makes their partner tick, they tend to assume the worst. Certainly they hang back from communicating, and make more use of the contract to manage the interfaces.

Measuring how well each party understands the other's culture and ways of working is another good leading indicator of how close partners are becoming and when to take another step toward more joined-up working.

When one company has a particularly strong culture, it's important not to overlook the impact this could have on its partners. When Disney merged with Pixar, the leaders knew they needed to keep the cultures distinct. Pixar managers were not sent to work shifts at Walt Disney World in Florida as other

Disney managers are expected to do, and Pixar switchboard operators weren't asked to end telephone calls with the words 'Have a magical day'. The key is to measure your understanding of your partners' culture, not the speed of your absorption into it.

Cross-cultural difference: sample statements for a survey

- We adapt our way of working to accommodate the needs of the other partners.
- I am aware that other partners try to accommodate how my organisation operates.
- I understand the positive and negative impact of my organisation's culture on other partners.
- Partnership behaviours are clearly documented and agreed by the leadership.
- Partnership behaviours are communicated regularly to all staff.
- I recognize and respect the different pressures on each of the different organisations involved in the partnership.
- The partnership invests in activities to encourage an understanding of the cultures of each of the partners.
- I observe partners trying to help each other to succeed.
- Partners are aware of the pressures on each other and try to give a hand.

Behaviours: How Good Is Joint Problem-Solving?

Do you manage to solve problems jointly or do you each take to the hills – separately – whenever a challenge surfaces? Measuring this will give you a lot of information about the health of the relationship. If parties are desperately trying to sort things out on their own, it's a sure-fire sign of impending trouble – and often on a grand scale.

When joint problem-solving isn't working, problems are left to fester and grow, and conflict is buried. A blame culture rapidly develops, and the different sides become trigger-happy – all too keen to use the contract to punish their opposite numbers.

The measures here are simple but easy to overlook. They're the sort of things that prompt unease – they give you a gut feel that things aren't right. However, they should also prompt an intervention, and the earlier the better.

Joint problem-solving: sample statements for a survey

- Staff from across the partnership regularly come together to solve problems.
- My organisation has demonstrated that it has been open to new ideas proposed by other partners.
- There is evidence of effective listening in partnership meetings.

- The conflict resolution process defined by the partnership is used effectively by all partners.
- The partnership can come to consensus about the best way forward when it experiences a serious problem.
- The partnership actively looks for best practice when defining the way it achieves its objectives.
- The partnership actively encourages all partners to adopt best practice where appropriate.
- There are high levels of constructive challenge across the partnership.
- There is evidence of good 'chemistry' among partners when they are required to solve problems together.

KNOW WHEN TO ESCALATE A PROBLEM

In 2006, a scandal erupted in the Home Office. Some foreign national prisoners were being freed at the end of their sentences without being considered for deportation. Since 1999, over 1000 foreign prisoners had been released into the UK. Now this wasn't a secret – many people in the Prison Service, the Home Office and the National Audit Office had known about it for all that time. The issue wasn't that it had never been escalated sufficiently in order for the scale of the risk to be evaluated and dealt with. The report of the House of Commons Home Affairs Select Committee makes it clear that warnings were ignored.[6]

Home Secretary Charles Clarke was forced to admit that the Department had taken its 'eye off the ball'. A rapid growth in the number of foreign prisoners had led to the collapse of the monitoring process. 'The arrangements for identifying them and considering removal from the UK have not kept pace with that growth', Clarke admitted in his statement.

The National Audit Office had warned ministers nearly a year before that preparations for prisoners' removal from the UK should start much earlier, and Clarke promised that deportation procedures would now begin 12 months before a prisoner was to be released. However, his changes came too late. Although Prime Minister Tony Blair refused to accept his resignation, Clarke was eventually fired from his post and returned to the back benches.

Good measurement systems should be able to stop small problems from turning into big ones. Escalation procedures need to be specified at the start of any partnership, but not to such an extent that they become unwieldy or unresponsive. They're about getting information to the decision-makers when it matters, and letting them act on it – not gathering data for a management bureaucracy. To make sure this works effectively, partnerships need to be able

---

[6]*Home Affairs Committee report HC 58-I, Fifth Report of Session 2007–08 – Volume I: The Stationery Office*, July 2006.

to review the trigger points and the processes specified in the procedures in the light of practical operations.

But good escalation procedures are worth their weight in gold. Rather than over-specifying every detail in a contract, collaborative leaders would do well to rely on simple rules on escalating problems. The ability to nip impending trouble in the bud is considerably more valuable than tit-for-tat point scoring.

ALL IN GOOD MEASURE

Measurement within partnerships has had a poor history. Some partnerships have winged it without proper measurement, while many – particularly in the public sector – have been overburdened with hundreds of petty measures that seem guaranteed to create conflict.

As people take on the lessons from the failures, a new approach to measurement is emerging. Looking back is no longer enough – partnerships have to be able to predict what's likely to happen in the future and adapt their behaviour accordingly. We've found that measuring each area of governance, operations and behaviours, as well as the more usual balanced scorecard, gives collaborative leaders a mass of data on past and future performance to highlight the risks and help them to focus their time and activity on the areas that count in the relationship.

Partnerships are complex, and measuring them isn't easy. But that doesn't mean measures need to be heavy-handed. The experience of some of the most enlightened partnerships shows that the way forward is a relatively light touch on measurement, combined with greater responsiveness to both opportunity and challenges. Measurement shouldn't create problems. It should help you solve them.

Chapter 6

The Grit in the Oyster

THEY JUST DON'T UNDERSTAND US

The commonest complaint in any partnership is a clash of cultures. 'They just don't understand us', cries each side, and most of the time, they're absolutely right. It's natural for differences to crop up – after all partnerships reach out beyond comfortable boundaries into new and sometimes strange territories. The problems come when different partners start seeing each other only in stereotypes. We're transparent, *they're* secretive. We're fast, *they're* bureaucratic. We're thoughtful, *they're* nothing but show. We're smart, *they're* dumb.

Cultural mismatches cause big problems. According to research by Accenture, they're a significant factor in the failure or underperformance of business alliances.[1] With public–private partnerships, the problems are only too obvious. One look at the press reporting of healthcare PPPs highlights the cultural difficulties the NHS faces in working with profit-making enterprises. Meanwhile a PPP guidebook published by the US Department of Transportation in 2007 warns that cultural differences between public and private agencies are one of the major impediments to successful implementation.[2]

We believe that differences in style and values within a partnership are a tough hurdle for would-be collaborative leaders – but not an impossible one. As we saw in Chapter 1, people collaborate more easily when they perceive themselves as being alike. And culture clashes tend to bring out the worst in people – prejudice, ignorance and suspicion. We're hard wired to understand our own style, and it's by no means intuitive to understand someone else's.

However, partnerships are not about finding clones of your own organisation – if that were so, there would be no need to partner in the first place. Successful collaboration is about understanding difference, not creating sameness. Leaders need to find ways of getting beyond 'they don't understand us'.

GRIT CAN MAKE A PEARL

Of course, partnerships are likely to run more smoothly if you share similar values. Many successful partnerships are formed because there's a natural fit.

---

[1] 'Grasping the Capability: Successful Alliance Creation and Governance through the "Connected Corporation"', *The Point*, Vol. 2, Issue 1, 2002.
[2] *User Guidebook on Implementing Public-Private Partnerships for Transportation Infrastructure Projects in the United States*, US Department of Transportation, 7 July 2007.

And as Rosabeth Moss Kanter has shown, some leaders use highly romantic language about their partners – 'love at first sight' or 'the company of our dreams'.[3]

'Business pairings aren't entirely cold-blooded', writes Kanter. 'Indeed successful company relationships nearly always depend on the creation and maintenance of a comfortable personal relationship between the senior executives'. Nor is it limited to the leaders feeling comfortable with each other. Kanter also believes it's important for potential partners to share 'compatibility in legacy, philosophy and desires'.

However, love at first sight is far from a universal experience in partnerships. In fact, some are forced marriages where partners have to learn to make the best of it. Most, however, are formed precisely because the partners have different things to offer, and hope that pooling skills and expertise will create new value that neither could produce on their own. The Sony Ericsson mobile communications joint venture, for example, unites Sony's creative, brand-driven and consumer-led expertise with the more traditional Ericsson's technological leadership. Together they create innovative products beyond the expertise of the individual companies.

The truth is that difference can be fruitful in all sorts of ways. It's well worth getting over the initial difficulties that cultural diversity causes in order to understand each other's working style and point of view. Difference is the grit in the oyster – develop it properly and it can turn into a pearl.

THREE COMMON REACTIONS: DENY, IGNORE, OBLITERATE

Few leaders, however, know how to nurture the grit in the oyster. In fact we see many partnerships busily pretending the differences aren't there at all. Partners forge on, bravely ignoring the festering resentments springing up at every level, and blind to the need to adapt and change.

Another reaction is to recognize the difference in cultures, but do nothing to tackle them. Partners shrug their shoulders, shake their heads and get on with things as separately as possible. In some cases they just walk away. In others, where a contract forces them to stay, the partnership may become completely dysfunctional. As many PPP or PFI deals last for 10 years or more, small irritations can grow to become major problems if they are not dealt with.

Finally, many leaders seek to stamp out difference altogether in the belief that conformity will make things easier to manage. One way is to make everything as transactional as possible to squeeze out any room for frustration. But reducing everything to process and contract, as we saw in Chapter 2, saps morale and certainly destroys initiative and innovation.

Go the other way, however, and try to make your partner part of a team, and you create a different set of problems. When a UK county council entered into

---

[3]'Collaborative Advantage', Rosabeth Moss Kanter, *Harvard Business Review*, July–August 1994.

partnership with an engineering design firm to build local transport infrastructure (roundabouts, bridges and so on), a clash arose between the designers on each side. The leaders' response was to put the designers in the same office and manage them under the county council structure. The result: three of the best designers promptly left. In the end the remaining designers settled down, but tensions still reigned and standards dropped to the lowest common denominator. Squashing out the difference had destroyed the potential value of the partnership.

And therein lies the problem. Culture clashes can be extremely damaging to a partnership. But if you try to deny, ignore or obliterate differences, you risk ruining what brought you together in the first place. Instead you have to face them – and learn to use them effectively. First, however, we'll take a more detailed look at common clashes.

WHEN CULTURES COLLIDE

Cultural differences can take many forms. Trans-national partnerships wrestle with potentially huge language and cultural barriers, but these tend to be anticipated and accommodated, with partners at least making some effort to learn about each other in advance. Yet while Western businesspeople will take the trouble to try and understand, say, a Japanese counterpart, they don't always invest the same time in getting under the skin of a UK government department.

For many partnerships, the differences between cultures are not immediately visible, and the effort to understand is correspondingly low. Sooner or later, however, the problems will surface. Below we've outlined some typical flashpoints.

A Clash of Values

Differences in values can take a while to emerge. Often it's the seemingly small things that become major stumbling blocks. For each side they can acquire symbolic status and get talked about again and again as proof that the other partner is 'not like us'.

One example we witnessed was a partnership between an engineering consultancy and a building firm. At the building company, the culture was about solving problems, dealing with the unexpected and doing whatever was necessary to get the job done. The consultancy company, however, believed in the mantra 'time is money'. New recruits were drilled into accounting for every hour of their day, and if they couldn't charge time to clients, they needed to allocate it to some internal project code on their weekly timesheets.

In the early days of the partnership there were considerable problems. Finally, in a spirit of collaboration, the building firm set up working groups and joint problem-solving sessions to find innovative ways round the difficulties. These worked well and everyone felt the partnership was making progress. Then at the end of the quarter the consultancy company presented their bill, including several thousand pounds of fees for participating in these working sessions. They added a note to say that they had discounted the fee rate by 50% in recognition of the partnership.

The building firm was outraged. For them it wasn't just the money, but the principle. Common reactions were: 'How dare they charge for something like that? Whose side did they think they were on'? Meanwhile the leaders of the consultancy company were thoroughly confused. They thought they had been generous in discounting their fee rate.

Working at Different Speeds

Making decisions at different rates can also cause serious misunderstandings. One example we witnessed was a large high street bank and a small software house in a long-term partnership to develop Internet banking systems. The relationship was going well and producing some award-winning results. Then one day the joint steering group decided that in response to customer concerns they wanted to put a whole new layer of security into the system.

The software house quickly went into action. They put forward an innovative idea to solve the issue, but pointed out that this would mean moving the software to a different (and more secure) development platform. The bank agreed in principle to the plan, so the software house immediately started retraining their developers and went out to the market to recruit some new and highly expensive staff.

Imagine their frustration at the next steering group a month later, when the bank's head of technology announced a delay. Before going ahead, he wanted a review of possible software development platforms, to see what was available that answered both the new security requirements and the bank's technical standards. Suddenly everything was on hold pending the review.

For the bank it made perfect sense. Although they'd agreed in principle to the software house's recommendations, they hadn't yet gone through a lengthy process of approvals. The software house, however, felt they had been put in a difficult position, and resented it. It wasn't just the cost of the delay that frustrated them – they felt the bank just 'didn't get it' and wasn't operating in the same world as them.

Mismatched Communication Styles

Often a difference in culture can show up as a difference in communication style. An organisation that is used to working by informal channels and expecting important messages to cross the company on the grapevine, for example, may have real difficulties in working with a partner that is used to minuting all its meetings formally and keeping a printed audit trail of all communication. This difference in communication style is often raised as one of the classic symbols of a culture clash between traditional public and private sector organisations and so often surfaces as an issue in public–private partnership deals.

Mismatched Leadership Style

Leadership style is generally a strong indicator of organisational style, so when leaders approach things from very different perspectives, cultural clashes are likely to follow.

We once worked with a partnership between a private sector technical consultancy company and a government agency to help them out of one such clash. The leadership style of the consultancy was to expect leaders to delegate to the maximum possible degree. The people below were then used to stepping up to the mark and thriving on seizing extra responsibility – or leaving the organisation if they couldn't take that pressure.

The government agency, meanwhile, had a much more paternalistic model of leadership, which was all about protecting junior staff and placing great value on fairness and equitable opportunity. The result was that what was seen as model leadership behaviours on one side was seen as either threatening or stifling by the other. Leaders on both sides lost the respect of their partners, and over time, relationships at every level suffered.

More often than not, simple prejudice is at the root of clashes like these. If organisations delve a little deeper, they may find that the crude stereotypes are often way off the mark. 'Bureaucratic' organisations like government departments, for example, have to move extremely fast in response to political changes. 'Creative' organisations can sometimes be as hidebound as traditional ones.

Getting past the simplistic labeling is essential if partners are to learn to collaborate effectively. As we've seen, that doesn't mean pretending everyone is the same. Nor does it mean trying to change either yourself or your partner – cultures tend to be deep-seated and difficult to alter. Besides, the culture may well be the driver for an organisation's success.

Make the cultural difference explicit and obvious to all partners, however, and you have the basis for an effective and productive partnership.

GETTING TO GRIPS WITH CULTURE

Our Ipsos Mori survey[4] found that accepting and understanding each other's culture was rated a critical success factor in partnerships (second only to having a common purpose). In addition, 85% of survey respondents said that cultural fit was a significant criterion in selecting a partner organisation.

However, when respondents were asked how they analyzed potential partners to see if there was a good alignment of cultures, the techniques they used appeared fairly haphazard. In fact most leaders assessed culture mainly on personal chemistry. And while this is undoubtedly important, it doesn't get to the heart of understanding culture.

---

[4]'Making Partnerships Work: A Survey of UK Senior Executives', Ipsos Mori and Socia, February 2007.

In fact, organisational culture is notoriously difficult to pin down. We need a way of describing in detail what makes Apple's culture so different from Microsoft's, or why an NHS trust is so different from the Prison Service. But before we get to our method of analyzing culture, we'll take a brief look at three very different models that have influenced the way we think about it.

William Bridges and the Concept of Character

William Bridges pioneered the use of personality type testing for organisations. In his groundbreaking book, *The Character of Organisations*,[5] he proposed that they differed in character in the same way that individuals do. Basing his work on the Myers-Briggs Type Indicator®, he developed a way of analyzing and articulating that character.[6]

For Bridges, there is no 'right' answer for organisations. He compares character to the grain in a piece of wood – no grain is inherently good or bad, but each type behaves differently. Some can take great pressure, some can withstand bending, while others take a fine polish. Each is well fitted to a particular purpose.

Self-knowledge, Bridges believes, can bring great benefits for organisations. If they come to understand their character and the strengths and weaknesses that run through it, they can avoid and compensate for weaknesses and capitalize on and develop their strengths. Rather than fighting the grain of their character, they should learn to work with it.

Charles Handy and the Four Organisational Structures

By contrast, management guru Charles Handy looks at organisational cultures in terms of structure, and is interested in what it feels like to work in each structure and in what circumstances they thrive. He divides structures into four types: power cultures, task cultures, role cultures and person cultures.[7]

Power cultures (or club cultures) look like a spider's web, with the leader at the center and ever-widening circles of others around that center. The closer to the center you are, the more influence you have. If you're part of the club, they can be a great place to work, and often rich in personality and passions. However, their weakness lies in the character of the boss – his or her failings are mirrored throughout the rest of the organisation.

---

[5]*The Character of Organisations,* William Bridges, Davies Black Publishing, 2000.
[6]The Myers-Briggs Type Indicator was developed in the early 1940s by Katharine Cook Briggs and her daughter Isabel Briggs Myers. Based on Jungian archetypes, it is widely used for personal and team development in business settings.
[7]Charles Handy first used this classification in his book *Understanding Organisations*, Penguin, 1976, although the four types were at that time given the names of Greek gods. The names are simplified in a later book, *Inside Organisations: 21 Ideas for Managers*, BBC Books, 1990.

Role cultures are like organisation charts – pyramids of boxes with job titles against each box. When the individual departs, the box remains. They're formal, procedural and logical, and thrive on stability. However, they have difficulty in coping with change.

Task cultures look like nets that can be pulled this way and that according to need. Pooling a team of talents or resources to respond to specific projects or solve particular problems, they're less individualistic than power cultures and faster than role cultures. They're forward-looking and usually warm, friendly and questioning, but they're expensive in terms of time.

Finally, person cultures are like stars loosely grouped in a constellation. They put individual talent at the center, with minimal structure to service it. Professionals who possess this talent are given high status, while administrators tend to be accorded lower status and have little control. It's hard to manage the professionals – they can be persuaded but not commanded.

Fons Trompenaars, Charles Hampden-Turner and National Cultures

Fons Trompenaars and Charles Hampden-Turner approach the issue from a completely different angle. In their book *Riding the Waves of Culture: Understanding Cultural Diversity in Business*,[8] they take as their starting point an analysis of the characteristics of different national cultures and then apply these to organisations.

The pioneering work in this area was done by Geert Hofstede, who first looked at cultural differences across a sample of IBM employees in different countries some 25 years ago and identified a model of cultural difference.[9] It identified five variables of national culture:

- attitude to hierarchy
- attitude to predictability of the future
- the balance between individual rights and freedoms and collective responsibility
- the degree to which expressing emotions is desirable or acceptable
- the balance between a belief in the rule of absolute and universal truths and the need to take account of the context of a specific situation.

Later Trompenaars and Hampden-Turner expanded on his research, adding two further variables: is the culture past-, present-, or future-orientated, and does it emphasize working with nature or trying to control it? They then took this

---

[8]*Riding the Waves of Culture: Understanding Cultural Diversity in Business*, Fons Trompenaars and Charles Hampden Turner, Nicholas Brealey Publishing Ltd, 1993.
[9]*Culture's Consequences: International Differences in Work-Related Values*, Geert Hofstede, Sage Publishing, 1984

analysis even further to analyze the culture of a business (irrespective of the country it is based in) and to resolve cultural dilemmas when two organisations of different cultures have to work together.

DON'T FORGET THE SUB-CULTURES

Of course, it gets even more complicated. Cultural mismatches are not just about different organisations in a partnership, but also about sub-cultures within a single organisation.

Different functions within a business often have their own character. Accounts departments recruit very different people from IT or the legal team. Creatives in an advertising agency are worlds apart from account managers. Academics at a university often find themselves at odds with administrators. The sub-cultures have different skills, different educational requirements and different mores. Putting them together can create unexpected behaviour and have huge impact.

Sub-cultures may be also based on different locations – the Manchester office and the London one, for example. When each location has a different business or customer base, the differences are even more marked. There may be significant variations in the type of people recruited, or in their length of service. The offices may even have started up as different organisations entirely – sometimes locations are the remnant of a past merger, and the old culture may well linger on.

Finally, leaders often influence the cultures of the parts of the organisation for which they're responsible. Charismatic leaders will create cultures in their own likeness. And a small business unit with a strong leader may have a more influential culture than the rest of the business.

ANALYZING COLLABORATION STYLES: THE ORGANISATIONAL PARTNERING INDICATOR

You can't tie down an organisational culture fully. There will always be something unexpected – just as an old friend or partner will sometimes surprise you by acting out of character. However, you *can* go a long way toward understanding the distinctions between organisational types and their preferred ways of working.

The model we use for analyzing organisational cultures and sub-cultures owes much to the work of William Bridges. We've built on Bridges' thinking so that not only do we describe the character of an organisation or function, but we also identify its collaboration style and indicate how other groups might experience working with it. The resulting tool – the Organisational Partnering Indicator (OPI) – helps leaders predict the challenges when different types of organisations have to work together, and gives them the knowledge to start addressing those challenges effectively.

The OPI uses terminology from the Myers-Briggs Type Indicator®, which describes an individual's personality preferences on four dimensions:

- Where, primarily, do you direct your energy?
  Introvert (I) – Extrovert (E)
- How do you prefer to process information?
  Sensing (S) – iNtuition (N)
- How do you prefer to make decisions?
  Thinking (T) – Feeling (F)
- How do you prefer to organize your life?
  Judging (J) – Perceiving (P)

It applies the same concepts and language to the culture of an organisation, analyzing the way culture is expressed in terms of an organisation's process, ways of working and habits.

The result of this analysis goes way beyond amorphous feelings of 'chemistry', giving a detailed picture of what makes an organisation tick – and importantly, how it's likely to collaborate with organisations with a different culture.

The following four tables are based on the model used in *The Character of Organisations*[10] and also on standard MBTI® terminology. They give an indication of the characteristics of each dimension used in the OPI.

Where Does the Organisation Direct Its Energy?
Introvert (I) – Extrovert (E)

The first dimension of the OPI explores whether the organisation looks outwards toward its customers, stakeholders and regulators (Extrovert) or inwards toward its own systems, leaders and culture (Introvert).

Extroverted organisations	Introverted organisations
Are open to influence from external bodies	Are not often open to influence from external bodies
Act quickly in response to changing situations	Respond to changing situations only after some consideration
Tend to put trust in spoken face-to-face communication	Tend to put trust in written communication
Ask others for guidance and new ideas, and seek assistance when in trouble	Believe that the best guidance comes from within the organisation and close ranks when in trouble
Have an approach to new opportunities dictated by their reading of future trends in the market	Have an approach to new opportunities dictated by their own values, capabilities and resources

[10]Ibid.

What Information Does the Organisation Pay Attention to? Sensing (S) – iNtuition (N)

This dimension looks at whether the organisation pays most attention to details and facts (Sensing) or to future trends and the 'big picture' (iNtuition).

Sensing organisations	Intuitive organisations
Strongest with specific detail	Strongest with the big picture
Record and analyze large amounts of data	Quickly spot emerging trends and implications in data
Aim to build solid routines and prefer incremental change	Tend to be a little careless about routines and prefer transformational change
Understand the future as an extension of the current situation	Believe that a new future can be created
Like their partners to operate precisely and to keep to procedures	Like their partners to be creative and respond quickly to new demands

How Does the Organisation Take Decisions? Thinking (T) – Feeling (F)

The third dimension looks at how the organisation makes its decisions: mainly by impersonal logic based on clear principles (Thinking), or more personally, based mainly on its values (Feeling).

Thinking organisations	Feeling organisations
Policies and principles drive decision making	Values and beliefs drive decision making
Focus on rules and exceptions	Focus on particular human situations
Encourage partners to live up to expectations	Encourage partners to do their best
Trust solutions that appear logical and financially sound	Trust solutions that appear to fit with the organisation's beliefs
Believe that criticism leads to greater efficiency	Believe that support leads to greater effectiveness

How Does the Organisation Plan and Structure Its Work? Judging (J) – Perceiving (P)

The last element of the OPI model focuses on whether the organisation prefers to close down decisions (Judging) or to keep its options open for as long as possible (Perceiving).

Judging organisations	Perceiving organisations
Focus on decisions and quickly lock into them	Stay flexible and seek more information
Are often moralistic – see fairness and justice as cornerstones of their culture	Are loose and fairly tolerant – often see personal freedom as a cornerstone of their culture
Never like to sit on the fence	Never like to miss an opportunity
Value others who deliver to the plan and give no surprises	Value others who think on their feet and take the partnership in new directions
See the creation of a stable plan and clear instructions as the basis for high performance	See the gathering of good market intelligence and flexible responsive processes as the basis of high performance

THE 16 TYPES OF ORGANISATION

To obtain a detailed profile for an organisation, a representative sample of staff need to complete a questionnaire, and their scores are taken for each dimension, just as a Myers-Briggs profile is obtained for an individual. The result is a four-letter profile, for example, ISTJ or ENFP. Alternatively, partners can work out their preferences together, using the statements listed under each dimension discussed above.

There are 16 possible combinations of the four dimensions, and we have developed detailed profiles for each organisational type, describing the collaboration habits and pitfalls for each. These profiles provide reliable predictors of how an organisation is likely to behave in collaborative situations.

Summaries of the two elements of the sixteen profiles are given on the following pages.

The 16 Types

ISTJ	ISFJ
Contribution to a partnership	**Contribution to a partnership**
• They are responsible partners, always fulfilling their responsibilities to other parties • They are able to bring the necessary governance and formality to a collaborative situation • They ensure that a partnership is planned and avoids getting deflected into new and 'interesting' areas • They will ensure that all parties pay attention to the essential details required to make delivery assured	• They are loyal partners who take care to keep their promises to other parties • They focus on implementation and want the partnership to deliver tangible results • They are concerned that relationships work effectively and that conflicts do not take place • They put a great deal of effort into delivering jointly agreed practical outcomes
Potential collaboration pitfalls	**Potential collaboration pitfalls**
When entering into a partnership, these organisations will need to:	When entering into a partnership, these organisations will need to:
• Avoid a tendency to increase the risk of introducing unhelpful bureaucracy • Consider the long-term demands and plans of the partnership, not just the short-term challenges • Take care to be patient with partners and their different ways of working • Put effort into communicating their decisions and activities to other parties	• Consider the long-term demands and plans of the partnership, not just the short-term challenges • Take care not to avoid addressing issues when there is conflict between parties • Put effort into communicating their decisions and activities to other partners • Avoid becoming disorientated if the ground rules of the partnership change quickly
Typical organisations	**Typical organisations**
Most IT companies, finance and admin departments	Hospitals, insurance companies

ISTP	ISFP
Contribution to a partnership	**Contribution to a partnership**
• They enjoy troubleshooting and are technically competent and enthusiastic problem-solvers • They are adept at finding the flaws and difficulties in current plans, and ingenious at finding practical solutions • They don't spend time talking, but like contributing through practical action • They are relaxed partners who do not make demands on others, preferring to provide the freedom that encourages experimentation	• They can be versatile and resourceful when circumstances demand a fresh approach • They can be very effective in a crisis, where their calm and easy-going manner can be reassuring to others • Their listening skills can help to discover new customer needs or to get early warning of tensions in a relationship • They avoid conflict and seek to understand others' points of view
Potential collaboration pitfalls	**Potential collaboration pitfalls**
When entering into a partnership, these organisations will need to:	When entering into a partnership, these organisations will need to:
• Resist the temptation to do it all on their own – they should use the skills of others • Consider the long-term demands and plans of the relationship, not just the short-term challenges • Put effort into communicating their decisions and activities to others – even if it means attending what might be seen as time-consuming meetings • Be careful not to shy away from others who become unexpectedly passionate about a situation	• Be aware that their partners may need long-range plans than they are used to working within • Be prepared to make their voice heard in lively or combative meetings • Seek to develop individual relationships across the partnership to create in both a sense of belonging • Make sure their own desire for independence doesn't mean they ignore the needs of others who are trying to establish rules and standards for a partnership
Typical organisations	**Typical organisation**
Construction and building companies	Professional practices which often work best when part of larger group

INFJ	INTJ
Contribution to a partnership	**Contribution to a partnership**
• They notice when relationships start to go wrong and want to help fix them • They bring fresh perspectives to the partnership, challenging other organisations to think about the long term and the fundamental aims of the arrangement • They tend to encourage other parties to participate and to deliver more than they thought possible • They provide a degree of innovation and clear thinking to the partnership, provided that others listen to their quiet input	• They act as the brains of the partnership, understanding the total situation before coming to conclusions • They rigorously test the ideas and strategies of other parties • They provide structure and process to the mechanisms of collaboration • They challenge traditional ways of working and encourage others to innovate
Potential collaboration pitfalls	**Potential collaboration pitfalls**
When entering into a partnership, these organisations will need to:	When entering into a partnership, these organisations will need to:
• Be more detailed about how they brief others than they would be internally • Create whatever recording and control mechanisms work for them and meet their own needs • Realize that on some occasions they will have to respond to other parties' requests immediately without time for consideration • Ensure that their creativity does not become too inward-focused and they are not seen as 'invisible partners'	• Avoid communicating too little and not explaining the rationale for their conclusions • Avoid appearing to hold fixed and inflexible views, particularly when changes are forced on all parties • Give particular consideration to the people impact of their style and approach • Put time into building consensus with other parties where this is necessary to gain commitment
Typical organisations	**Typical organisation**
Think tanks	Research organisations and academic institutions

INFP	INTP
Contribution to a partnership	**Contribution to a partnership**

Contribution to a partnership (INFP)

- Their contribution depends on the extent to which they trust others and believe in the shared values and ambitions of the partnership
- They can demonstrate inspirational leadership to all parties when times are tough
- They are willing to share knowledge and expertise in order to develop the skills that other parties need to succeed
- They are prepared to be flexible in their ways of working – but only if this flexibility contributes to meeting the shared goal

Contribution to a partnership (INTP)

- They act as the brains of the partnership, understanding the total situation before coming to conclusions
- They listen carefully and offer quality analysis and insight
- They encourage the partnership to be original and innovative
- They use the skills of other organisations to complete the tasks that do not interest them

Potential collaboration pitfalls (INFP)

INFP organisations are usually small, so they are likely to be partnering with organisations that are much bigger than they are, meaning that they have to adapt to a degree of process formality that is not their natural style. They will need to:

- Recognize that their expectations of the depth of the relationship are likely to be greater than most other types of business
- Communicate any issues and concerns early and formally – to avoid the development of later crises
- Be more formal about how they brief others than they would be internally

Potential collaboration pitfalls (INTP)

When entering into a partnership, these organisations will need to:

- Resist the temptation of only communicating when they are being critical of others
- Put time into building relationships with partners to avoid being seen as aloof by others
- Take care that other parties do not take their lack of apparent engagement as indifference or even agreement
- Pay particular attentions to facts that might be important to other organisations but can appear trivial to them

Typical organisation (INFP)

Social reform and environmental advocacy groups, small fast-growing companies

Typical organisation (INTP)

Experimental, entrepreneurial new technology companies

ESTP	ESFP
Contribution to a partnership	**Contribution to a partnership**
• They are the fixers of the partnership, identifying ways to address urgent problems that are holding up progress	• They are adaptable partners in a crisis
• They bring great energy to bear to achieve the task, often in innovative ways	• They encourage parties to bond through their ability to focus on the social aspects of a relationship
• They work to turn strategy into practical and implementable activity	• They work to turn their contribution into a service to the whole partnership
• They bring a flexible and sometimes informal approach to a partnership	• They bring a flexible and sometimes informal approach to a relationship
Potential collaboration pitfalls	**Potential collaboration pitfalls**
When entering into a partnership, these organisations will need to:	When entering into a partnership, these organisations will need to:
• Resist the temptation to do everything themselves	• Resist the temptation to do everything themselves
• Balance the focus on short-term tasks with spending time working with partners on defining future plans	• Be careful not to irritate others by appearing to be more interested in their organisational cultures than in the task in hand
• Be careful not to alienate partners by 'taking over'	• Take care that their communication is not perceived as too informal – invest in partnership governance
• Take care that their communication is not perceived as blunt by partners – they should invest in building relationships	• Act in an expedient way when times are tough rather than worrying too much about the impact on others
Typical organisation	**Typical organisation**
Central government department	Organisation involved in health and beauty treatments, such as health resorts

ESTJ	ESFJ
Contribution to a partnership	**Contribution to a partnership**
• They are tenacious problem-solvers for any partnership • They bring great energy to bear to achieve the task • They take deadlines and accountabilities seriously (both their own and those of other parties) • They pay attention to the detail and won't leave a job until it's done	• They are solid and dependable partners and are good at delivering regular tasks to a high standard • They will encourage a co-operative approach to tackling problems and will listen to everyone's opinions • They will work to define clear roles and structures • They will take care of people throughout a partnership
Potential collaboration pitfalls	**Potential collaboration pitfalls**
When entering into a partnership, these organisations will need to:	When entering into a partnership, these organisations will need to:
• Resist the temptation to take action on their own when they see relationships becoming too complex or political • Balance the focus on short-term tasks with time spent working with others on defining future plans • Give their partners room to operate – and avoid giving too much detail when specifying requirements • Invest time in understanding other parties' needs to agree on some of the less immediately tangible aspects of the relationship such as shared vision and values	• Make sure their great loyalty to their own staff doesn't create barriers to working with people from their partner organisations • Adapt their normal slow-moving and stable style in novel or rapidly changing situations • Take care not to be too accommodating of the needs of other organisations • Be careful to avoid promoting unsatisfactory compromises which try to keep everyone happy
Typical organisations	**Typical organisations**
Traditional military-style big corporations	Outgoing people companies, for example, small communications companies

ENFP	ENTP
Contribution to a partnership	**Contribution to a partnership**
• They support the process of developing vision, values and shared objectives for a partnership • They can function well as change agents, which draws on their characteristic positive outlook and their ability to engage others in the vision • They enjoy taking the role of coach or facilitator in any cross-organisational situation • They are good at picking up external trends	• They tend to engage others in new ideas and lateral problem-solving • They are willing to experiment with new untried courses of action • When and if they respect the other organisations' competence and contribution, they are able to collaborate and to partner • They enjoy the complexity of making a multi-party structure work
Potential collaboration pitfalls	**Potential collaboration pitfalls**
When entering into a partnership, these organisations will need to:	When entering into a partnership, these organisations will need to:
• Balance their enthusiasm for starting new lines of work with the necessary persistence and follow through • Take the necessary time and effort to make realistic plans and to be specific about roles and responsibilities • Be wary of going off on too many tangents and getting distracted by new opportunities • Be aware of their discomfort with conflict and make sure that difficult relationship issues aren't avoided	• Recognize that collaborative relationships need good governance and process to hold them together • Take care not to over-delegate the detail to others • Avoid giving up when results take time to deliver – as they often do in multi-party relationships • Be careful not to overwhelm or distract other parties with too many novel or lateral ideas
Typical organisation	**Typical organisation**
PR, training and marketing departments	Technical engineering consultants

ENFJ	ENTJ
Contribution to a partnership	**Contribution to a partnership**
• They tend to articulate the mission or vision for what a partnership is trying to achieve • They identify and try to resolve conflicts and problems between all parties • They will be sensitive to the needs of other parties and the individuals who work for them • They ensure that plans support the joint mission	• They take the lead in establishing strategy and direction for a partnership • They can quickly bring structure and organisation to the chaotic early days of a new relationship • They bring clarity to decision-making • When they see there is a problem, they can deal directly with conflict
Potential collaboration pitfalls	**Potential collaboration pitfalls**
When entering into a partnership, these organisations will need to:	When entering into a partnership, these organisations will need to:
• Be concise and avoid taking too long to express their requirements to other parties • Avoid investing too much time trying to involve all parties and keep them all happy • Avoid taking on all the tasks of the partnership and overloading their own people • Take care that their high principles and aspirations can realistically be implemented by other parties	• Resist the temptation to take over too much of the running of the partnership • Take time to listen to the views of others and check that their own communication has been understood • Be aware of small dissatisfactions or potential conflict that may be bubbling under the surface • Be prepared to flex their plans to meet new demands or changes to stakeholders
Typical organisation	**Typical organisation**
Creative value-driven organisations – some in the third sector	Most common types of large American organisations

HOW TO USE THE PROFILES: GET UNDER EACH OTHER'S SKIN

Understanding your own organisational profile and those of others sheds remarkable light on the frustrations within a partnership. It also allows you to use cultural difference effectively by tailoring your approach toward partners of a different type and taking their preferences into account.

To illustrate the profiles in action, we'll look at an example of three different organisational types in partnership together. A large engineering and project management consultancy is in a long-term contract with a government department to deliver a major infrastructure project. In addition, a small hi-tech start-up company is supplying some innovative touch-screen technology as a key part of the overall contract.

However, things are beginning to go wrong. Decisions get reversed and ideas blocked, the right people aren't consulted at the right time and there's no evidence yet that the pilot system is going to work. A team building day has had no effect. Something needs to be done.

Finally, the partnership assesses each partner's organisational type using the OPI. This throws up some interesting results.

The engineering consultancy has the profile ISTJ – introvert, sensing, thinking and judging. Its people are focused on implementation and want the partnership to deliver tangible results. They're also good at rules and procedures, and at putting the right governance in place. As partners, they need to be given time to digest ideas and come back with an analysis of the challenges. But they're pretty demanding. They want evidence and precision. And if someone makes a commitment, they expect it to be delivered in full.

The government department is ESTP – extrovert, sensing, thinking and perceiving. They're single-minded and task-oriented. They like to take charge when time is critical, and they're good at unblocking bottlenecks. They'll get involved in the detail of their partners' work, but want partners to communicate concisely and stick to the point. However, long-term planning doesn't come naturally to them and they're likely to spring some surprises on their partners.

Finally, the hi-tech start-up is INFP – introvert, intuitive, feeling and perceiving. They're passionate about what they do, though not always articulate about it. They hate bureaucracy, and sometimes rebel against it. But they're happy to be flexible and to share knowledge and expertise in the pursuit of shared goals. As partners, they need to be given freedom to get on with what they do best, and to question the beliefs and values of their partners. Tying them down to processes too early is a big mistake – they'll jib at it. Probably the best way to get to know them is to spend some social time with them – they don't believe life is all about work.

Understanding each other's culture is a vital first step to tackling some of the clashes that have characterized the three way relationship to date. Once each partner understands a bit more about the others, they can start accommodating their preferences far more than they have in the past. Armed with the profile results they run a set of three-way joint planning workshops, and they agree to a number of changes. For examples, they will now hold pathfinder meetings where the government department can talk about a range of possible future requirements without having to commit anything to paper. The hi-tech start-up can respond to these with creative ideas of its own. Meanwhile the consultancy can take note of possible implications for their core infrastructure. There's a long way to go. But it's a strong basis for effective collaboration.

SHIFTING THE CULTURE

Although organisational type tends to be deeply ingrained, it is not immutable. Organisations change over time. A start up will gradually settle down into a more process-driven organisation, and over time, a process-driven organisation can ossify into a slow-moving bureaucracy. Even a change of CEO can herald a new culture, since many CEOs build a culture in their own image, whether consciously or unconsciously.

One organisation that has successfully shifted its culture is Royal Parks, the body in charge of Hyde Park and other historic London green spaces. When Mark Camley took over as CEO in 2005, the prevailing culture was inwardly focused, concentrating on preserving the landscape and heritage. The park's many stakeholders were not seen as a high priority, as did balancing the budget. And while marketing staff had ideas for using the spaces in new ways to generate income, the horticultural staff were vetoing these initiatives.

'We were often on the back foot, governed by the seasons rather than a business plan', says Camley in an interview in *HR Director*.[11] 'We needed a new culture of decisive planning and implementation – a more proactive and extrovert approach based on information gathered from the outside world, not just horticultural issues'.

Using the OPI, we helped Mark Camley analyze Royal Parks' culture at the outset of the process. This score gave him a baseline measure for his process of change, and was followed by training in collaborative leadership for senior managers.

One of the insights from the training was that different functions were working on radically different timescales. When one horticulturalist was asked for his view of the long term, his response was: 'See those trees we're planting right now? We'll see whether we planted them in the right place in 100 years. Governments come and go, but trees remain'.

A year on, however, the different functions were able to understand each other far better, and to look externally as well as internally. Royal Parks hosted Live 8 and the London stage of the Tour de France, as well as won Green Flag Awards for all eight parks under its management. Meanwhile plans were under way for hosting seven events for the 2012 Olympics.

---

[11]'Changing Culture in the Royal Parks', *HR Director*, February 2008.

The second OPI measurement confirmed that the culture had shifted signifi-cantly toward planning and implementation. According to Camley, the detailed analysis helped 'unstick' the organisation. 'Understanding your organisational type helps you convince even the most sceptical people that you're making progress', he says. 'We're still in the process of changing, but we've managed to make a major shift'.

MAKING DIFFERENCE WORK FOR YOU

Cultural differences can be a huge problem for collaborative leaders, but an opportunity too. They can turn people tribal, circling their territory and tak-ing potshots at the enemy. They can bring out fear, prejudice and distrust. Yet they're a fact of life in partnerships. Most partnerships involve a degree of dif-ference in values and preferred working methods – and some indeed are forced marriages. Pleasant though it might be, you can't always create cozy relation-ships with like-minded organisations, and nor would you want to if you're try-ing to create something new.

All in all, we view cultural difference as a good thing. As we've seen in this chapter, it can be highly productive. Often the very reason for entering a partnership is to harness that difference in order to achieve something nei-ther partner could accomplish alone. Innovative Sony needs logical Ericsson. Traditional banks need whizz-kid software companies. And every organisation needs extroverts and introverts, accountants and marketeers, look-at-the-facts-people and people–people.

For collaborative leaders, the issue is how to get beyond skin-deep. It's not an instinctive skill to be able to read organisational character. Yet if you're entering into collaborative partnerships, you need to acquire those skills, and fast, because they really matter. Don't underestimate your own influence as a leader in this area. Your behaviour (collaborative or not) will have a dispropor-tionate influence on the behaviour of your own organisation and on the behav-iour of your partners. Collaborative leaders cannot stand outside the culture of the organisations that have to work together.

If all partners truly understand what makes each other tick, they can use that knowledge to build better relationships. The essence of collaboration lies in knowing each other's skills, likes and dislikes, trigger points and support needs – and not only accommodating those differences but employing them to the full. That way you can turn the irritating grit in the oyster into a pearl – and quite possibly one beyond price.

Chapter 7

The Secrets of Successful Leaders

STRAIGHT FROM THE TOP

Theodore Roosevelt once said that 'the most important single ingredient in the formula of success is knowing how to get along with people'. For a cowboy-hero president, those are highly collaborative sentiments, and it's pertinent advice for leaders today. To collaborate well – and to achieve ambitious goals – you need to be part politician, part psychologist. The question is how?

So far we've looked at the building blocks of collaboration in terms of the processes and tools you can use to analyze and guide you through the difficult task of managing a partnership. But there's no simple formula to applying these tools – making any partnership or other collaborative relationship work is a learning process. And it's not just about instilling the principles of collaboration into your organisation – it's also a journey of personal learning for you as a leader.

In this chapter we've chosen four successful leaders from very different fields, whose own journeys to collaborative leadership bring out some important lessons. Spanning both public and private sectors, they're experts in joint ventures, alliances, public–private partnerships and cross-departmental government collaborations, and all have made collaborative working a way of life. We ask them what qualities it takes to lead effective collaborations, and what they've learned along the road.

- Charles Jamieson is the former chief executive of Premier Oil, in an industry where joint ventures are the only way to operate. He now helps to develop fledgling companies and is chairman of two fast-developing oil companies.
- Moira Wallace has spearheaded cross-departmental collaboration in Whitehall, first as the head of the Social Exclusion Unit under the Blair government, and then setting up and leading the Office of Criminal Justice Reform, a joint venture delivery vehicle owned by three Whitehall departments. She is now Director General for crime and policing in the Home Office.
- David Sterry is chief executive of the support and construction services firm May Gurney, which builds and maintains infrastructure ranging from utilities to highways and bridges. He led an MBO of May Gurney in 2001 and has pioneered innovative public–private partnerships for over 10 years.

In 2005, he was awarded an OBE for services to civil engineering for his approach to partnership and innovation.

- John Yard led the biggest government outsourcing project in Europe in the 1990s, when the Inland Revenue transferred the management of its IT systems to technology services giant EDS. He went on to manage the IT aspects of the merger of the Inland Revenue and Contributions Agency, which had outsourced its IT to Accenture. He now advises organisations on collaborative ventures.

All four leaders have achieved extraordinary things through collaboration (for a mini-biography, see the boxes on each). When John Yard took on the leadership of the Inland Revenue's outsourcing project with EDS – at that time the biggest in Europe – his move was widely seen, he says, as a 'hospital pass'. Yet the project ended up being a model for governmental collaborations. Charles Jamieson headed Premier Oil for 13 years through all the ups and downs of volatile oil pricing and uncertain rewards, and increased both its market capitalization and oil production fivefold over that time. Moira Wallace led the highly successful Social Exclusion Unit in Whitehall, which dramatically cut the numbers of rough sleepers, school exclusions and teenage pregnancies. And David Sterry, chief executive of May Gurney, has achieved long-term relationships with public sector partners in an industry famed for its confrontational tactics.

While they're very different in character, these leaders share a common philosophy: in today's world, collaboration is not just desirable but essential in delivering their business.

Charles Jamieson: Joint Ventures in the Oil Industry

When Charles Jamieson realized he wasn't cut out to be an accountant, he took an MBA at INSEAD and went to work in strategic finance in the oil industry – probably the most collaborative business in the world.

His first job in the industry was at Gulf Oil, where his role was to travel in Europe evaluating investment projects for its various businesses. Although he enjoyed the experience, he felt the company operated as a collection of fiefdoms, often doing battle with each other. 'It put me off big companies', he says.

Instead Charles Jamieson accepted a job as finance director of what was then a small oil business – Premier Oil. In a risky and expensive industry, joint ventures were the only way to get things done, and he entered into scores of partnerships with governments, oil companies and contractors, particularly in Southeast Asia. He was made chief executive in 1992 and remained there until 2005. In his time as leader the company increased both oil production and value by more than 500%.

Since retiring from Premier, Charles Jamieson helps incubate start-ups and acts as chairman of two fast-developing oil companies, Salamander Energy and Vostok Energy.

THE DRAW OF COLLABORATION

What attracted these four leaders to collaborative careers? For David Sterry, a practical engineer by training, it's a practical solution to a problem: partnership is quite simply the most efficient way to get things done. The construction industry was – and to a large extent still is – traditional and unprogressive, relying on unforeseen extras to inflate low-margin prices, and generating huge confrontation along the way. Opting for long-term partnerships changes all that.

'In reality I don't like confrontation', says Sterry. 'It just got in the way of solving problems and I got very frustrated. It's a waste of effort bringing in the consultants and the lawyers. I'm looking for any way I can to avoid that'.

When he was headhunted by May Gurney, it was an opportunity to do something more constructive. 'They were passionate about solving problems together, and working in teams with the client to build a better, safer product', he says. 'Now I wouldn't like to work in any other way'.

In the capital-intensive and highly risky oil industry, collaboration is nothing new – it has long been a necessity. Oil companies enter joint ventures with each other, work alongside governments and employ a vast array of skilled contractors. 'For every exploration well you drill, only one in twelve has a chance of leading to commercial success', says Charles Jamieson. 'You can spend tens of millions of dollars. Even big companies will need to offload some of the risk by being in partnership'.

But beyond the inevitability of working in partnership within the industry, Jamieson is also naturally drawn to the personal relationships on which collaboration depends. 'I'm not particularly gregarious but I enjoy meeting people from different cultures', he says. 'Business school is all about strategy, but when you get down to it, it's personal. You get people to help by helping them'.

For John Yard, the attraction is – in part at least – the novelty of swimming against the tide. When he took on the Inland Revenue outsourcing project, he found himself in his natural element. Instead of changing jobs at the end of a 4-year stint (the norm in public sector management) he chose to keep on heading partnerships. 'Successful organisations are ones that can find ways to work across corporate boundaries', he says. But for him, partnership is more than a route to being successful. The real excitement lies in having to approach problems in completely new ways. 'I like coming at things where the solution is counter-intuitive', says Yard. 'If you're going to make partnerships work, you have to do things a bit differently'.

Moira Wallace sees collaboration not just as useful but indispensable. 'The Social Exclusion Unit could not have come up with solutions to the problems it was asked to look at without working in partnership – with those experiencing social exclusion, front line workers, and other Whitehall departments. And the Office of Criminal Justice reform was set up because it was only by working in partnership that the police, prosecutors, and courts could achieve the PSA targets set for them – to make justice more efficient and give the public a better service'.

She was immediately drawn to the idea when the Social Exclusion Unit was mooted. 'Although it was political, it was also managerial. It told me something about the structure of government that was getting in the way of things that needed to be done', she says. 'I thought "why didn't I think of that"'?

John Yard: Public Sector Outsourcing

Originally a tax inspector, John Yard became a senior manager in the Inland Revenue and found himself mediating between the IT division and the rest of the business. In the drive for market testing in the early 1990s, the Revenue responded by deciding to outsource IT. John Yard agreed to run the outsourcing project – at that time the biggest in Europe.

Finding it natural to work across corporate boundaries, he chose not to apply for the post of Director of Operations and instead stayed on to manage the highly successful IT partnership with EDS for several years. When the Inland Revenue merged with the Contributions Agency (taking on 10 000 new people), he then took over its IT partnership with Accenture. National Insurance is now seen as one of the fundamental databases in the UK.

John Yard now acts as what he calls 'a corporate Relate', advising organisations on collaborative projects.

MAKE IT MATTER – FOR EVERYONE

One of the most important attributes of a leader in any partnership is being able to engage people in what you're trying to achieve. 'Communication is the most important thing', says Charles Jamieson. 'Any leader needs a simple, clear vision. When I first started giving presentations to the City for Premier Oil, the strategy was a bit complex, and fund managers tended to nod off before it had been fully explained. You have to go in there and within one minute be able to say, "this is my strategy, this is what I'm going to do". Being simple is just amazing'.

Of course, this is true for leadership in general. But in collaborative ventures, you don't have captive audiences of staff whose salaries you pay. You've gone beyond your own power block and now have to win people over for a living. And there are many more stakeholders to deal with, 'Anything to do with partnership is invariably going to be more complex', says Moira Wallace. 'If there isn't sufficient clarity about what people are there to do, they just drown'.

Not only do you need clarity, but also the ability to flex the message according to your audience. The great communicators are ones who can relate the overarching vision to the needs of different partners and different groups. John Yard tells the story of going to a partner's organisation and giving a rousing talk to the staff there, taking a good look at things from their side of the fence and being candid about what the Inland Revenue was getting wrong. It won a standing ovation. 'There was some concern about whether I should have been so open and said all that', says Yard. 'But it was important in order to win trust'.

It's also important to inject some energy. Moira Wallace believes that you have to 'make it matter – otherwise partnerships are just so draining'. She thinks cross-government working is given a bad name by those 'oh, we had to send someone' meetings. 'Better not to have the meeting at all if it's just for form'. Her experience is that partnerships are energized by a measurable and challenging goal. 'When I see a partnership that has got lost in the fog, I try to boil down what we're asking for, bring it to life and increase the amount of electricity for the hour that we're together – so that people see how much it matters and want to put something of themselves into it too'.

Moira Wallace: Joined-up Thinking in Whitehall

A career civil servant, Moira Wallace was a private secretary at Downing Street when a more holistic way of thinking about social problems began to gain currency. Attracted by the new analysis, she won the job of setting up and leading the Social Exclusion Unit when the Labour government came to power. The unit's remit was to address major problems such as rough sleepers, school exclusions, teenage pregnancy and deprived neighborhoods – all challenges that cut across many government departments. The unit brought together staff from different disciplines and worked closely with people on the front line and those experiencing social exclusion, giving a voice to both. In a very short period of time, the solutions it put in place achieved notable successes.

Moira Wallace went on to set up the Office of Criminal Justice Reform, a joint venture owned by the Home Office, the Ministry of Justice and the Crown Prosecution Service. She is now Director General for crime and policing in the Home Office.

DON'T BLAME WHEN THINGS GO WRONG

'If you think collaborative partnerships are going to go swimmingly, you're wrong', says oil industry leader Charles Jamieson. It's a sentiment that strikes a chord with all the leaders we've spoken to. Not that they are pessimists – far from it. They simply know from experience that partnerships are complex and fraught with difficulty. It's far better to acknowledge this up front and prepare for the worst, than to come to blows further down the line.

'I sit down with customers right at the beginning and say "let's look at how to deal with something that goes wrong"', says May Gurney chief executive David Sterry. 'You have to build a relationship that allows you to deal with difficult things'. In the past, he believes, people were trained to trip each other up and catch each other out. Collaboration requires a very different approach, where you can admit to weakness in your own organisation without becoming defensive. 'If you're always trying to score points, it doesn't help. It just makes people behave as if they're under attack', says Sterry.

Of course, this doesn't always work: sometimes the customer doesn't want to drop the defences – or won't ease off on the attacks. 'Sometimes you can only conclude that their whole life is like that', says Sterry. 'And if they're not going to recognise the benefits of change, it's best not to work with them'.

'We need a greater recognition that things do go wrong on complex projects', says former Inland Revenue boss John Yard. 'We need to get people off the blame culture. The natural reaction of both sides when something goes wrong is to get the contract out, argue about how the terms haven't been met and seek penalties wherever possible, instead of working out how to solve the problem in order to achieve the outcome both sides need. It's all very well winning an acrimonious contractual debate, but how do you get both sides focused on the real issue afterwards? And there are always problems on both sides'!

When John Yard headed the Inland Revenue's IT outsourcing project in the mid-1990s, the IT provider, EDS, hit a performance problem early on in the deal and failed to deliver all of the targets specified in the contract. The natural reaction of the Inland Revenue board was to seek penalties from EDS, particularly given the difficult financial position at the time, but Yard argued that this approach on its own would not solve the underlying problem. He persuaded the board to allow him to work with EDS to ensure that the real causes of the problem were understood, before looking for a solution that was acceptable to both parties.

This revealed that the structure of the contract was causing problems, and the terms needed to be adjusted to make the deal more commercially viable, in return for delivery improvements and clarification of the way the contract would work in the future. Despite the difficulties of getting this accepted by the board, John Yard secured their agreement to what was in effect a counter-intuitive decision. 'The easy thing is to agree with all your peers', he says, 'but to make partnerships work across corporate boundaries, you have to recognise that there are times when you need to stand up and be counted'. The decision put the partnership back on an even keel, and it became a model for government collaborative projects.

'Too often people focus on the wrong thing', says Yard. 'The focus shouldn't be on winning the short-term penalty battle but on winning the long-term delivery war'.

David Sterry: Public–Private Partnerships

When David Sterry began his managerial career in a northern-based firm, the construction industry was mired in the 1980s confrontation. Construction firms took on contracts on low margins, but were experts at maximizing profits when specifications changed.

Sterry believed there were better ways to work, and as ideas on partnership came in from America in the early 1990s, he looked for more opportunities to work collaboratively. In 1996, he joined May Gurney, a firm specializing in highways and utilities infrastructure and maintenance, but with a reputation for a relationship-led approach. Already it had established the first partnering contract with the public sector.

After taking over as chief executive in 2000, David Sterry led a management buy-out – another step in building long-term relationships.

Under his leadership, long-term partnerships have increased from 10% of May Gurney's business to 70%, and public–private partnerships are increasingly run on innovative lines.

PUT YOURSELF IN OTHER PEOPLE'S SHOES

Building trust starts with service delivery. In the early days of building a relationship, doing exactly what you've promised is the way to convince partners they've made the right choice. May Gurney's David Sterry recalls a partnership where trust was decidedly lacking because the original architects of the deal had moved on. 'We just concentrated on delivering what was required', he says. 'As soon as you fail to deliver, you lose the relationship. Then progressively we managed to break those barriers down. Trying to maximise the contract always comes undone. So we take a long-term view'.

John Yard agrees that delivery is key. When he took over the National Contributions Agency partnership with Accenture, the relationship was going through major difficulties. 'I had to persuade Accenture I was serious that I could find a way that would work for both parties', he says. 'I said to the senior partner "give me three weeks and I'll do these three things. If I do them, then I want you to sit down with me and solve this problem"'. Yard duly delivered – and the relationship began to improve.

Keeping your promises is the first step. But to build truly collaborative relationships you need to go further and put yourself in other people's shoes. Our four leaders have become remarkably good at thinking through what motivates other people.

'We spend a lot of time trying to understand what the customer's drivers are – how they're encouraged to succeed and how they're incentivised', says David Sterry. 'Sometimes incentivisation can drive the wrong behaviours, and you need to get the issues out on the table'. John Yard is equally diligent. 'I need to understand why x gets his bonus and how I help him get it. What you're looking for is a mutuality of objectives – they're not the same'.

The problem is that this is a time-consuming business and can't be rushed. 'I learned a lot about how to enlist supporters, some of it the hard way', says Moira Wallace. She freely admits that she and her colleagues stepped on toes in the early days of the Social Exclusion Unit, taking ministers with them but failing at first to build sufficient support among the equally important Civil Service officials. 'So I learned about sharing control, and thinking about it from the other person's position. We put a lot of emphasis in the early days on understanding what life was like for people experiencing social exclusion. We hadn't been as good at thinking through how our recommendations impacted on those who would have to implement them in other departments. It's not easy when you're running a big and difficult programme in a department and then someone comes in from left field and says, "Do this as well". We all discovered a bit more about how to acknowledge the pressures that were on some of the people we were working with. We managed to find some critical friends, and meet them half way. We learned a lot'.

It's something that Charles Jamieson excels in. The polar opposite of a typical Texan oil supremo, he quietly goes about forging real and lasting relationships all over the world. At the beginning of his career in the oil industry, when he was evaluating investment projects for different businesses owned by Gulf Oil, he had to convince people that he was on their side. 'People hate accountants and people from head office. I tried to make them see I was someone who could help them', he says. 'It was the first time that I saw that personal relationships are the most important thing'.

At Premier Oil, he had to work with government officials all around Southeast Asia. 'They're often poorly paid civil servants, and you're not going to bribe them. How do you get work done? The only way I know is by being human and decent – understanding and appreciating their position. You need to be interested in people as people'.

'Glad-handing skills' are of course part of it, but there's far more to it than that. Charles Jamieson is a great believer in 'just pitching up and talking to people on a regular basis' to maintain a true personal connection. 'There was one senior bureaucrat in a country in South East Asia I used to visit seven or eight times a year', he recalls. 'Whatever time I got in the previous night, I would meet him on the golf course at six o' clock in the morning and we'd play nine holes and have breakfast and talk through business before we had formal meetings in the rest of the day. It meant that he was aware of everything I was going to say beforehand, and he would say, "I can't do it that way, but we can do it this way". So we built up a strong degree of trust – and frankly I don't think we'd have been able to do all that we achieved if we didn't have that relationship'.

This isn't just negotiation, although finding something for each stakeholder is important. It's genuinely getting on with other people and putting the effort in to maintain relationships, however time-consuming and difficult it may be. And when things go wrong – as they always do in partnerships – there are many, many people Charles Jamieson can call upon for help.

PATIENCE IS A VIRTUE

Collaborative leaders need patience. While aspects of the original deal may force leaders to make decisions at breakneck speed, getting to the contract can take ages and the actual partnership is likely to last many years. It can take a long time to yield results. So it's important to be flexible enough to have both a fast and a slow mode.

In addition, when you work outside the bounds of your own authority, everything takes longer. You can't simply tell people what to do, as you could if you led your own organisation – you have to bring them around. And sometimes you have to bite your tongue and let things happen in their own sweet time.

'Early on you need to listen a lot, and not form opinions too quickly', says David Sterry. 'You need to understand why the other party is how they are. Then you need to test it to make sure you understand. Try to ensure that they own the solution. People are willing to move if they can contribute to change'.

Moira Wallace agrees that big changes may need to emerge gradually. 'When we were working on criminal justice, it took us a while to work out that we needed to set up a joint venture to drive change. We started as a loose partnership and ended up realising that if we wanted to achieve our targets we had to be a single team, working for three different Ministers. The realisation was slow to dawn – in fact it was someone outside the team who first suggested it. And then it took a bit of patience to test that out and make sure everyone was on board'.

Building the coalition is more important than speed. And sometimes, says Wallace, 'it just takes a bit of time for people to get used to a new idea'.

SHARE THE CREDIT, SHARE THE LOAD

Building a genuine partnership means that you have to share leadership – something that the Social Exclusion Unit discovered along the way. 'There was a time when we realised we were holding the work too much in the team, and we needed to share the leadership – and the credit – with other departments', says Moira Wallace.

In the course of work on deprived neighborhoods, they developed 'policy action teams' with a mix of people both from the front line and from Whitehall. Senior people in Whitehall were asked to lead each group.

'It meant we had less control, which was unnerving', says Wallace. 'But it was really quite powerful. We didn't have to do everything ourselves. And people reacted to it in a very personal way, so they were firing on all cylinders. For years later, I saw people put it on their CV – it was a big experience to be asked to help shape government policy. It was a great way of generating common purpose and lots of brilliant ideas that would have taken much longer to emerge, or never have come to light'.

Modesty is important here – the ability (and self-confidence) to stand back at times and let others take the glory. It's a characteristic of all the collaborative leaders in this chapter: while well aware of their achievements, they're apt to credit their teams, their managers and their partners for many of their successes.

Moira Wallace believes it's a balance: 'I wanted people in the Social Exclusion Unit to have a strong sense of achievement, but I didn't want us to go out and throw our weight around', she says. 'I wanted the ownership to be shared wherever possible'. By refraining from hogging the limelight, collaborative leaders get things done.

EXERCISE YOUR INNER STEEL

'Partnership is not a soft and fluffy approach', says John Yard. 'It's hard and difficult. You need to have a backbone of steel'. Although collaborative leaders have to form strong personal relationships, they also need to be direct when necessary. Developing both the skill and stomach for difficult conversations is a key skill.

'It's about getting the emotions on the table – telling a supplier that you think they're being greedy, for example – and not getting people's backs up', says John Yard. 'You need to defuse the emotion and start looking at the real issues. Both sides need to state the problem and be prepared to listen and understand problems from the other party's perspective'.

It's important to get this right from the outset. 'You need to establish early on in a relationship that it's OK to do that', says Charles Jamieson, 'so you can put your hand up and say "I think you're talking rubbish" without destroying everything'.

Leaders also need to be able to fight their corner when it counts. 'I believe you shouldn't shy away from challenging, fact-based debate', says Moira Wallace. 'Sometimes you just have to say "well, we could all come out of this meeting very happy, but we wouldn't have solved the problem, so we can't stop still we get it right"'.

In fact tenacity and persistence are strong features in all four leaders' careers. For Charles Jamieson, sheer persistence has achieved some extraordinary results. Premier Oil is a small company, but it won and completed the Myanmar Project, two of the largest offshore gas development projects in Southeast Asia, as operator of the consortium. And in the UK, it was part of a record-breaking consortium that succeeded in drilling for oil under Poole Harbour in Dorset. 'The residents of Poole Harbour wouldn't take kindly to oil rigs and platforms right in the harbour, even if they were useful to sail round', says Jamieson. 'Instead we had drill laterally from the sea to the land. At the time the record was two kilometres. In the end we went to ten kilometres'.

THE ART OF QUIET CONFIDENCE

We started this chapter with Theodore Roosevelt, but the collaborative leaders in this chapter are a far cry from the charismatic cowboy-style president. Machismo and old-style heroism don't come into it. In fact, all four leaders are markedly thoughtful and reflective, highly self-aware and surprisingly modest. They lead less by authority than by persuasion, building coalitions, developing close personal relationships and learning to understand what motivates their partners and stakeholders.

What they all have, however, is strong self-belief. They don't demand recognition all the time – they're confident enough and relaxed enough not to need positional authority as leaders within a single organisation. Instead, they are happy with complexity, intangibility and shades of gray. All of them are more than willing to share or give away control in order to secure what they're after. They know what they want, and they know that the only way to achieve it is through slow, complex collaboration.

They're also brave enough to stand up for what they believe in. David Sterry led a risky management buy-out in order to build the kind of company he wanted to lead. Moira Wallace will always ask the difficult question. John Yard has frequently put himself in situations where people would like to have seen him fall flat. And Charles Jamieson is unfazed by asking Premier to punch above its weight, including taking on the challenge of managing billion dollar developments for the first time.

Five Attributes of Collaborative Leaders

- **Empathy**: Understand what drives others and causes them to respond in a particular way.
- **Patience**: Stick at what you believe in, taking the time to bring people along and not walking out on important relationships.
- **Tenacity**: Care enough about the outcome to keep going, however hard the negotiations.
- **Holding difficult conversations**: Confront issues honestly and early in the process so things don't fester.
- **Coalition building**: Build networks of support, find critical friends and pull together the necessary coalition of disparate groups to get the job done. It's a truism, but collaborative leaders don't do it on their own.

THE CHANCE TO MAKE A MARK

Just because the leaders in this chapter are confident about giving away control, it doesn't mean they're driven by altruism. For each the gains are considerable – it's just that they win more by giving power away than by holding tightly onto it.

'In my early career I could be as commercial as anyone else', says David Sterry. 'It was great fun and a bit of a game – how could you outwit the next guy? But it's not very constructive. This isn't how I want my approach to the built environment to work. I want to be more innovative, and I want to achieve more'.

For John Yard, the real kudos lies in making organisations work better in a complex world. 'How do we move away from an environment where giving of my best stops you giving of your best'? he asks. 'Most organisations have hierarchical models – people have to compete against each other to get the best jobs. So they're competitive, not collaborative – they're about personal gain and sometimes doing down colleagues. But delivering success for an organisation with complex services or products depends on a whole set of skills in the team, not just the skills of one person'.

Charles Jamieson believes a spirit of collaboration allowed Premier Oil to do things the bigger players could not. 'You can't just walk into a foreign country and say, "if it's good enough for Houston, it's good enough for Outer Mongolia"', he says. 'We were offering a packaging of treating people the way they wanted to be treated, building relationships, and managing projects the way they should be managed'.

And for Moira Wallace, collaboration is the chance to achieve something that couldn't be done by any other means. 'In the Social Exclusion Unit we were able to have an impact on social problems that had been going in the wrong direction for years, such as school exclusion, teenage pregnancy and rough sleeping. And in criminal justice we got agencies working together to achieve much greater efficiency and a better public service, and met targets that seemed impossible when we started'.

They're impressive legacies. And in a world where everything is inter-connected, it's increasingly hard to make a lasting mark unless you learn to collaborate.

Ten Lessons of Successful Collaborative Leaders

1. Find the *personal* motive for collaborating. It's not just about the hard business case – you also need to work out what's in it for you at a personal level. Our four leaders' personal motivations are very different, but they matter to each one.

2. Find ways of simplifying complex situations for your people – the implementation will often be difficult and messy but the principles or the policies you follow need to be elegant and simple to communicate.

3. Prepare for how you are going to handle conflict well in advance. Start with the assumption that some conflict will occur and look hard at your own habits and the typical reactions of your organisation to conflict situations. Will they help or hinder the long-term progress of the partnership? And what can you do in advance to build a mutual safety net?

4. Recognize that there are some people or organisations you just can't partner with. If a high degree of collaboration is vital in a particular situation, you may just have to rule those people out as potential partners.

5. Have the courage to act for the long term. Good collaborative leaders look at success over the whole lifetime of the partnership. In the private sector, financial models are often built with a payback period of many years, and leaders are prepared to take a short-term hit if they are confident of the long-term health of the relationship. In the public sector (paradoxically) it can be harder to take a long-term view, because the reality of the political cycle means that goal posts will move as election time comes around.

6. Actively manage the tension between focusing on delivery and on building a relationship. Recognize that imposing financial penalties on your partner can

be counter-productive. It just takes money out of the system and can reduce willingness to collaborate in the future. Penalties should therefore be used carefully and be proportionate.

7. Invest in strong personal relationships all the way through the partnership, and externally with stakeholders. Nothing can beat real human connections when things go wrong.

8. Inject energy, passion and drive into your leadership style – partnerships can be complex, interminable and draining, so they need to be kept from flagging.

9. Have the confidence to share the credit generously – partnerships are not about single stars but constellations and galaxies.

10. Continually develop your personal leadership capabilities, in particular the five key attributes of collaborative leaders: empathy, patience, tenacity, skill in holding difficult conversations and coalition building.

LEADERS MAKE THE DIFFERENCE

The four leaders we've seen in this chapter are largely natural collaborators – they're drawn to collaboration and they've chosen it throughout their careers. But that's not to say it's always been an easy ride for them. They've had to learn some of their skills the hard way, like patience, coalition building and empathy. And in some cases they've had to dissolve partnerships that just weren't working. However, all four are passionate about collaboration and the possibilities it offers to achieve things they couldn't do on their own. And to a large extent it's their character and abilities that have made the partnerships they enter a success.

You don't need to be a natural to collaborate well. But you do need to understand what it entails and master the steps, processes and skills. In the next chapter, we look at four leaders who neglect to do this, and see what happens when collaboration fails – not because of external factors, but because of the character and actions of the leaders themselves.

Chapter 8

Why Some Collaborative Leaders Fail

PAST PERFORMANCE IS NO GUARANTEE OF FUTURE SUCCESS

Around half of all of alliances break down prematurely, resulting in financial damage for both partners. As we've seen, research on alliances between American firms found that 48% ended in failure in less than 2 years.[1] The picture is equally gloomy in public–private partnerships – although there are fewer outright failures, public–private partnerships are recognized by government to have performed poorly over recent years. And though it's hard to prove a single cause for collaborative ventures that fall apart, the leader bears a heavy responsibility.

Why do so many leaders go wrong? The simple answer is that they just don't understand the nature and complexity of collaborative working. While they might have a great track record in leading a single functional area, department or organisation, the distinctly different challenges of running a highly collaborative venture leave them all at sea. Habits developed over years of success in a situation where they could exercise positional control become major barriers to working effectively in a partnership. Like the warnings about choosing high-profile fund managers to manage your nest egg, past performance is no indicator of future performance – or not unless recruitment boards start looking for proven collaborative skills instead of prowess in a single-lane role.

For leaders who find themselves in charge of a partnership or other collaborative relationship without being prepared for the change in leadership style required, it can be a stressful and unsettling experience. Suddenly the approaches you've used for years don't work any more. It's almost as if you've landed in a foreign country where nothing is quite as it seems. Some leaders learn rapidly from the experience and quickly start to pick up bits of the language and customs. But others stick to their guns and either try to bluster their way through, or gradually lose self-confidence and withdraw into themselves.

In this chapter we'll look at four types of leaders – the control freak, the idealist, the incrementalist and the selfish fast-streamer. In each case their

---

[1] 'When to Ally and When to Acquire,' by Jeffrey H Dyer, Prashant Kale and Harbir Singh, *Harvard Business Review,* July–August 2004. The authors studied 1,592 alliances that US companies formed between 1993 and 1997.

actions (or inactions) manage to ruin partnerships – failing to achieve the hoped-for value, leaving acrimony and chaos in their wake or, at the extreme end, forcing the contract to be abandoned and started afresh. This is not a random sample. These four portraits illustrate typical leadership styles, which in the right circumstances can take someone a long way in their career, but which prove disastrous in collaborative ventures.

The portraits are fictional, they are caricatures, but we hope you will find lessons to learn in each of them. In our many years of working with partnerships, we've seen aspects of all of these leadership behaviours and the risks they pose to building effective organisational relationships.

THE CONTROL FREAK

The Context: From Consulting to Corporate Leadership

Kevin was the new IT director of the largest division of a major manufacturing company. With a long and successful track record as technologist and a middle manager, he now wanted to cement his reputation for fast delivery of complex IT systems in a very different environment. He was approaching retirement and this was his most senior perhaps last corporate role, providing him an opportunity to work at board level in an established company, and in the manufacturing sector where he had started his career.

In taking up the IT director post, he quickly became aware of two factors that were to define his tenure in the company. The corporate center of the parent company was becoming more powerful, and its demands were increasingly in conflict with those of the largest division for which Kevin worked. At the same time there was a move toward company-wide single source contracts for corporate services. Procurement planning on one such IT outsourcing contract had already started before he arrived in his new post. The work was being led by the corporate shared service function, supported by members of IT staff from each division, and already Kevin was finding faults with it.

The Leadership Challenge: Turning Round the Reputation of IT

Kevin was a man with a lot to prove. He was fiercely keen to ensure that his IT function improved its reputation within his division. The history of IT throughout the company was one of poor investment and user disappointment, and the current supplier was widely considered to be providing a terrible service. Kevin realized that the new contract – for company-wide IT desktop services was critical to his achieving his own objectives.

He also knew that his fellow directors on the board of his division were concerned about the move to concentrate services at the corporate center. They had little faith that this approach would improve service. This view was reinforced when HR was moved to a corporate shared service model and service levels deteriorated significantly.

Kevin was expected to deliver significant improvements in service and knew that he could only do this if the new contract and new supplier delivered for him. In addition, he had to manage at the center of a complex web of relationships (the current IT suppliers, the bidders for the new contract, his new department, his director colleagues and the corporate IT function). And finally, he had something personal to prove – could he cut it as a 'proper' IT director?

Kevin's Character: The Expert Loner

Kevin was a technical expert. He really knew how to implement IT systems, and the more complex the better. He understood how to set up IT service centers and make an outsourced IT contract work. After all, he had implemented outsourced arrangements in the past, although not in a corporate leadership role.

However, for all his technical knowledge and experience, he was a bit of a one-man band. He tended to work on his own, and when in the lead he would select the most competent people to work with him and then direct them closely in the detail. He had no time for what he saw as incompetence, and found it quite acceptable to criticize others in public using very direct language. He liked people that he had worked with in the past – they were predictable and they understood and tolerated his style.

Kevin was highly committed to his work. He had little private life, living on his own without forming strong personal relationships. As a consequence he had lots of time to give to work issues. It was not unusual for him to send emails or make calls in the middle of the night if there were IT problems. No issue was too small to avoid his comment or involvement.

This energy and commitment was welcomed by his colleagues in the senior team in his own division. After his predecessor, who was considered lightweight and indecisive, Kevin was a breath of fresh air. If another director called with an IT problem, he was on to it immediately. Soon his reputation for 'driving IT forward' attracted the positive attention of his peers, although his impact was somewhat different with his own staff and his stakeholders in other parts of the manufacturing group.

The Consequences: Obstruction, Bullying and Conflict

Unhappy with the outsourcing contract, Kevin spent several weeks delaying its completion. At each stage he wanted more and more changes to the details. These delays caused frustrations to his own staff, who were increasingly unsure of their authority to define the contract. The goalposts constantly moved. The frustration also extended to the heads of the IT functions in other divisions of the company. They saw Kevin's behaviour as obstructive and selfish. Concern grew among all parties (including bidders) that the delays in letting the contract were eating into the planned transition period.

The contract was eventually placed, but immediately Kevin wanted to deal with the new suppliers on his own, outside the collective governance arrangements. The demands of his division were paramount and he intended to get rid of the incumbent supplier as quickly as possible. However, he also had wholly unrealistic expectations of the service improvements he could achieve with the new one. He expected significant improvements from day one – and when these did not happen, he demanded ever more detailed involvement in the supplier's business.

Things went from bad to worse. Service levels did not improve in the short term. In fact, with a reduced transition period, work on defining new roles and training users was inadequate and some high-profile failures of service occurred. With every new problem, big or small, Kevin's behaviour became more aggressive. He felt he knew the answers to the deteriorating situation, but no one was listening. His IT colleagues in other divisions were publicly criticizing him, and the new suppliers began to get different messages from different people.

As the commercial impact of Kevin's behaviour became apparent, disputes arose between the heads of IT across the company, and the problems were escalated to CEO level. At first the directors at Kevin's division supported him – after all, he was looking after their needs. But this support did not last. Service levels failed to improve and costs escalated at a frightening rate, as claim and counter-claim were made against the contract. Communication between the various parties broke down, with Kevin holding his own crisis meetings with suppliers in conflict with the corporate governance meetings.

Finally, there was a formal complaint from a supplier regarding Kevin's behaviour toward one of their members of staff. At the same time, a grievance was taken out by one of the corporate directors on the same issue. Kevin's approach could no longer be supported, even by his divisional colleagues. He was paid off and an interim IT director was quickly brought in to stabilize the situation.

However, Kevin's impact lasted much longer than his relatively short tenure in post. The relationship with the suppliers was in tatters, and costs were out of control. In the end the decision was made to break the contract, bring in an interim supplier, redefine the outsourcing requirement and start the whole contracting process again – from the start.

This was a disruptive and enormously costly exercise for the company, resulting in a dramatic change in the structure of IT across the divisions, with the corporate center now taking a strong lead. Relationships between the center and the divisions were significantly damaged and the impact of this situation could still be felt in the organisation some 3 years later. There were no winners – except the lawyers!

Lessons for collaborative leaders

- The successful operation of any partnership is ultimately dependent on productive relationships between the leaders involved. Leaders are role models for the behaviour of the rest of their organisation, and the way they act is particularly important at the start of the partnership – early experience forges the behaviours and habits that others will adopt.
- The risks – both perceived and real – for any organisation entering a partnership are high. Failure has a huge financial impact, and perhaps just as importantly, an impact on reputation. The personal stakes for the collaborative leader in any partnership are also high. This pressure is real and corrosive for those who find the complexity of collaborative relationship building a challenge.
- You can't do it all on your own. Not only do you have to share control with partners, you need the special skills of others in your own organisations (perhaps from other functions like procurement, commercial, legal or HR) to help you build the partnership constructively.
- You can't always pick the personalities of your partners, and bullying behaviour unfortunately does take place. You need a strategy to manage such situations:
  - Agree the ground rules on how to treat each other from the start.
  - Build strong relationship governance to deal with inappropriate behaviours.
  - Avoid colluding with a bully just to have a quiet life – it never works in the long term.
  - Address the first signs of bullying behaviour – don't let a problem become a crisis.
- Be aware of your own need for control – when things are going well, most people behave reasonably, but when the pressure is on, it's easy to lose flexibility and the need to control everything and everyone can become destructive.

THE IDEALIST

The Context: Delivering Complex Public Initiatives

Tony had spent his whole career in public service, working up through the ranks of the Civil Service. At last he achieved a long-held ambition to win a director-level post in a central government department, where he led an initiative to reduce the cost and improve the care of several chronic conditions. These were all complex challenges with high political priority, and each initiative involved many different stakeholders. In most cases, these included several central government departments (Health, Education and Pensions) along with organisations from the voluntary sector and some private sector drug companies.

This was the challenge that Tony had been waiting for. At interview he had impressed the panel with his commitment to the issues, and the energy and zeal he had demonstrated in driving his previous team to deliver. References from his colleagues and stakeholders had also been impressive. Many mentioned his inspirational leadership style and how he created and motivated a very close, committed team.

The Leadership Challenge: Making a Difference in Well-Trod Territory

Tony had no time to lose. He now had the remit and authority to drive this forward and he intended to make every minute count. Making a difference was his mission, and he was sure everyone else would be equally committed. However, Tony was not the first person to try to address the cost and management of these chronic complaints. Many had tried before him and failed to get the various parties involved to collaborate. Although aware of past failures, Tony felt that sufficient passion and commitment had been missing. All you needed, in his view, was one team with a single-minded focus on a clear objective.

Tony's Character: A Driving Passion

Tony passionately believed in the public service ethos and, in particular, in the values of the NHS. This was not surprising given his background – long-term chronic illness had afflicted several members of his family, and his own childhood had involved many trips to the hospital, visiting his mother who had died when he was a teenager.

His new role took him into unfamiliar cross-functional health policy issues and away from the simpler functional leadership he had exercised in the past. Tony was not a technical expert in the specific chronic complaints that he was now to address, but he knew how to get a team to deliver and he had boundless energy.

His style was to lead his team from the front. Membership of the team was rather like a club where only fully paid-up members were trusted completely. All others were outsiders. Tony took time to trust individuals – but when he did trust them; his loyalty to them was absolute. When things went wrong, he could see no fault with members of his team – the fault was always with other people or organisations. His loyalty to his team was returned by his own staff, who gave him their complete devotion.

When Tony was successful, everyone knew about it and his team loved it.

Behind the scenes, however, the impact of this charismatic, driving style was more evident. Tony's family life suffered as he worked long hours, often away from home. And there was an illness a few years ago that was put down to stress and overwork. But these problems were not discussed openly by Tony in the office.

The Consequences: Dwindling Trust and Commitment

Within a few weeks of taking on the new role, Tony had gathered his team around him, selecting several members from his previous job. They spent considerable time together understanding the challenges they faced and the objectives that they had to achieve. They drew up a detailed plan describing how they were going to deliver the healthcare outcomes and cost savings, with such ambitious timescales that even members of Tony's own team were skeptical. However, their belief in Tony's ability and leadership meant that these doubts were never aired in public.

The next step was to launch the project. This was done with some fanfare. All potential partners were invited to a conference where Tony took center stage. The challenge was laid out and the gauntlet thrown down. Either you were with him in his mission to improve chronic illness, or it was quite clear that you were making a choice to work against the project. In fact, this was no choice for most of the parties present. It was inconceivable for the other government departments not to sign up to the plan – any other approach would have been political suicide. The drug companies saw the potential damage to their reputation if they did not join in, and charities believed the initiative might help them deliver their own long-term aims.

The project started well but quickly hit problems. Relationships between the leaders of the various organisations involved in the partnership quickly became strained. Tony either dominated discussions at partnership meetings, or decisions were made in private with partners being told about them afterwards. As time passed, Tony's passion was undiminished, but the rumblings of discontent from other parties grew louder.

Tony's response was to initiate a team building event over 2 days in a country house. All the leaders from all the parties were invited and – under some pressure – they attended. Conversation was polite until the director of another government department criticized Tony's decision-making style and 'autocratic approach'. The department's officials explained that they felt excluded from direction setting and planning and did not see how the current project could be successful. Several other parties then supported this argument.

Tony was shocked and hurt by their response. Did they see the importance of the mission they were on together? Had he not made this absolutely clear at the launch meeting? Wasn't it obvious that the project needed one overall leader to drive it forward? The discussion became a quiet stand-off. It was evident that Tony did not have the support of his partners but also that he was not about to change his approach to any great extent. Although he regrouped his team after this event and altered the governance of the project to try to involve other parties more, his style remained much the same. Levels of trust slowly dissipated.

The voluntary sector organisations were first to walk away from the project – they didn't have to be involved and the effort of getting their voice heard was too great. The drug companies sent more junior members of staff to meetings, watching developments but becoming less active. Their promises of funds and support did not materialize. The other government departments did not change their involvement on the surface, but meetings were less well attended and deadlines were missed.

Tony and his team worked harder and harder to compensate. They pulled the drawbridge up and focused their efforts on forcing through change – but with little impact. In the end the funding was reduced, then quietly removed for the project and the team disbanded. Tony had a recurrence of the stress-induced illness and was off work for 3 months.

Lessons for collaborative leaders

- For a partnership to operate effectively, there has to be a common agreement among partners about the objectives and the operation of the relationship. However, the alignment of the leaders is most important, and without this agreement from the start, the partnership is under threat.
- Not all parties enter a partnership with the same level of enthusiasm. Some may see it as something of a forced marriage – and leaders of all parties need to recognize this at the outset.
- When things begin to go wrong in a partnership, it is important that leaders have an open relationship where difficult issues can be discussed and resolved. Most difficulties in a partnership are evident to the leaders if they listen to their people and ask the right questions. Leaders who are overly enthusiastic can discourage difficult feedback from others.
- Charismatic leadership might be engaging and motivating in some circumstances, but in a collaborative relationship, there is more than one person in a leadership role. A single leader cannot influence all the parties and stakeholders equally.
- Ambition and drive for the partnership are important, but so are realism and planning. Things will inevitably change and problems emerge, and mature collaborative leaders should be able to recognize when other parties are losing engagement with the objectives of the partnership, stop and listen to difficult messages, and change their approach to deal with the concerns of others.
- Collaboration is about sharing control. Driving all parties forward without thinking about the consequences demonstrates unhelpful control of others. It will create conflict throughout the partnership.
- As a leader, you should listen to your own motives – what you personally want out of the collaboration and why. This is important information, as it will drive your behaviours. Share this information where possible with your partners – it is an important enabler to building trust.

THE INCREMENTALIST

The Context: The Leader in Waiting

John was and lifelong engineer and had recently been appointed Director of Works in a local authority in the north of England. Several years before he took up post, people had talked about him as 'director in waiting' – doing most of the work in the role of deputy, and waiting for Jim, the old director, to retire.

Jim's swansong had been to negotiate a 12-year contract to outsource much of the local authority's building and property maintenance to a private sector contractor in a public–private partnership deal. This involved transferring 150 members of his department's direct labor force over to the contractor, as well as bundling up a number of existing sub-contracts and managing them through the PPP. It was widely seen as a groundbreaking contract, with terms ensuring that any savings made were shared between the public and the private sector.

In taking up the director post, John was faced with the task of making the contract work and delivering value for money, as well as hitting all the authority's maintenance targets. The problem was that the contract was failing to live up to the expectations of the architects of the original deal. They had believed that on top of achieving efficiency savings, importing best practice ways of working from the private sector to the council would generate internal cost savings. They also assumed that as both partners got used to working together, the number of inspections and the amount paperwork needed to manage the contract would also reduce, in a virtuous spiral of increasing joint efficiency. But none of this was coming to pass.

The Leadership Challenge: Taking Decisive Action

John wanted the same goals as his predecessors, but the means of achieving them posed big challenges for him. The internal cost savings would necessitate staff cuts, but the people he wanted to lose were those least keen to take early retirement, and the unions were out to protect them at every step. Meanwhile he was getting conflicting messages from his senior stakeholders – one group of councilors were forever pressing him to deliver the savings, but another group (including some councilors from more marginal wards) was anxious that he should do nothing to cause unrest among the staff or more bad news stories in the papers.

In addition, the managing director of the private sector contractor had been supportive at first, but was now saying openly in the steering group that the council was failing to live up to their side of the contract and needed to press ahead with internal changes if the partnership was going to hit its first-year targets.

Finally, John's own management team was behaving defensively, with each member of the team withdrawing into their own area of technical specialism and leaving John to make all the decisions about cross-departmental issues.

John's Character: A Safe Pair of Hands

John was an incrementalist – his character and his career as an engineer and a civil servant had taught him to check his ground at every step. He was uncomfortable with uncertainty and with plans that hadn't been fully worked through and documented from every angle. Most of all, he wanted to be sure of the details before he started.

John was a popular and respected leader, but the foundation of his leadership was his grasp and control of the details of the task. His staff trusted him because they knew he wouldn't act until he was sure of all the consequences of those actions.

He genuinely respected the private sector contractor, and believed they had most of the technical capability to do the job, but deep down he was convinced that they didn't understand the realities and constraints of the public sector – and that could make them a risk. He needed to hedge his bets.

The Consequences: Lackluster Performance and Lost Potential

Time passed, and very little changed within John's department. The old control structures remained. However, the cost of administering the contract and managing orders and payments was going up, not down, and John's managers complained that the private firm was reverting to type and becoming 'old-style contractors' rather than the profit-sharing partners they had hoped for.

On the other side of the partnership, the contractors were increasingly frustrated at the lack of progress. Their best managers started asking for transfers onto other projects where they could have more responsibility and impact. They had put forward some radical ideas, but these had all been squashed or 'bludgeoned to death by bureaucracy'. The cautious approach of the authority was holding back innovation, which in turn meant that the managing director was less prepared to invest more senior management time and money in the relationship.

For a while none of this was particularly visible outside of the management team of the partnership, but then project milestones started to slip and some early delivery dates were missed. This started to raise wider concerns. However, when John was challenged on these points, he asked colleagues to consider the risks in any alternative approach – possible industrial action, political risk in giving a contractor more responsibility when they were perceived to be delivering poor quality work and financial risk in removing some of the control and inspection structures without totally understanding how the contractor would respond.

Most of his colleagues agreed that these points were valid and that on balance John should stick to his guns. Eventually, some 2 years after taking up the post, John was able to complete the long-promised reorganisation – which on the whole was greeted with a sigh of relief. However 3 months later, there was a local election and a change of the political complexion of the council. New councilors were appointed to chair the major committees, it was clear they had very different priorities to their predecessors and they wanted to see change. John had to tell his management team that a further, costly, reorganisation might be on the cards.

The contract rolled on. The private contractors did a reasonable job but not a great one – and they didn't make as much money from the contract as they had been expecting. John's reputation as a 'safe pair of hands' within the authority was, if anything, strengthened by the experience. The contract had failed to deliver the savings that had been predicted, but it hadn't been a disaster either and all sides could point to lots of politically inspired changes in priorities as the reasons for the overspend. But when John and his old boss Jim met up for their annual lunch, as was their habit, John was the first to confess that the last couple of years hadn't added up to half as much as he had intended.

Lessons for collaborative leaders

- The successful operation of any partnership usually means that both sides have to change to get the best from the new relationship. In public–private partnerships, this often means significant organisational and managerial change for the public sector side of the partnership.
- Making these changes for the benefit of the partnership will often be seen as risky and unpopular. The constant complaint leaders hear is 'why should we change just to fit in with the private sector'?
- Driving through this sort of change takes personal leadership courage – daring to be unpopular in your own organisation because you can see the long-term benefits for the whole partnership. But self-confident, driven leaders are not often found in these public sector roles. A two-speed approach to change across a partnership, with one partner wanting to go much faster than the other, will create tensions and can often lead to one of the partners disengaging from the process.
- Control means different things to different people. A leader who is used to incremental change and being sure of every step will struggle with partners who are used to making a leap of faith in the confidence that they will thrive in any situation.
- Incremental leaders can get caught in the vicious circle of their own lack of confidence with radical change:
  - team members who expect them to be on top of all the detail,
  - colleagues who would rather collude with risk-averse behaviour than have a radical role model in their midst,
  - external stakeholders who are risk-averse by nature and demand an audit trail of all decisions and actions.
- Frustrated partners who offer increasingly radical suggestions to try to break the log jam will only reinforce the belief that they need to have strong controls on them to prevent them from doing something stupid.

THE SELFISH FAST-STREAMER

The Context: Bringing Private Sector Drive to the Public Sector

Rachel had recently been appointed as the finance director of a large central government agency. She was ambitious and saw herself as on a fast track career within the Civil Service as a whole. Her background was in the private sector – she had worked her way up through a number of finance director positions in smaller privately owned companies. Her recruitment into the Civil Service was part of a Whitehall initiative to improve the financial capability of agencies and to bring private sector commercial awareness to the role.

As finance director, she had responsibility for procurement and commercial contract management as well as for the conventional central finance function. When she arrived, one of the highest-profile items in her in-tray was the immanent procurement of a complex facilities management and building maintenance deal. The scale of it was enormous – much bigger than the organisation had ever attempted before. Progress to date had been led by a project manager from inside the property function and was painfully slow. There was a project board that was supposed to be chaired by the agency CEO to indicate the significance of the deal, but so far it had only met once.

Within weeks of Rachel's joining she had volunteered to take over the chairing of the project board until the end of the procurement phase. In addition she promised the CEO that under her guidance the deal would be done and the contract ready for signature on the original timescale – even though the project was running several months behind schedule.

Rachel threw herself into her new task with a passion, recruiting a 'heavy hitter' finance project manager who had led the procurement of a similar outsourcing deal for a pharmaceutical company in the previous year. She also made personal contacts with the managing directors of the three or four most likely bidders in order to demonstrate the agency's strategic commitment to driving through this deal.

The Leadership Challenge: Building Alliances

Getting this job was a big step up in responsibility for Rachel. Her salary wasn't much higher than the one she had been earning in the private sector, but the scale and breadth of her role were much bigger than anything she had experienced before. The reputation of the finance department across the agency was poor, and some of that was justified – capabilities within the team were not very high – but the department had also made enemies over the years among the heads of other parts of the business. Rachel needed to make a positive impact fast.

She also needed to build alliances with the existing head of facilities management and the heads of the biggest divisions, whose budgets would be funding the ongoing costs of the contract. They saw the whole thing as a major risk and a bit of a distraction from their day job. They were rather pleased when this new high flyer came along and offered to take the difficult decisions out of their hands.

Meanwhile the major facilities management suppliers were delighted – on paper this looked like a long-term profitable deal, with someone driving it who was prepared to take decisions swiftly.

Rachel's Character: Ambition Without Flexibility

The first impression Rachel gave was of a confident, ambitious leader, with a high need for status and recognition. Her career trajectory was one of rapid promotion and moving on – she had rarely stayed in any job for more than 2 years. Now she wanted a job close to the heart of government and this role looked like a good stepping-stone along that path.

Underneath this confident exterior she was scared. Scared that she had made a mistake in taking this job, and fearful that she could get stuck in a morass of public sector bureaucracy that would slow down her career. She was used to working in businesses small enough for her to have her fingers in most of the pies and a high degree of control. She was also used to working with dynamic and highly capable businesspeople who understood the commercial implications of business decisions as a matter of course.

Rachel found it very difficult to cede control of the details, and especially difficult to cede control to people she did not rate as particularly competent.

The Consequences: Apparent Success, Actual Disaster

The deal went through on schedule, and was feted in the trade press as highly successful, with a groundbreaking procurement process. Rachel herself was featured in much of the press coverage and she was quick to point out the benefits of bringing her commercial expertise to the aid of a public sector procurement process in all her interviews.

Under the surface, however, the few months leading up to the signing of the deal had been very stressful for all involved. As the contract paperwork was finalized, the heads of the main operating divisions finally engaged in the detail and didn't like what they saw. One declared that he wouldn't sign up for his share of the budget, and two others formed a hasty alliance with the head of facilities management to try to delay the procurement process by 6 months in order to give all parties time to reconsider. It took all Rachel's belligerence to force the deal through, and she had to persuade the CEO to lean on his other directors so that the procurement timetable to which they had both publicly committed wasn't totally compromised.

Rachel was triumphant when the deal was signed, and made sure most of the limelight fell on her. After all, it seemed a personal vindication of her hard-driving and commercially savvy approach. But signing the deal was only the start. As soon as the new suppliers came on board, it was clear that the transition and implementation timetables were completely unrealistic. In one area, the original plan had been for a 3-month transition, but after 12 weeks' hard work, there weren't even any transition plans on paper that everyone would sign up to, never mind an end date in sight. All the internal and external relationships that needed to work with a degree of give and take in order to make a complex transition operate properly had been strained to breaking point by the antagonistic atmosphere created throughout the procurement. And although few would say it openly, most people put Rachel's leadership style at the heart of the problem.

By refusing to share any of the decision-making during the procurement, and taking all the credit for the deal being done on time, she had also personalized the whole situation to a high degree. When the situation became difficult, her colleagues weren't going to put themselves out to help her succeed. Six months later, Rachel applied for and, somewhat to her own surprise got, a high profile job as global finance director for a major charity, which was about to embark on procuring a major IT outsourcing deal and needed a successful director with private and public sector experience to guide them through. But in the press, stories were already emerging about her 'abrasive' management style, and amongst her peers her reputation was beginning to tarnish.

Lessons for collaborative leaders

- Ambitious leaders move roles and organisations frequently as they further their career. The developing collaborative leader should use these moves to learn from the experience of others and build new relationships quickly. This is challenging because it means being open about your lack of knowledge, and willing to accept advice and ideas from people you don't know well and who may work in a different way to you.
- Building an effective coalition at the start is crucial. If it is not built early, leaders will have to spend time attempting to salvage it at the later stage – with inevitable delays in the timetable.
- Many partnership projects have distinct phases of procurement, transition and operation, and although these may be led by different people from different functions, the tone and style of the relationship will be carried over from one phase to the next. You can't have an antagonistic procurement and then expect a co-operative transition.
- With large collaborative projects, organisations need to build governance and processes that avoid placing all the power with one person, who may then choose to move on when the going gets tough.
- Leaders need to share the plaudits as well as the pain. If a leader is seen to be drawing all the praise to themselves and acting as a personal figurehead for the program, then don't be surprised if others are less than willing to throw their own weight behind the wheel.

WISING UP TO WHAT IT TAKES

Sadly, these four stories of floundering leaders are not that unusual. Anyone who has been around partnerships for a time will have their own story of isolationism taken to extremes, over-cautiousness that stifles innovation, passion unchecked by realism or ego unchecked by humility and patience. And these experiences are unlikely to end happily.

However as the fictitious accounts in this chapter illustrate leaders in these situations are not often viewed as failures. Even when others in the partnership are well aware of their shortcomings, the outside world is not. The selfish fast-streamer can be celebrated for the success of 'doing the deal' and move on to her next high-profile post, quite possibly to wreak havoc once again, before the consequences of her previous actions are all played out. Yet all four destroy both the goodwill and the value of the partnerships they lead, costing huge amounts of money and setting the tone of the relationship in years to come.

If organisations are to avoid failures like these, they need to put the right governance in place to ensure that decisions are taken for the good of the whole partnership. If a leader is failing to collaborate effectively, this should be noticed early by others in authority and action taken to change the situation or the people involved. In addition, partnerships need the right operational processes and measurement to ensure leaders get the data to do their job effectively, to capture lessons learned along the way and feed them out to the whole organisation. Finally, the right leadership behaviours need to be encouraged at every level to get real value from the interaction of different parties.

We need to get much better at teaching collaborative skills and understanding what to look for in potential leaders – especially in partnerships where there is a lot at stake. When you go back to the words of the successful leaders in the previous chapter, you realize the extent of their wisdom and experience. Some of that needs to go into the training of would-be leaders if we are to get past the 50% failure rate to the point where a respectable majority of collaborative ventures can create real value. That point isn't yet in sight.

But we'd like to believe it's somewhere just over the horizon.

Chapter 9

Risk and Opportunity

TWO AND TWO CAN MAKE EIGHT

Partnerships are risky things. Because they're more complicated than single enterprises, risk is inherent in their structure and needs to be managed carefully. Yet at the same time, partnerships are all about opportunity – creating possibilities for growth, innovation and change. And the opportunities are only there for those who grab them with both hands.

Leaders have to strike a balance, then, between mitigating the risks and going straight for the prizes. Too much emphasis on controlling the risks, and you stifle opportunity, as we saw with the incremental leader in Chapter 8. Too little and you squander the potential of a collaboration and expose it and yourself to unforeseen danger.

The consequence is that collaborative leaders must be both pessimists and optimists, creating a culture of strong risk management, yet injecting enough drive, ambition and openness into the partnership to have a chance of claiming the opportunities. Once again, it's a bit of a paradox. You need to get people to think through the worst scenarios that could happen and to keep a close watch on the main sources of risk so they don't spiral out of control. But you also need to encourage people to try out new ideas and encourage innovation in the space between the different organisational cultures. This in turn means encouraging people to take risks at an individual level – and of course being prepared to take them yourself.

In her book, *Beyond Authority*, Julia Middleton, chief executive of community-based leadership development charity, Common Purpose, describes leadership as a series of circles emanating outwards.[1] At the center is your inner circle, your circle of authority, where you have the control to reward or sack people. Beyond that is the circle that bounds your organisation. Beyond still is the outside world. And the further away you get from your inner circle, the tougher and riskier it gets – personally, as well as organisationally. Yet some things can only be achieved by creating coalitions and working beyond your authority. For Middleton it's the chance to strengthen democracy and build civil society. But whether your partnership is about making money or changing the world, you're out there in the dangerous space. The risks are bigger – and so are the potential rewards.

'What I love is helping to develop leaders who operate across worlds,' says Middleton. 'Who counteract the forces of fragmentation in organisations and society. Who – together – make two and two make eight (or even ten)'.

---

[1]*Beyond Authority: Leadership in a Changing World*, Julia Middleton, Palgrave, 2007.

WHY PARTNERSHIPS ARE RISKIER

When HMRC outsourced its data management to EDS and its internal postal service to TNT, it's unlikely that leaders imagined a risk scenario in which the combination of some unthinking actions by a junior official and lost piece of internal mail would get senior officials and ministers on the front pages of all the papers. Yet all it took was a security failure in 2007 where two disks containing names, addresses, national insurance numbers and, in many cases, the bank details of all the Child Benefit recipients in the UK were put in an unregistered package and delivered by couriers TNT. The disks never turned up – and the ensuing scandal led to the resignation of the chairman of HMRC and even threatened to topple government ministers.

Risks in partnerships are legion. They crop up where they're least expected, and they often have huge consequences. Partly that is because partnerships are complex systems where small changes can trigger large effects. And as many different parties are involved with different interests at stake it's much harder to keep any problems 'inside the family' and out of the public eye. Just consider British Airways in 2005. One of its suppliers, Gate Gourmet, a maker of in-flight meals, took on extra workers to cover the holiday peak. This wasn't in itself a major problem – except that Gate Gourmet was also in the process of renegotiating pay and working conditions for its staff. The workers took unofficial action in protest, and 670 people were summarily dismissed. Staff at British Airways then walked out in sympathy. The result: 900 BA flights from Heathrow grounded during August – and tens of thousands of holidays ruined. You can share risk with your partners in theory, but you can't give away the responsibility for managing it, nor the accountability for the consequences if it all goes wrong.

So why is it so hard to manage risk in partnerships?

There isn't Enough Trust

One of the reasons is that there's a higher level of uncertainty built into the relationship, particularly when partners are relatively new and haven't yet established trust. To assess risks properly, you need openness and honesty on all sides. It's hard enough to talk about potential problems at the best of times, but it's of a different order of magnitude when you don't wholly trust your partners across the table, and are unsure about how they will use the information you're about to give them. And it's only too easy to view risks incurred by another partner as 'not my business' – even though the consequences are likely to affect the whole partnership.

Partners have Conflicting Takes on Risk

The difficulties are compounded when partners have different attitudes to risk, especially if one partner is risk-averse and the other more gung ho. Polarized perspectives can lead different sides to retreat behind stereotypes of each other – for example, grasping developers versus slow, pedantic bureaucrats. Besides creating tension and misunderstanding, this makes it difficult to generate a joint sense of ownership of risk within the partnership. And should a risk turn into reality, it's likely to lead to deeply unhelpful behaviour, with each side pointing the finger at the other.

While it's not always possible to match outlooks toward risk within a partnership, it's certainly something to consider during the selection process. At the very least all parties need to discuss their appetites for risk openly from the beginning and agree on an approach that works for everyone.

A Collaborative Risk Checklist

(Taken from a joint HM Treasury and Office of Government Commerce publication *Managing Risks with Delivery Partners*[2])

Partnership arrangements

- Alignment of objectives: is there sufficient buy-in to the department's objectives? Have strategic objectives been communicated sufficiently well in order to identify common interests?
- Aligning authority with responsibility: are those responsible for managing the risks empowered to do so?
- Incentives: are there incentives for partners to manage risks effectively (or, e.g. are the consequences of failure felt primarily by the department)? Is the risk/reward balance right for each partner?
- Resilience of the partnership: how resilient to unexpected events is the supply chain?
- Approach: has the right approach been chosen (e.g. the risks of taking a partnering approach rather than an 'arms length' approach potentially include lack of clarity; getting too close to one partner at the expense of others; risks of improper relationships developing; higher cost with less value for money)?
- Is the partnering approach understood by those operating it? And have any tensions been resolved between the need to agree clear contractual arrangements and retaining flexibility for partnership working?

Partnership management

- Monitoring: is there prompt, relevant, high-quality performance information? Is this clearly embedded in robust performance management arrangements?
- Skills, experience and culture: is there sufficient understanding of the whole picture (departmental staff responsible for working with partners often have little experience of working in delivery bodies and so are not always well placed to understand the priorities and risks of partners; conversely, staff in delivery bodies often have little experience of working in the center of departments)? Are any cultural barriers to joint working being overcome?

---

[2]Available to download at http://www.ogc.gov.uk/documents/cp0013.pdf

One Partner is Expected to Shoulder All the Risk

Contracting arrangements in PPPs and PFIs have been particularly prone to clashes like these. They also have a history of over-optimism about how much risk could be transferred to private companies. The public sector traditionally emphasized an arm's length approach to risk, and in the early days of public–private partnerships, private contractors were expected to carry the lion's share. Often, however, this was politically naive – a private company could not be solely responsible for delivering a fully functioning hospital, for example. In addition, private sector companies charged a high premium for taking on risk, but when something went wrong, it often proved to be outside the original assumptions.

A more sophisticated concept of risk-sharing in PPPs is to transfer the risk to the people best able to manage it and for other partners to pay for this service. Under this model, a private contractor in a roads maintenance contract, for example, might take on responsibility for estimating how much road salt is required for the winter and keeping a sufficient supply in stock for the gritting lorries in case of bad weather. They'll incur a financial penalty if it runs out. It makes a certain amount of sense, but some problems still remain with the arrangement. If the gritting lorries run out of salt on a snowy day, the public will blame the council, and not the contractor, whatever it says in the contract. There's no getting away from sharing the burden.

The Risks aren't Visible from One Perspective

The very nature of shared ownership also creates risks of its own – and the points where two or more partners are most dependent on each other are where things are most likely to go badly wrong. Remember the platform edge example from Chapter 2? Managers at London Underground have to concentrate their greatest collaborative efforts at interchange stations like Green Park. If the management of tube lines, trains and stations is not properly coordinated at these points, there there's a very real risk of disaster at the platform edge – people could get hurt.

In any partnership, these points of interdependence between different functions or organisations are usually the areas of highest risk. One of the main problems is that the risks aren't visible from just one perspective. All parties need to work together and share information effectively if they're to prevent risks from becoming major incidents. At points of interdependence, you can't afford to do it alone.

Risks can Spiral out of Control

Even more worrying is that risk in partnerships can have disproportionate consequences. As we saw in Chapter 1, partnerships are complex systems – admittedly not as complex as nervous systems or the stock market, but complex nonetheless. And complex systems are non-linear, so a small perturbation in one area can cause a disproportionate effect in another. In other words, actions may have unpredictable consequences. The lost disks at the Inland Revenue and the Gate Gourmet strike are dramatic examples of this principle in action: unforeseen errors with huge and dramatic results. Pinpointing risks like these – and dealing with them fast – is a skill any leader wishing to avoid disaster should take care to master.

EXPECT THE UNEXPECTED

Kate Nealon is an American ex-corporate lawyer and now a non-executive director on several corporate boards involved in numerous joint ventures and alliances. She's also a government and risk management expert. Her advice is simple: expect things to go wrong – and in a major way. 'You need to bring in all the Eeyores of the world right at the beginning', she says. 'And you need to do thorough scenario planning – if you're a bank, for example, what if the World Trade Centre blows up and clearing doesn't work'?

Some potential risks are obvious – handling successions, preparing exit strategies or dealing with conflict, for example – and careful planning in advance will make each one far less painful to handle. Diageo supply chain director Gerry O'Hagan recalls how he entered a 15-year partnership with a multinational utility company 'just before it all went pear-shaped' and went into liquidation. However, he had a good exit strategy and a workable plan B. 'We managed a very productive exit from the partnership when things went awry', he says. 'A few months later we were up and running with a new partner, and working even better, because of the lessons we had learned and the plans we'd had in place for unexpected eventualities'.

While it's impossible to foresee every risk, it clearly pays to expect – and discuss – the unexpected. 'You can't predict the future, but you need to talk about it', says former Inland Revenue leader John Yard. But this isn't as easy it sounds. To communicate effectively about risk, leaders must have the courage to admit potential shortcomings and vulnerabilities in their own organisations, well before they start causing problems. They need the patience to understand each other's operations thoroughly to find out where the crucial interdependencies lie. And as a leader you have to own the risk and take a judgment about what constitutes an acceptable level. Remember John Yard's words from Chapter 3 on setting up a partnership? 'It takes self-confidence to put your foot down', he says. 'I'm straight with procurement – I say, "you're advising me, but I will decide what to do, and I will decide the level of risk"'.

So listen carefully to the Eeyores. And then make up your mind.

PUT THE RIGHT GOVERNANCE IN PLACE

Managing risk is a relentless process. You have to keep on doing it – at regular meetings, and informally by constantly going to the coal face and finding out what the issues are.

You also have to make sure you get the governance right. The most senior leaders from all parties should come together to talk about risk on a regular basis – perhaps once a quarter – in a mandatory meeting that no one can miss or delegate. At this meeting, it's worth scheduling two or three key issues that you know are worrying people, and gathering survey data in advance of the meeting (e.g. on staff morale and customer perceptions – both areas that give you leading indicators of future risks). But you should also take care to devote at least part of the meeting to 'the things that keep you awake at night' – which may not be the obvious issues, and may well be vague and nebulous. Good risk management isn't always about examining the obvious – sometimes it's the subtle things that can trip you up.

A governance meeting for the partnership to rebuild the ticket hall at Kings Cross Underground station threw up one such worry. Although each partner had developed their own plans for closing the Thameslink railway for maintenance over the Christmas period, none of the leaders had confidence that it would actually work. It emerged that some partners were worried about risks belonging to their partners – for example, whether Kings Cross station could cope with the extra traffic generated by closing the Thameslink line. It was only by raising these half-formed worries that they started working together to check the interdependencies thoroughly – and to make the plans join up properly. Caring about each other's risk was essential in making the line closure go smoothly – which it did.

Good governance is even more necessary when things go wrong. At that point, all parties have to refrain from blaming each other, because blame merely encourages everyone to clam up the next time. It's also important not to seek advantage for your own team out of a risk that has come home to roost, even if the contract makes changes expensive to one party and profitable to another. If the impact of a problem falls unequally, affecting one partner more than others, it could jeopardize the partnership as a whole.

BEWARE THE RISK REGISTER

Risk registers, with their red/amber/green coding for each risk, are the traditional way to categorize risks and plan how to mitigate them. They're certainly simple, but all too often they degenerate into simple-mindedness – a mechanistic box-ticking exercise with no roots in the reality of the collaboration. And when risks are coupled by trivial plans to mitigate them (e.g. 'insufficient sponsorship by leaders' being coupled with 'get sufficient sponsorship'), the alarm bells should start ringing.

One government department we know of dutifully produced a risk register with a huge list of around 150 elements. This labor of love was then consigned to a desk drawer where it languished for several months. To be honest, this probably didn't make much difference, as some of the ideas in the register for risk mitigation were entirely toothless – for example, one key figure in the partnership was known to be likely to leave, but the mitigation for this eventuality went along the lines of 'brief new Director' – it's not wrong but it's hardly a thought-through strategy.

Risk registers are a useful tool, but only if you make them so. There's no point in bundling every possible risk into one interminable document to which no one will ever pay attention. Instead a risk register should list a manageable number of risks and highlight a handful of the truly scary ones at any one time. 'I start by writing down the three things I'm worried about – and then see if they're on the risk register', says former Inland Revenue outsourcing chief John Yard. 'Then I look at the management information, and ask, "What does it feel like? Is it measuring the wrong things"'?

To do this, of course, you first have to know which issues to worry about – and that means keeping an ear to the ground. 'Failures are often because of an inability to see the warning signals', says oil industry leader Charles Jamieson. 'You need to tell people that if they make a mistake you want to know right now. Lots of people don't tell you bad news early enough'. Board adviser Kate Nealon goes further. 'When things get bad, staff start hiding things', she warns.

'Even if you try to legitimise the telling of bad news, you are still fed what people think you want to hear', says Julie Baddeley, a non-executive director on the board of several major partnerships. 'And the Red Amber Green traffic light report just doesn't tell you enough. The very first time you see it switch to amber you need to go round asking questions – you have to go and ask people what's keeping them awake at night'.

Most importantly, leaders need to own the risk register. There's no point in sticking rigidly to one dreamed up at the start of the partnership, possibly by a different set of people, if it doesn't match what's going on in the partnership from day to day. And you certainly shouldn't delegate the responsibility for it. Managing risk is a priority leaders can't afford to duck.

DON'T LET RISK DESTROY OPPORTUNITY

It's clear that collaborative leaders need to pay a lot of attention to risk, because the stakes are so much higher in partnerships. But equally you can't afford to let caution get the best of you. We've seen leaders so afraid of being out of control that they can't act when it matters, and won't let others either. They effectively kill all innovation. So if you're going to make collaborations work, you have to be prepared to take some chances.

As we've seen, the greatest risks in a collaborative system are often found at 'the platform edge' – the points of high interdependence between different parties. Yet the greatest opportunities are often found at precisely the same points. Here different organisations have to work closely together, and while that can be tricky, the friction can also be creative: people challenge each other's assumptions, ask apparently stupid questions that make people see in a new light and posit different ways of doing things. And every so often break-throughs get made.

Trusting your partners in those high-pressure, edge-of-the-platform situations is hard, but the point of greatest criticality is often the point of greatest creativity. And as Bill Joy, one of the co-founders of Sun Microsystems says, 'There are always more smart people outside your company than inside it'. The challenge is whether you can recognize what they have to offer if they speak a different language or bring with them a whole set of different assumptions about your business.

It's a balancing act – cultivating a healthy respect for risk, without letting it turn into a fear, and exploiting the opportunities of partnership without being reckless. But timidity is not an option. Common Purpose chief executive Julia Middleton believes that in the outer circles where you have to lead beyond your authority, you need 'sensible courage' – 'so as not to go back, especially when everything you know fails to match the situation'.[1]

In fact, the business world can learn from the voluntary sector in creating opportunity through collaboration. Voluntary sector organisations are often highly skilled at getting a lot done in tough circumstances and on a small budget. They understand only too well how joining forces can help them make a far greater impact.

FIND YOUR INNER ENTREPRENEUR

In some ways entering a partnership is akin to being an entrepreneur. You're chasing a particular opportunity and a set of potential returns. And unless you put everything into it, there's no chance of it coming off. It's no place for the faint-hearted.

The oil industry takes this to extremes. As we saw in Chapter 7, only one in twelve exploration wells drilled will make it to successful use. Exploration is so eye-wateringly expensive that it has to be a joint enterprise. Of course, all the players involved do what they need to do to mitigate the risks. They pour everything into information, analysis and expert advice. But in the end they're taking what is in effect an informed bet – which in most cases they're likely to lose. Naturally, the occasional wins have to be worth the effort.

Many private sector collaborations are on built the entrepreneur model – it's a way of starting up a new market without committing the whole organisation to the project. Take Ocado, a UK partnership between start-up firm Ocado and Waitrose, which has pioneered online grocery shopping. An idea hatched by two former bankers at Goldman Sachs, Ocado was launched in 2000. It attracted huge investment from backers – more than £277 million – although few people at the time believed it would catch on. But with a highly automated central warehouse and a strong service philosophy, Ocado is finally beginning to make money. And while Waitrose accounts for only 4% of the British grocery market, Ocado has cornered 18% of the online market. One of the UK's most successful and creative online grocery businesses has been created by a collaborative venture rather than by a conventional powerhouse of the retail world.

But what about other partnerships? Is there an element of entrepreneurship in different kinds of collaboration? The language may be different – but the principle remains the same.

When nature conservation charity WWF agreed to a partnership with the world's biggest cement manufacturer Lafarge (discussed in Chapter 4), there was a high element of risk. Accepting sponsorship is an implicit endorsement, and it would have been easy for WWF to be seen as a corporate collaborator (in the worst sense) by the rest of the voluntary sector. In fact at one point the partnership risked being derailed entirely by a conflict over a proposed Lafarge quarry in an area of outstanding natural beauty on Harris in Scotland.[3]

For Lafarge, too, there were risks in entering the partnership. The company was publicly committing to stringent targets on rehabilitating quarries and cutting CO_2 emissions. And there were plenty of critical voices within Lafarge complaining that the partnership was a waste of resources. Yet the opportunity – to create partnership that really worked between a major corporate and a global NGO – made the very real risks worthwhile.

With government projects, the risk lies in incurring public wrath and losing credibility (as well as public money). Moira Wallace's Social Exclusion Unit, a cross-governmental and community collaboration (discussed in Chapter 7), was highly publicized from the start, with clear and measurable objectives. The results couldn't be fudged. But the chance to do something about chronic social problems was a goal that inspired everyone to take the risks, go out on a limb and come up with real answers.

Even the self-regulating networks like Wikipedia and Linux, discussed in Chapter 1, have risks for participants. If you submit something to Wikipedia, you seek the satisfaction of writing a definitive entry to the world's biggest online encyclopedia – but at the same time you risk having it publicly contradicted by another editor. And as a Linux programmer, your code is scrutinized by the whole community, and any flaws dissected. Yet entry to the community has big rewards – you're part of an elite band of hackers who are challenging the supremacy of corporate software.

KEEP THINGS OPEN

Leaders of collaborations like these don't spend all their waking hours worrying about risk mitigation. Instead they let the air in. They encourage openness in their organisations, so that people feel free enough to challenge each other,

---

[3] *Tough Dialogue Pays Off: How Lafarge and WWF Make Their Partnership Work to Help Preserve the World's Ecological Balance*, by Claudia Heimer, Roger Pudney, Jean-Paul Jeanrenaud, Luc Giraud-Guigues and Michel Picard, Ashridge Practitioner Paper, 6 October 2006.

confident enough to risk making mistakes and engaged enough to change things for the better if they're not working well. They nurture new thinking and innovation. They constantly open the doors to the outside world, bringing in ideas from other sectors, industries and nations. And above all, they believe in what they're doing, and make others believe it too.

Creating this kind of environment means that you can't run everything according to the perfect project plan. Attempting to tie things down too fast is counter-productive – there has to be some space for creativity and innovation. And given that it's a collaboration, there also has to be space for backtracking and catching up, going round the houses and getting everyone on board. So how do you build this kind of flexibility and openness?

Create Tight Roles and Loose Tasks

One way is by defining roles tightly but leaving tasks loose. Back in Chapter 4, which examined the three-legged stool framework for collaborations – governance, operations and behaviours – we looked at how staff in television crews have clear and unambiguous roles that everyone understands and respects. This allows teams to work smoothly and efficiently in what would otherwise be stressful situations. But where the tight role and loose task definitions come into their own is in dealing with the unexpected. Since no one has to worry about their individual role, the team can focus quickly on how to deal with a changing situation. They have wide latitude on how to deal with their task, so they think on their feet, respond quickly to a new situation and come up with creative solutions. Keeping the task open leaves space for innovation.

Use Diversity to Encourage Innovation

The other key tool is tapping into diversity and harnessing the power of many ideas. Diverse teams are better at innovating – they look at things in different ways, make new connections and see unusual angles. And here collaborations are at a natural advantage – unless you've chosen a partner that's a clone of you, diversity is almost certainly built in to the fabric of the partnership.

In *The Wisdom of Crowds*, James Surowiecki describes how the SARS virus was isolated in a matter of weeks instead of years when the World Health Organisation assembled eleven research teams from around the world in March 2003 and asked them to collaborate to find the cause of the disease that was claiming hundreds of lives in Southern Asia.[4]

Each team was allowed to pursue their own line of discovery, but instead of guarding the results closely in the hope of winning personal glory, all agreed to share their emergent findings daily by email. The collaborative process allowed

---

[4]*The Wisdom of Crowds: Why the Many are Smarter Than the Few*, James Surowiecki, Little, Brown, 2004 [first published in USA by Doubleday, a division of Random House, 2004].

the teams to follow multiple directions, build rapidly on each other's research and determine which leads were fruitful and which were blind alleys in record time. Within a month of starting the collaboration, the virus that caused SARS had been found and confirmed. Although no one team or individual could claim its discovery, everyone contributed – and everyone won.

Of course, to make diversity work to your advantage within a partnership, you need to get beyond the misunderstandings and stereotyping that can arise from putting together groups from different cultures. Chapter 6 explains how to build awareness of each other's organisational characters and to use the differences effectively. Those differences should be gold dust in a collaboration. After all, if you wanted a group of people who think the same, why bother to collaborate in the first place?

Inject a Bit of Fun

Finally, innovation and creativity also need an element of playtime – a free-flow interplay of ideas, without censoring, checking or organizing – just letting ideas go wherever they want. It's very much like having fun – and Common Purpose chief executive Julia Middleton sees sheer enjoyment as an important factor in leading coalitions. In her book *Beyond Authority*, she writes: 'I reckon that people will volunteer authority to all kinds of leaders – as long as they are brave – and fun'.

When Moira Wallace was head of the Social Exclusion Unit with a brief to tackle rough sleeping, school exclusions and deprived neighborhoods, the project was driven and intense. But the unit also managed to make it light-hearted – appointing someone they called 'the air traffic controller' to 'stop everyone landing in Bradford on the same Wednesday in the same estate'.

A sense of humor, the ability to laugh at oneself and the ability to surprise people – they're often overlooked, but they make collaborations happier, easier and more creative.

MAKE THINGS FEEL SAFE

For openness and innovation to flourish in a partnership, you first need to make people feel secure. It's a bit like composing music or writing poetry: in order to be free you need to know the rules and the structures inside out. And in any group, you need a framework in place before you can let yourself loose on the possibilities.

In his book, *The Truth Option*, Will Schutz describes how group formation follows three clear stages – inclusion, control and openness.[5] First people need to feel that they're legitimate players with a right to be included in the group.

---

[5]*The Truth Option: A Practical Technology for Human Affairs*, Will Schutz, Ten Speed Press, 1984.

Second, they need to be able to exercise sufficient control over what they need in order to operate. This is the point where people establish their independence in the group, and if there are problems here, there may be jostles for power or even turf wars. Finally they reach a stage of openness or collaboration – but only if they've gone through the first two stages successfully, and haven't got stuck there. We talk more about what happens if you get these stages wrong in Chapter 10 (page 167).

To reach the openness stage, then, you need to get the fundamentals right – things like the basics of the contract, governance of the partnership, the role definitions, the performance data and all the arrangements for money. If people spend all their time worrying about big issues like these, there's no chance that they'll ever be able to free up their minds to think creatively about how to make the partnership deliver. So build a strong framework, based on the three-legged stool of governance, operations and behaviour described in earlier. That will help you sort out the accountabilities, the shared systems and the tensions caused by cultural differences – all obstacles you have to get over if people are to feel a sense of inclusion and control.

Even if the partnership has reached a state of openness, this won't apply to new recruits. Each time an individual or a group joins the partnership, they need to go through the same stages to ease themselves into collaborative working. If you don't make this possible, they will be operating under par.

Also Remember that people will have varying perspectives on what constitutes a safe environment. This is where different organisational characters come into play. Staff who have built their careers in a public sector organisation may well set a lot of store by clearly defined procedures in every area. But for a small and innovative company, a long list of procedures is unlikely to feel like safety. Getting invoices paid on time will probably be far more important.

BALANCE OUT THE ASYMMETRIES

One barrier to developing opportunities within a partnership is a lack of symmetry in the rewards they offer. An innovation in one area may produce great benefits for one partner but few or none for other partners. Unless you address the unevenness, you're limiting your possibilities.

But when you start a joint R&D investment program to create innovative opportunities for a partnership, you don't know where the benefits will accrue. You need a trading mechanism, agreed in advance, to balance out the asymmetries in the costs and value of any innovation. And where this isn't possible, you need to exercise fairness and generosity in sharing the rewards of innovation.

For a clothing distributor, for example, the idea of transporting clothes from the warehouse on hangers and running rails produces minimal savings. For the supermarket that buys the clothes, it has enormous advantages, saving both time and space on arrival. But for ideas like these to flourish, partners need to be rewarded well. If you're squeezing the lifeblood out of your suppliers, you can't expect collaborative behaviour to happen naturally.

Another example, again from retail, underlines the point. One of the most important things that a retailer can do to increase its sales of clothing is to ensure that all sizes of all lines are never out of stock on the shelves (one typical supermarket found that a 4% improvement in stock availability can drive a 15% increase in customer sales). This usually requires a complex network of manufacturers, wholesalers and distributors to make it happen. New technology and new work practices may all help the process – but at a cost – and at first sight the majority of the benefits end up in the retailer's profit margin.

Of course many retailers have the power to lay down the law on this, and beleaguered suppliers often have no choice but to comply. However, a more positive spiral is created when the retailer works collaboratively with suppliers. To take the example above, we've seen one retailer jointly funding a pilot project with a clothing supplier and a distributor to generate new ideas to increase stock availability and then later sitting down together to work out how to share profits effectively. This joint approach makes it more likely that suppliers will invest time and creativity in innovation – and stores up goodwill for harder times.

CULTIVATE INCURABLE OPTIMISM

Innovation is not the whole of the picture, however. To seize the opportunities a partnership offers, leaders need incurable optimism to drive through their plans, and the courage and ambition to take risks when necessary. The best leaders are both resilient and tenacious. They don't let adversity knock them off course. They're not overwhelmed by the often labyrinthine process of building coalitions. And when it matters, they don't take no for an answer.

It's a question of self-belief. Common Purpose chief executive Julia Middleton says that in the outer circle beyond authority, 'if you don't set out with enough determination and self-belief, you will come unstuck, come what may. You have to muster up an enormous amount of determination because you are in unfamiliar territory'.[1]

She quotes filmmaker David Puttnam, a skilled operator in the outer circle, who learned the art of the long game by trying to get his films off the ground. 'Chariots of Fire took three years – and a stream of insulting letters (some of which I then framed just to remind me)', he says. 'I am very patient. If I get blocked off here, I'll try something different there, but I will always come back. Someone once said of me: "Don't waste your time saying no to him". Maybe he did not mean it as a compliment, but I took it as one'.

Not only do you need drive and determination as a collaborative leader, but you also have to carry people with you all the way. And it's a never-ending task. In a process that can last several years and suffer many setbacks, you keep open to opportunity by injecting urgency and excitement, and by bringing the vision to the forefront and making sure it's kept alive, whatever the problems and challenges along the road. You need to make stakeholders feel included, and to leave the outcome open enough for people to feel they have a genuine part in building it. And of course you need to share the credit generously and selflessly whenever you achieve your goals.

The last thing you require in all this is an over-developed sense of risk. The collaborative leaders we admire have a healthy respect for it. But they certainly don't let it get in the way of achieving their goals.

How to Manage Risk: A Ten-Point Plan

1. Get the most senior people together across the partnership regularly to talk about risk.
2. Make this a mandatory process – no party can duck out and no one can delegate their role.
3. Ask people to talk about their worries – the intangible and perhaps irrational things that keep them awake at night, not just the tangible and quantifiable risks.
4. Build trust to a point where people are prepared to share their fears (and challenge others) about weaknesses in their own organisations that might damage the partnership.
5. Get everyone to talk about fears relating to things they do not control (or understand) in other partners' organisations.
6. Go out looking for what people are worried about at the coal face. Hold joint visits to each partner's organisation and listen to what people are worried about on the ground. That way you can counter misplaced fears as well as find out about things you hadn't thought of.
7. Keep assessing the risks relentlessly and put joint plans in place to handle them.
8. Develop realistic plans to deal with the high-likelihood, low-impact risks as well as the low-likelihood, high-impact ones.
9. Care about your partner's risk as well as your own. Sometimes supplying resource or expertise to help them avoid a risk within their organisation can save you all a lot of time and money at a later date.
10. Try not to seek advantage for your own team when things go wrong. If a risk comes out of the blue that affects one partner more than others, it may destabilize the whole partnership.

GO FOR IT

There's no doubt that partnership entails extra risk – it's part of the fabric of collaboration. By joining forces, you multiply the risks – and they can have disproportionate consequences. So as a leader you have to take them very seriously.

Yet at the same time, collaboration makes opportunities possible that are not within your sights as a single player. The trick is not to let awareness of the risks ruin those opportunities. A culture of endless mitigation won't generate enough drive to embrace the chances the partnership throws up. People will get discouraged, and all the drive, energy and innovation latent in the partnership will gradually dissipate. Over-control is a certain killer.

So we believe you can't afford to be timid as a collaborative leader. If you're a ditherer, it's not the job for you. In fact, as a leader, it's better to err on the side of optimism. Be shrewd about the risks and focus firmly on the ones that could cause most heat. And keep the Eeyores close by, because you need to spot trouble before it gets out of hand. But when an opportunity arises, you need to be ready to go for it – because that, in the end, is what collaboration is all about.

Chapter 10

Conflict and the Collaborative Leader

CONFLICT COMES WITH THE TERRITORY

When we speak to leaders of major collaborative ventures about the lessons they have learned, top of their list is often the need to prepare for and handle conflict. It's the same when we run training programs for leaders. At the start of a new partnership, their number one concern is not being able to deal with a serious dispute.

Most organisations see conflict as something to be avoided at all costs. Avoidance and collusion are common coping strategies: people tend to ignore the problem for as long as possible, and if that doesn't work, they pass it up the line. The underlying fear is that relationships may break down – and possibly result in litigation, which is damaging for all concerned.

But it doesn't have to be this way. Instead, leaders can learn to handle conflict, and see the early signs of conflict as a useful warning and an opportunity to take the relationship forward into new and more creative territory.

It's especially important for collaborative leaders – because in many collaborative ventures, conflict is inevitable. There are a number of reasons for this. For a start, there is often more at stake. However good the contract, the success of a partnership is built on trust between the parties. If conflict escalates and that trust breaks down, you can quickly get into a downward spiral of litigation, delay and cost overrun. The saga of the new Wembley stadium and the long-running battle between the Football Association, its main construction contractor, Multiplex, and the steel work firm, Cleveland Bridge over delays in the construction shows just how bad it can get. Cleveland Bridge originally took Multiplex to court in 2004 alleging non-payment of some of the costs it was owed. Multiplex then issued a series of counterclaims totaling over £25 million. In February 2008, High Court Judge Mr Justice Jackson described the process as 'grim and ghastly', and said that he believed the whole row should have been sorted out years before.[1]

Individual leaders also have less control in a partnership. When a dispute arises within an organisation, a leader can use personal authority or positional

---

[1] 'Multiplex court case a "grim and ghastly" saga', *Contract Journal*, 20 February 2008.

power to force through some sort of resolution, however painful or expensive that solution may be. In a partnership, however, you've given away some of that power, and if your partner doesn't like your solution, you have to look to different methods of dispute resolution.

In addition, more leaders are likely to be involved as peers in the debate. For example, in a road maintenance project carried out in-house by a local authority, a single director is ultimately responsible for resolving the outcome of any design disputes that occur along the way. But in a typical public–private partnership arrangement, there will be a partnership board with a mix of public and private sector leaders representing the interests of different organisations. There is no one guiding mind, and although that difference of perspectives should in the end produce a better result, the process of getting there can create a lot of conflict.

Finally there are just more organisational interfaces and interdependencies in a partnership – and each one is a potential source of friction and frustration. Well handled, these frictions can generate creative and resilient solutions to problems. Badly handled, they sow the seeds of eventual breakdown.

CONFLICT CAN BE HEALTHY

'Clashes between parties are the crucibles in which creative solutions are developed and wise trade-offs among competing objectives are made', says Jonathan Hughes, a partner at Vantage Partners, a consulting firm affiliated to the Harvard Negotiation Project.[2]

Hughes outlines 'three myths of collaboration': first, that giving people the skills to work in teams prepares them for collaborative working; second, that the right incentives guarantee collaboration and third, that the ideal structure makes it happen naturally. These myths, Hughes believes, 'all overlook the central role of conflict in collaboration – the fact that collaboration requires actively engaging differences, that differences generate conflict, and that unless people and organisations are equipped to deal constructively with conflict, collaboration will break down'.[3]

For the collaborative leader this reality has a number of consequences. Partnerships are multi-faceted and long term, so you have to play the long game and find ways of making progress in some areas, while being in dispute in others. What's more, you can't change partners easily or without incurring major costs, so relationships matter and you have to be prepared to make compromises and accept some give and take. Not only do you need to see conflict as part of the process, you also need courage and sophistication in handling it.

[2]'Want Collaboration? Accept – and Actively Manage – Conflict', Jeff Weiss and Jonathan Hughes, *Harvard Business Review*, March 2005.
[3]'Collaboration Advantage: An Interview with Jonathan Hughes', *Effective Executive*, March 2008.

EQUIP YOURSELF TO HANDLE CONFLICT

As a collaborative leader, then, you have to be able to handle conflict person-ally and directly in order to defuse the disputes at the top and provide role models for the rest of the partnership. You also have to be able to help your staff and colleagues in the partnership deal with conflict when it happens.

However, in our experience few leaders are well equipped to do this. Most of the skills for handling cross-organisational conflict aren't in the normal man-agement armory. Coming down heavy simply doesn't work. And marching in to solve other people's disputes can be downright counterproductive. At the other end of the scale, over-stressing alignment between partners can leave conflict simmering beneath the surface, storing up serious trouble for the future.

Some leaders are naturally more attuned than others to dealing with conflict. If you've had to cope with a lot of arguments in your early life, you may well have developed skills to defuse disputes effectively. However, for many leaders, dealing with conflict requires a set of skills that have to be learned. At the heart of these is a strong awareness of self. You can't deal with conflict unless you truly understand how and why you're reacting to a particular situation.

In this chapter we look at the common causes of conflict in partnerships, examine the skills and other attributes collaborative leaders need to develop, and look at the structures that need to be in place for partnerships to function well in the face of conflict. We don't cover legal resolution or litigation – such specialist areas are outside the scope of this book. Instead, we focus on every-day conflict within partnerships.

There's a caveat, however. Most of the necessary skills and attributes are best absorbed experientially – by practice, rehearsal and reflection on your feelings and responses to conflict. It's an area where formal training can really pay off. And if you're trying to build collaborative leadership capability within your organisation, handling conflict is an area well worth investing in.

DON'T IGNORE THE EARLY SIGNS

While a jogger on a treadmill at the gym may see pain as something to be ignored or a barrier to be broken through, elite athletes are trained to see pain as their friend. It's a valuable warning sign of a flaw in technique, an imbal-ance in effort or a training regime that has gone too far in one direction.

The same goes for attitudes to conflict in a partnership. When we are asked to do a health check for a collaborative venture, we are immediately suspi-cious if the senior players all report that there is no conflict anywhere in the system. That's because in any healthy collaboration there will be evidence of conflict being actively managed in different parts of the relationship or having been resolved in the past. We'll also see honest learning from the conflict, and knowledge of where the potential hot spots are for the future. And in the best of relationships, this evidence and learning is available and used by all the sen-ior people across the partnership.

It can be pretty obvious when conflict is brewing. Deadlines are missed. Communication gets strained – key individuals don't speak up, or don't even turn up to meetings. And meetings are characterized by bad behaviour, for example veiled or overt aggression.

Other symptoms are cynicism, silence or withdrawal. People may find themselves making inappropriate jokes. At other times, conflict may be suppressed, with individuals strenuously denying that anything is other than perfect.

A key symptom to look out for is when people start going back to their own territories and circling the wagons, making sure that no one invades their space. Sometimes this is accompanied by a profusion of identity building. Just before two primary care trusts were due to merge, for example, we saw a massive outburst of business plans, mission statements, values statements and the like from each organisation. The implications were clear. Neither side wanted to work with each other, and their defense mechanism was to create logos and symbols, stamping their identity on the areas they could still control. It was an unmistakeable sign that they felt out of control in everything else.

A key attribute of a collaborative leader is the ability to recognize the signs of conflict for what they are – to put aside their own emotional response to the situation and to find out what is going on behind the scenes. Whatever the presenting symptoms, underlying them all is some genuine source of conflict, which must be understood and handled if a partnership is to work effectively. And by handled we don't always mean resolved. Sometimes the causes are deep rooted and intractable – they may even be written into the contract that all parties signed up to, but now find is flawed. However painful, those causes still have to be uncovered and examined in a healthy manner – they cannot be ignored.

DIG UP THE ROOTS OF CONFLICT

The role of a collaborative leader is to be clear about the presenting problem, but then to help people across the partnership address the causes beneath it. In the sections below we look at four broad types of causes. It's not an exhaustive list, but in our experience they are at the root of a large number of conflicts in partnerships or joint ventures.

Differences in Objectives or Values

If there are real differences in objectives or values within a partnership, the ingredients are there for serious conflict. Unless those differences can be aligned satisfactorily, the partnership risks implosion. Sweeping the conflict under the carpet is the worst thing you can do here. Attempting to sort out differences on this scale will take tough and honest debate if you're to have any chance of reaching a resolution.

You could say that at one level, every public–private partnership has within it a fundamental difference in objectives. The private sector partner has objectives about profit and financial growth, while the public sector partner needs to serve the needs of its political masters and deliver within budget. This can (and often does) lead to a degree of conflict. But if both sides can align around a common purpose of building their reputation with the public and with their government paymasters, then all can find a way to benefit and achieve their different objectives from the partnership.

Differences in values may prove more difficult to deal with. A joint venture between a major US food manufacturer and a UK supplier is a case in point. The UK firm was somewhat paternalistic, with a long history of caring for its employees. Meanwhile, the American company had much more of a 'hire and fire' mentality. The leaders had discussed this at the outset and even drawn up some ground rules between themselves about the circumstances in which they would or would not dismiss staff. But when they hit competition from a totally unexpected source, they needed to move fast. With the UK supplier lacking the skills and equipment to change their products, the leadership team had difficult choice to make – move production to a new site with a new workforce or buy in new equipment and try to train the existing staff. The American partners saw it as a simple business choice – a trade-off of time and cost. But for the UK leaders, it was a moral decision: how would they look after the interests of their staff, customers and shareholders? At that point, effective decision-making broke down, conflict erupted in several areas and the whole venture was stuck for many months.

Holding honest and detailed debates about where objectives and values differ and overlap is a fundamental part of setting a partnership off with the right expectations. It may not be possible to resolve all these differences, but you will know where you stand and have a clearer idea about the areas of risk for the future.

Differences in Organisational Character

As we saw in Chapter 6, clashes in the character of organisations is also a frequent source of conflict. John Yard, former leader of the Inland Revenue's massive IT outsourcing project, recalls how the differences in character between the Revenue and technology services giant EDS were incubating conflict. 'EDS came in with a clear view – let's fix the problem', says Yard. 'But civil servants are very different in their approach. They get scrutinized and crucified by the press. They have to explain things – they can't just do them'.

His answer was to put in place a 3-week process in which each side shared their perceptions of the other. In the first week, EDS presented their feelings about the Inland Revenue to the Inland Revenue team. 'The rules of the process were that they didn't need to give evidence for their perception provided they felt it inside – and we couldn't respond', Yard recalls. 'So we were told we were bureaucratic, that we were covering our backs, and that we didn't believe in delivery'. The next week the Revenue staff did the same, explaining the anger they felt at overcharging for extras after an initial low bid, and complaining that EDS didn't listen. In the final week, both teams went away together and spent the evening socializing. The following day they had to identify the differences and agree on a set of actions. 'There were about ten areas and I nominated an EDS owner or a Revenue owner responsible for each', says Yard. 'You weren't allowed to say, "I can't do this because my partner won't do xyz, although if you wished you could blame the management. In the end we created a culture where people started to believe that, as a leader, I was genuinely going to get people to work together"'.

Differences in the Leaders' Personalities

The press would have it that the most common source of conflict in business relationships is a clash of personality between the people at the top. Over the years, the business pages have been littered with lurid tales of personality clashes in the boardroom bringing down a company that was once a household name.

The DaimlerChrysler merger was one of the biggest transatlantic mergers in history, and carried with it many sources of potential conflict, but the one the papers liked to focus on was the dispute between Thomas T. Stallkamp, the top American executive in charge of integrating Chrysler into its new German parent, and Daimler's chairman, Jurgen Schrempp. Eventually the American was forced out and the joke went round the US media, 'How do you pronounce DaimlerChrysler? Daimler – the Chrysler is silent'. In a similar manner, when the AOL Time Warner merger was announced, the press saw the biggest source of risk as being the 'different personalities' of AOL's Steve Case and Time Warner's Gerald Levin, which were thought to personify the cultural differences between the two firms.

Personality clashes occur at the top of partnerships too, but in some ways, resolving them is even more difficult. If two executives within a single organisation don't get on, and this escalates to pose a threat to the performance of the whole company, then mechanisms exist to get rid of one (or both) of them. Shareholder pressure can be brought to bear and non-executive directors have the power to force executives out. But in a partnership, it's just not possible to sack the director of one of your partners just because you don't get on with them.

However, the quality of the personal relationship between the senior players often sets the tone for other relationships all the way down the partnership. If the people at the top are in conflict, leaders at other levels have a hard task on their hands to build an effective and trusting relationship between the different parties. And to that degree, the press have got it right.

Differences in Resources

Finally there are resource conflicts – the stuff of major wars. And while partnerships don't generally come to grief over land, water or oil, other inequalities in the way resources are distributed can lead to fierce disputes. Resource conflicts can come in many forms, but we see three subjects crop up on a regular basis – critical skills, finance and technology.

Conflicts over critical skills are legion. After many years of relative decline, the UK rail industry is currently in the middle of a boom in new design work. Upgrades to the London Tube network, extensions to lines to cope with the 2012 Olympics, the development of Crossrail, and a number of new light rail and tram systems around the country have led to a national shortage of railway signaling engineers. Conventional recruitment drives aren't filling the gap and so companies have taken to poaching engineers from their competitors. But it's a small industry, and a competitor for one contract is likely to be a partner in another. If you have just poached a number of key signaling personnel from a company you are about to enter a partnership with, then the seeds of conflict are already sown.

Money, of course, is a key factor in disputes. Perhaps the truth is that disputes about money are a simple proxy for other conflict. But in a downturn where money gets tight, a lot of things in a partnership become harder to manage. Instead of being able to help your partner out of a short-term cash flow crisis, you have to delay paying invoices until the last minute. And instead of being able to take a risk and be generous in contributing toward your partner's R&D costs to investigate the potential of a money-saving idea, you may end up asking your partner to fund it all but still want to take a share of the savings. Money can oil the gears of a partnership, but when it's in short supply, things can begin to grate or seize up altogether.

Lack of technological resources can also cause serious problems. In one public–private partnership we know, the whole process of inspection and approval of a contractor's work could have been dramatically speeded up if the inspectors had remote access to the contractor's database of works orders. However, incompatible technology got in the way, the hand-held PDAs used by one partner couldn't talk to systems used by the other, and what could have been a useful means of improving efficiency became a festering source of conflict at partnership meetings for months to come.

FIVE LEADERSHIP SKILLS IN DEALING WITH CONFLICT

You've read the signs, and know what the real reasons for conflict are. But as a collaborative leader, how do you tackle it? Sometimes you're part of the conflict and have to negotiate a way through. At other times you're outside it, but you may need to step in and mediate a successful outcome.

In all cases we believe there are five essential skills or attributes that a leader needs to develop when dealing with conflict in collaborative relationships:

- understanding your own relationship to conflict
- understanding the needs of groups

- holding difficult conversations
- finding the greater good
- mediating in other people's conflict.

Understanding Your Own Relationship to Conflict

As a collaborative leader, you're going to be dealing with a lot of conflict, and some of it will be aimed directly at you. For many people, this is stressful and unpleasant, and it engenders intense and sometimes uncontrollable emotions. But to deal well with conflict you need to be able to disentangle the emotions from the situation. And to do that, you need to understand two things – first, how you habitually react to conflict, and second, how you behave under stress.

People's habitual behaviour in situations of conflict is shaped by their past experiences, and especially by their early life. That informs whether they want to run away and hide, smooth things over and make everything all right, step in and square up to a perceived assailant, or use the situation to their advantage. These four reactions to conflict – avoidance, denial, aggression and manipulation – are the most common ones we see in partnership conflicts. But none are particularly healthy.

- *Avoidance*: If you recognize conflict for what it is, but strongly dislike it, you may find ways to avoid it – for example, not turning up at a meeting where you know there will be a dispute, exercising silence rather than openly disagreeing, or even agreeing to things when you have no intention of doing them.
- *Denial*: If you're afraid of the consequences of conflict, you may deny that it's taking place at all. For example, you insist that the team is really happy (despite what everyone says), because everyone goes to the pub together each week.
- *Aggression*: Some people react to conflict by going to war themselves in a bid to protect themselves from being hurt. If someone is in conflict with you, then it follows that you're in conflict with them – and you'll raise the stakes each time to prove it.
- *Manipulation*: Another reaction is to see conflict as a weakness that you can exploit in others. You're able to stay outside the conflict yourself, but can use your power to your advantage. It's a classic 'divide and conquer' tactic.

If you adopt one of the first three reactions, you are effectively controlled by the conflict and allowing it to overwhelm your thinking brain, alienating colleagues and partners in the process. If you choose the last, you remain outside the conflict, but you risk losing people's trust if you're found out, and in the long game of partnership, there's a lot at stake. You may also seriously overestimate your power to control the situation.

In fact the healthiest reaction to conflict is to see it neither as good nor bad, but as an opportunity to get to the heart of things. Conflict may produce scenes of painful confrontation, but at least it's honest communication – even if people don't understand or can't articulate what's really bothering them, the feelings of frustration, disappointment and anger are genuine. And often it's the catalyst to getting things moving.

When you understand your habitual reaction, you can begin to change it, moving more closely toward the opportunity stance. But you also need to know how you behave under stress – because that's when you start functioning well below your best.

At times of stress, you can unconsciously change character. You find yourself behaving in ways that you – and other people – don't recognize. If you're naturally flexible and laid back, you become rigid and didactic. If you're logical and analytical as a rule, you get tied up in emotion and start accusing others of lack of appreciation. If you normally grasp the big picture intuitively, you start focusing exclusively on a few facts or details. It's almost as if you're taken over by a shadow of yourself – and not a very competent one. The Myers & Briggs Foundation, custodians of the Myers Briggs personality type tests, describe it as being 'in the grip'. You are suddenly in the grip of personality traits that you don't usually exercise – and unfortunately, you're not very good at them. Just when you need to be at your best, you're suddenly at your least competent.[4]

Developing a conscious awareness of the triggers that can push you into a stressed state, and knowledge of how you behave when under stress will help you to control your own actions in conflict situations. And of course you also need to be able to recognize the same things in other people too.

Understanding the Needs of Groups

To understand the dynamics of the group of people involved in a conflict, you need to know what stage of development the group is at. If people aren't getting their basic needs met at any point, conflict is likely to erupt. Attempting to miss out a necessary stage of group development will only make matters worse.

In Chapter 9, we touched on Will Schutz's work on the stages of collaborative group formation. There are many models of collaborative group dynamics but we find this one particularly strikes a chord with many of the leaders we work with. According to his model, newly formed groups go through three distinct phases of development: inclusion, control and openness (Figure 10.1).

In the first stage – inclusion – people are looking for legitimacy and significance. They need to know that they're noticed and accepted as part of the group. They're concerned about where they fit, and the unspoken fear is of being ignored or discounted. It may even bring back fears such as not being picked for a team in the school playground. And of course, you can't force a group to include you – they have to let you in.

---

[4]*In the Grip*, Naomi L. Quenk, CPP Inc., 2000.

Behaviours	Inclusion	Control	Openness
Feelings	Significance *Dependence*	Competence *Independence*	Likeability *Interdependence*
Fears	Will I be ignored?	Will I be able to cope?	Will I be rejected?
Signs	In or out	Boundary disputes	Flexibility

Three stages of collaborative group formation

FIGURE 10.1   Inclusion control openness.

So at this stage, the leader of the group needs to focus on ensuring that the right people are on board and everyone knows who is in and who is out. Key leadership tasks at this stage are things like getting the contract sorted out, running induction events and holding symbolic meetings where everyone can see that they're in the same boat together. If inclusion is mismanaged or left unaddressed too long, individuals may opt out of the joint enterprise, and the core group will blame this on the fact that they didn't fit in the first place.

Once people feel sure that they are part of the group they can move to the next stage and start addressing their needs for the right degree of control. In this second stage, people begin to assert their autonomy and independence. They need to establish what area of work belongs to them, and exercise control over it, with clear boundaries around their responsibilities.

In a collaborative system, this degree of separation isn't easy to obtain. During this stage, groups can spend a lot of time in disputes about boundaries and accountabilities. It can be healthy initially, but if they get stuck here, you see turf wars, fragmentation and sub-groups forming. As a collaborative leader you need to make some judgment calls about how much conflict is helpful, and to put energy into resolving the gaps and overlaps in accountabilities. The task is to help people to understand and accept where they need to be dependent on each other and where they can act independently.

The third stage – openness – is about people truly accepting their interdependence and being open with each other about their hopes and fears for the joint enterprise. It's only at this point that they can take off their guard and speak honestly, from the heart. But speaking openly has its dangers: the underlying fear at this stage is that they might have their views rejected, or even ridiculed. This is why there needs to be a strong foundation of inclusion (I know I'm part of this group and no one is getting rid of me) and control (I know I'm competent in my role and people recognize that I've got things under control in my area) before groups can take the risk of being really open with each other.

Only when the group has reached that degree of openness can it begin to wrestle with joint values and beliefs. These conversations can now be sincere and meaningful, because the members of the group have invested in each other and their joint future.

None of these stages can be rushed or skipped. They happen in this order, and every time someone new joins a group, each stage has to be repeated, albeit on a smaller scale. If people don't feel included, they won't take full responsibility for their areas of accountability. And if you're trying to sort out conflict over boundaries and competence issues from the second stage, you can't expect openness – the group hasn't got there yet.

Group dynamics is a big subject and we're only touching on one aspect here. But the progression from inclusion to control to openness is a key part of building a collaborative enterprise. Failing to recognize anxieties, skirmishes and full-blown conflict at each stage for what they are will slow the whole process – and collaboration will suffer as a result.

Understand Where You're At: Inclusion–Control–Openness in Action

Some years ago we worked with a leader in a bank that had recently outsourced its call center operation to a third party. He was frustrated at the terrible dynamics in meetings of his new 'team', which included representatives from the call center.

In a series of interviews with each member of the group, we used the inclusion–control–openness model to find out what might be driving their behaviours. It soon became clear that two people didn't feel part of the group at all.

Carol was representing the firm that now operated the call center, although she had originally been part of the bank and had been transferred over when the outsourcing deal went through. Despite the fact that she'd known many of the individuals round the table for years, no one had really listened to her when she tried to explain her new role. Often she didn't get copies of the papers ahead of meetings, because she was no longer on the bank's own email system. As a consequence, she felt she was there on sufferance, and contributed very little in meetings.

Meanwhile, Brian was a member of the inner circle – but that was part of his problem. Many of the old hands in the team expected him to sort out operational problems, as he always had in the past. But under the new outsourced arrangement he didn't have the power to do this any more. People were always asking him to take on things he couldn't – and it put him on edge. For Brian, meetings had just become a sparring match, and he now expected nothing more from them.

Over a number of weeks we guided the team through the three stages. We helped Carol to be more included by running sessions on the outsourcing contract where she could explain her role and others could talk about what they needed from her. We also made sure everyone received invitations and papers for all meetings well in advance. We then helped the team tackle boundary conflicts by mapping accountabilities so people could see what they could expect from their colleagues. Finally, with these foundations laid, we ran a 'working together' session where the team talked about what helped or hindered them in being open with each other.

It took time, but 6 months on, the management group had become highly collaborative – and highly effective.

Holding Difficult Conversations

Some business conversations are just plain hard. Telling someone their work isn't up to scratch. Tackling someone who has persistently put you down. Having to disappoint someone when they rely on you. They're the kind of conversations that trigger defensiveness and attack, blame and counter-blame. Sometimes they descend into bitter wrangling, or hurt withdrawal. And it's very easy to get them entirely wrong.

However, difficult conversation across organisational boundaries is a skill collaborative leaders need to cultivate. 'Being able to talk about what you feel is a key feature of people who are good at collaboration', says former Inland Revenue leader John Yard. 'We do it in our personal life, but it's harder to at work. It's all about trying to understand what someone is feeling. If you find out why people are under pressure and which triggers stress them out, you can empathise far better, and you have more chance of defusing the situation'.

If you've built strong relationships first, you're better equipped to enter into this kind of conversation. 'You can't just do it by parachuting in', warns Julie Baddeley, a non-executive director on the board of several major private and public sector organisations. 'If there's no relationship there already, it's hard to have difficult conversations. You need sensitivity and strong communications skills to have the conversation and come out of it positively, without everything falling apart'.

The techniques of conducting difficult conversations in a positive way have been researched extensively by Douglas Stone, Bruce Patton and Sheila Heen of the Harvard Negotiation Project, and their book, *Difficult Conversations*, is the best guide we know to recognizing the stumbling blocks and defusing the emotion in these situations.[5] 'Delivering a difficult message is like throwing a hand grenade', say the authors. 'Coated with sugar, thrown hard or soft, a hand grenade is still going to do damage'. Instead they map out a way of holding conversations more constructively, disentangling the intent from the impact and avoiding the painful process of blame and counter-blame altogether.

Fluency in difficult conversations is a sophisticated skill and takes time – and practice – to master. But if you're to deal with conflict effectively, you can't do without it. And your personal life and friendships will benefit immeasurably too.

Finding the Greater Good

In partnerships the key to defusing conflict is often to help people to find the 'greater good', or what Muzafer Sherif, the psychologist who did much of the early work in intergroup conflict, calls the 'super-ordinate goal'.

---

[5]*Difficult Conversations: How to Discuss What Matters Most*, Douglas Stone, Bruce Patton and Sheila Heen of the Harvard Negotiation Project, Penguin Books, 2000 [first published by Viking Penguin 1999].

If you can be clear about what you are all trying to achieve, you can then have a productive discussion about what may be getting in the way of achieving it. Without that understanding, each party is reduced to trading in an attempt to get the best deal for themselves. But this makes little sense in a partnership. If a negotiation looks at face value like a great win for you, but you know that in the long term your partner won't be able to afford it, you clearly haven't met your objective. In addition the adversarial process can take its toll on the relationship – a serious problem in long-lasting relationships.

Instead, negotiations should aim to achieve 'win–win' outcomes over the longer term, where each side obtains a useful result (though perhaps not the one they'd originally hoped for) rather than ending up 'splitting the difference' in a way that satisfies neither party. As Jonathan Hughes from Vantage Partners says: 'Trading offers and counteroffers may eventually produce agreement, but such haggling rarely results in an effective exploration of each side's underlying interests, many of which therefore go unaddressed'.[6]

Looking for 'win–win' outcomes entails finding creative solutions to conflict by uncovering different interests, needs or objectives that can be used to reframe a possible solution. After exploring their individual interests, the parties should then brainstorm multiple options for satisfying these interests – things like changing payment schedules, varying time frames, agreeing a solution contingent on performance in the future or something completely different that nonetheless matters to each party.

Partnerships simply aren't the place for hard-nosed negotiations of the old school. Aiming for win–win outcomes leaves relationships intact – and able to continue for many years to come.

Negotiating for the Long Term: An Example from the Oil Industry

Leaders in the oil industry are used to working in partnership, but that doesn't mean that things don't go wrong. On taking over as leader of an oil company offshore operation, Robert discovered that the contract for the design and delivery of gas turbines for the offshore platform was out of control. His predecessor had not specified his requirements clearly enough, the design had changed, and the project was now late and $10 million over budget. Robert needed to address the situation and get an acceptable cost agreed.

As an effective collaborative leader, Robert realized that he had to engage his partner in detailed negotiations, but to do it in a manner that preserved the relationships for the future *and* found a result that everyone could live with. After all, the same company was contracted to maintain the turbines for their life on the rig.

---

[6]'Negotiation, The Better Way', Jonathan Hughes and Jeff Weiss, InSpine, 1 October 2005 [on the Vantage Partners website].

Robert set up a clear negotiation process with the leader of the turbine company. Each company allocated time and prepared well. The meetings took place out of the office, and each party had time to explain their case and to listen in details to the other views expressed. The process was tense at many points, but Robert ensured that there was plenty of time for each group to reflect and talk. He also ensured that the process had clear ground rules so that people behaved well throughout the negotiations.

With time, patience, tenacity and compromise, the parties found a mutually acceptable way forward that involved agreed delivery dates for the equipment at fixed costs everyone felt were reasonable in the circumstances. And more importantly, by the end of the negotiations the parties wanted to work together again and indeed were already planning the next deal.

The lessons for the collaborative leader when negotiating are clear:

- A mutually acceptable 'win–win' outcome is even more important in collaborations where you will have to operate together in the future.
- The negotiation process must be agreed by all parties.
- The leaders must demonstrate the right behaviours if others are to follow.
- All parties must give the process time so that relationships can be protected throughout.

Mediating in Other People's Conflict

Sometimes relationships get stuck and need a third party from outside the system to help solve them. At this point, it may make sense to use an external facilitator or mediator who is agnostic about the outcome, but can steer each party toward some sort of resolution. If as a leader you stand outside the conflict, however, you may be well placed to play the role of a 'semi-independent mediator' or 'super-facilitator'. This role is possible so long as you're trusted by all parties, who see that you are able to intervene impartially because you care about the health of the whole system.

As a mediator you are responsible for making the process work well. Part of that is taking responsibility for providing a safe environment for the parties to come together, and setting up the ground rules clearly. You have to take care not to assume responsibility for the outcome or to negotiate for either side. Instead your role is to help the warring parties find common ground. You need to explore the issues and find creative ways to resolve the conflict, encouraging reciprocal gestures to get the process moving. A key role for a collaborative leader in these situations is to encourage honesty, challenging people if they're being less than candid, and highlighting areas where unspoken assumptions are getting in the way.

Mediating is tough – but if as a leader you can learn to intervene effectively in other people's conflicts, you can cut down on a considerable amount of grief, wasted time and escalating costs, and quite possibly save your partnership from the depressing fate that claims half of all alliances.

Mediation in a Consortium Breakdown

A central government department had entered into a 10-year technology outsourcing deal with a consortium made up of the strongest players in the market. Shortly after the contract was placed, the department's leader, Susan, observed tensions between the members of the consortium. However, she felt these were teething problems that they needed to sort out themselves, so she left them to it.

As time went on, the tensions developed into arguments (some in meetings, some reported back by staff in the department), although day-to-day delivery suffered no significant setbacks. Looking to the future, however, Susan could see that the conflict would have an increasing impact on the partnership, inhibiting the open communication necessary to meet some challenging timescales. She raised these concerns with her counterparts in the consortium, but their initial reaction was to paper over the cracks and assure her that there was no serious issue. Susan pointed out that she was keen to make a contribution to resolving the problem if they wished, and left it at that.

A couple of weeks later Susan walked in on another real row between the partners, and offered to help them sort out the situation. She set up meetings with each individual and then agreed a process where members would air their difficulties and resolve a way forward. Her role (and her value) was that she was an outsider to the consortium but was trusted by all parties. They also knew that she wanted success.

A plan of action was agreed, with Susan acting in a role of an ongoing mediator when problems arose. This enhanced Susan's credibility with partners and increased her knowledge and engagement with the consortium. And while conflict didn't disappear altogether, relationships between all parties became considerably smoother.

The lessons for the collaborative leader in such situations are:

- Don't assume that other parties' problems don't affect you – they will in the long term.
- The collaborative leader is often in an ideal position to mediate in the difficulties of other parties.
- Make sure that the rules of the mediator role are clear to everyone, and don't think that you have to find the solution for the other parties – your role is to manage a process and help the parties keep to their commitments.
- Be patient – it may take a long time to solve.

PUT THE RIGHT GOVERNANCE IN PLACE

Acquiring the personal skills to deal with conflict in a healthy manner is a major part of keeping a partnership on the road. But in many conflicts, the personal skills of an individual leader are not enough. You also need to make sure that you have the right escalation procedures and formal governance in place to deal with major disputes.

As we've seen, the starting point is to assume that conflicts will occur and to think through in advance the possible mechanisms for resolving them. Alternative dispute procedures should be written into the contract from the start, detailing how the partnership should recognize and escalate conflicts that cannot be resolved through the day-to-day operational channels.

The design of effective escalation processes is quite an art. They mustn't become too multi-layered, over-cumbersome or bureaucratic. Usually an important step is the formal mechanism to bring in a party from the parent organisations or a key stakeholder to mediate on a particular issue, before turning to legal intervention.

However, contractual dispute resolution should only be a weapon of last resort. If your first step is to call in the lawyers, the collaboration has zero chance of survival. Collaborative leaders need to build their own conflict resolution systems on top of the legalistic framework, allocating regular agenda items to conflict, creating enough space to air debates fully, being respectful with each other, examining the facts while separating them out from the feelings and then coming to a decision wherever possible.

Remember too that collaboration requires a healthy dose of give and take. 'Once that decision is made', says Jonathan Hughes of Vantage Partners, 'part of collaboration means that everyone lines up behind the decision, even if they would have preferred a different outcome, and does their best to implement it successfully'.[3]

MAKE CONFLICT-HANDLING PART OF THE CULTURE

As a leader you can attempt too much conflict resolution as well as too little. Given that collaborations are likely to spark disputes at all levels, it's important that staff throughout the organisation know how to resolve disputes themselves, instead of constantly referring them up the line. Not only does it save management time and effort, it also leads to better resolutions if conflict can be dealt with locally wherever possible. When managers step in to solve conflict below them, they're often not in possession of the full facts, or have been given a one-sided account of the situation. And sometimes different line managers end up attempting to solve things separately – creating a new conflict at a higher level.

Training staff in some of the skills we've discussed above, so that they have the vocabulary and techniques to tackle conflict themselves, is well worth the effort. And it's particularly useful if you can do this training in mixed groups with people from all organisations in the partnership.

When May Gurney – the highways and construction company run by David Sterry whose story we told in Chapter 7 – start up a new maintenance contract in partnership with a local authority, they run a series of joint development workshops in the first 3 months of 'mobilization'. In these workshops staff at all levels, from directors to gang supervisors, come together to discuss collaboration, conflict and their own habits when working with people who are 'not one of us'. They use tools like the Myers Briggs (MBTI) personality pro-filing questionnaire and the organisational partnering tool described in Chapter 6 to look at the differences between them and help them understand some of the potential causes of conflict. The workshops give people a safe environment to talk about their expectations of the relationship and about past experiences of similar situations, both good and bad, which may influence how they react. They also work through a number of simulation exercises and games about competition, collaboration and conflict, to build knowledge and skills of what do when difficult situations arise.

Making conflict-handling part of the culture is enormously powerful. It doesn't prevent disputes from arising. But it means that conflict is respected, rather than feared – and that means you are much more likely to build a long-lasting and resilient relationship with your business partners.

LEARN TO KEEP YOUR COOL

Working collaboratively creates conflict – and the more collaboration you need, the more conflict you're likely to see, at least until different parties have learned to appreciate each other's differences. As a collaborative leader, you need to develop a combination of strong self-awareness and a thick skin if you're not to be overwhelmed by it all.

The risk is that you become part of the conflict, and that your own reaction to the situation makes you all the less equipped to deal with it. But if you can treat conflict as honest communication, rather than a personal attack, you can begin to make effective use of what it uncovers. Get below the presenting symp-toms of conflict to the underlying reasons, and you start to uncover differences that may fuel innovation and productivity if they can be properly resolved.

The ten tips below are distilled from our own experience in mediating in conflict. We hope you'll find them a useful checklist when times get tough and you feel your own temperature beginning to rise.

Ten Conflict-handling Tips for Collaborative Leaders

1. Identify your own personal triggers – what tends to push you into bad behav-iour? If your partner then does something to trigger it, you may not always be able to prevent your initial reaction, but at least you can plan to deal with the consequences.
2. Remember the other side of the coin too – understand what it is that you do that can trigger unhelpful behaviour in your partner, and plan to avoid falling in to those habits.
3. Don't overreact to conflict – 'count to ten' and 'don't make any sudden moves' are old adages but wise ones.

4. Analyze the nature of your relationship and identify the potential points of conflict and the drives that could push these into a full-blown dispute.

5. Not all conflicts are equally important to the future of the partnership and its business success. Identify the situations where conflict really matters – and where it doesn't.

6. Intervene fast in those places where conflict matters most and has the greatest long-term consequences for the relationship.

7. Seek to understand the motives of all concerned. What do they get from being in conflict at this point and what therefore might be their incentive to resolve it?

8. As a leader, don't try to take the conflict away from those involved – it just creates an environment of avoidance or collusion. Make sure the people at the heart of the conflict are also at the heart of the work to find its solution.

9. Understand the limits of your own conflict resolution capability – some situations need you to seek help from third parties and from dispute resolution professionals.

10. Teach others to manage conflict in a sustainable manner – share your own knowledge, and not just within your own organisation. Your partners probably need to build their conflict-handling capability too.

Chapter 11

The Future of Collaboration

INTERCONNECTEDNESS IS CHANGING THE WORLD

Today the collaborative possibilities afforded by an interconnected world are transforming the way organisations operate. The new approach has already reached the world of politics. In the Democratic presidential primary campaign of 2008, Barack Obama became what *The New York Times* described as 'the first real "wiki-candidate"', with an online fundraising operation that operated in much the same way as social networking sites like MySpace or YouTube.[1]

'What's amazing', says Peter Leyden, director of the New Politics Institute, a California-based think tank, 'is that Hillary built the best campaign that has ever been done in Democratic politics on the old model – she raised more money than anyone before her, she locked down all the party stalwarts, she assembled an all-star team of consultants and she really mastered this top-down, command-and-control type of outfit. And yet she's getting beaten by this political start-up that is essentially a totally different model of the new politics'.[2]

The My.BarackObama.com site offered users a 'practically unlimited array of ways to participate in the campaign', writes Joshua Green in *Atlantic Monthly*. 'You can register to vote or start your own affinity group, with a listserv for your friends. You can download an Obama news widget to stay current, or another one... that scrolls Obama's biography, with pictures, in an endless loop. You can click a "Make Calls" button, receive a list of phone numbers, and spread the good news to voters across the country, right there in your home. You can get text-message updates on your mobile phone and choose from among 12 Obama-themed ring tones, so that each time Mom calls you will hear Barack Obama cry "Yes we can"! and be reminded that Mom should register to vote, too'.

Barack Obama's campaign is a sign of things to come. It involved and con-nected voters in new ways, allowing mass participation in politics (albeit in fundraising, not policy) on an unprecedented level. But interconnectedness isn't always quite so democratic.

One of the most dramatic and challenging manifestations of our intercon-nected world is the impact of global terrorism in the years since 9/11. Remote areas of Iraq and Afghanistan are now seen by many as the 'front line' in the

---

[1] 'The Wiki-Way to the Nomination', Noam Cohen, *The New York Times*, 8 June 2008.
[2] 'The Amazing Money Machine', Joshua Green, *Atlantic Monthly*, June 2008.

'war against terror'. And the results of elections in Pakistan can affect how safe commuters feel in London or New York. It's a remarkably small world.

The collaborative skills of a terrorist organisation like Al Qaeda go way beyond the 'Facebook politics' of a presidential campaign. Al Qaeda is a hugely resilient organisation because it does not run on command and control lines – it's largely self-organizing. The actions of interdependent agents are co-ordinated not by rules and orders from central command, but by their common passion and conviction. And with access to global news and the Internet, the dramatic act of one group in a distant country can inspire copycat actions across the world.

In a recently added postscript to her book, *Leadership and the New Science*, Margaret Wheatley writes, 'What appears as atomised and fragmented is in fact more lethal than an organized military force'.[3]

Al Qaeda's self-organizing structure is a harsh lesson in the effectiveness of collaborative methods. It remains to be seen whether the rest of the world can use collaboration equally effectively as a force for good. In this final chapter we examine why we believe collaboration has an even greater role to play, both in business and in the world in years to come, and what that means for leaders in the future.

GLOBAL THREATS NEED JOINED-UP ACTION

The biggest threats we now face are global ones – and they increasingly require global responses. If we are to make headway with the complex issues that threaten our security, we need to get a whole lot better at global collaboration.

The War on Terror

It's clear, for example, that the 'war on terror' won't be won by a display of force from a handful of Western nations. To begin to combat the power of an organisation like Al Qaeda, we have to understand the complexity of new forms of collaborative organisation. Louise Richardson is a Harvard professor of government who grew up in rural Ireland in the height of the Troubles in the 1960s and 1970s. In her insightful book, *What Terrorists Want*, she writes, 'I am struck by how futile counterterrorist policies are likely to be if they are based on the view of terrorists as one-dimensional evildoers and psychopaths'.[4] In her view, a war on terror is simply not a war you can win. 'We are going to have to learn to live with it and to accept it as a price of living in a complex world'.

But her message isn't entirely gloomy. Lessons from biology and ecology teach us that a self-organizing system will evolve to cope with changes in

[3]*Leadership and the New Science: Discovering Order in a Chaotic World*, 3rd edn., Margaret Wheatley, Berrett-Koehler, 2006.
[4]*What Terrorists Want: Understanding the Enemy, Containing the Threat*, Louise Richardson, Random House, 2006.

its environment. So if we want to limit Al Qaeda, we need to seek to defuse the sources of the anger and rage that fuel its development, and address the causes of discontent felt by groups of people across the world that give tacit or active support to would-be terrorists. This would require a huge coalition for change – aligning action across the police, the criminal justice system and the immigration authorities, and influencing local communities, governments, foreign policy and the actions of soldiers in remote countries. It's an enormous collaborative leadership challenge – one of the most important facing us today.

Global Epidemics

Some global threats are already inspiring concerted global action. Since the flu pandemic of 1918–1919, which claimed the lives of up to 40 million people worldwide, borders have opened and air travel has become routine. Yet as we saw in Chapter 9, the World Health Organisation effectively contained the SARS virus in 2003 by breaking the human chain of transmission, and by encouraging a global collaboration between 11 research labs that isolated the SARS virus within just 1 month. The WHO is also trying to build huge collaborative effort to plan for the possibility of a bird flu pandemic. 'In developing a WHO public health research agenda (on influenza) we are trying to push for a paradigm change', said Keiji Fukuda, co-ordinator of WHO's global influenza program at a 4-day WHO meeting on bird flu. 'What we hope to improve is the kind of sharing and flow of information and take it to another level'.[5]

Climate Change

The issue of climate change is already taking collaboration to another level. As acceptance of the problem reaches critical mass, it's become self-evident that global collaboration is the way ahead.

Although the Kyoto Protocol on reducing greenhouse gases is flawed by both limited goals and the refusal of the United States to participate, its coming into force in 2005 was an important step in international accord. And on the ground, mass collaboration is furthering our understanding of what we face as a planet. The most ambitious global climate modeling experiment in the world – climateprediction.net, or CPDN for short – was made possible by hundreds of thousands of individuals from all around the world donating processing power on their own computers to create a virtual supercomputer.

The project, started in 1999 and run primarily by Oxford University, has allowed scientists to explore the complex effects of continued increases of CO_2 on the climate. As of July 2008, CPDN had produced a mind-bending 33 million model years of data – something that would have been unthinkable without collaboration.

---

[5]'WHO Seeks More Collaborative Research on Bird Flu', Stephanie Nebehay, *Reuters*, 9 May 2008.

Blogging from the January 2008 Davos World Economic Forum on collaborative innovation, *Wikinomics* author Don Tapscott wrote: 'Climate change is quickly becoming a nonpartisan issue and citizens, businesses and governments each have a stake in the outcome. Indeed, the global consensus emerging on climate change is that solving the crisis will require leadership from every country and every sector in society. The "killer application" for mass collaboration may be saving planet earth – literally'.

The Credit Crunch

The global credit crunch that started in 2007 and exploded in late 2008, taking down numerous banks and other financial institutions that were household names across the US, UK and Europe, has made joined-up thinking seem inevitable even in the highly competitive world of banking. What began as a panic over subprime mortgages in the United States rapidly deepened into a worldwide financial crisis – and suddenly the notoriously independent banking sector was talking the language of collaboration. Josef Ackermann, head of Germany's largest bank, Deutsche Bank, announced that he no longer believed in the market's self-healing power, and called for a global watchdog. 'We need concerted action by governments, central banks and market participants to help stop this wave', he said. 'Globally operating banks need globally operating oversight agencies'.[6]

'In banking, it's now the case that if *anyone* sneezes – not just America – the whole world gets pneumonia', says corporate lawyer Kate Nealon, a non-executive director on the board of several major corporations. 'We're getting to the point where you'll see the heads of the Federal Bank, the Bank of England, the Bank of China and the EU sit down together and say, "How are we going to deal with it"'?

All of these threats have materialized in the last decade. In a short space of time, they have transformed the way we look at the world. Not only has it shrunk beyond recognition, it has also become a much more uncertain place. Small issues suddenly bloom into large problems; and national borders are no protection. What looks like a local crisis at first sight can swiftly affect the whole world.

In this newly joined-up world, a consensus is rapidly forming. We're going to need to collaborate in order to survive.

ISOLATIONISM DOESN'T WORK

So in this complex, interconnected and increasingly hostile world, how do leaders react? Given that we're tribal animals at heart, our first thought may be to protect our own tribe, look after our own people, batten down the hatches in our own business or defend the interests of our country against outsiders.

But isolationism doesn't work. America's response to the worldwide pressure on oil supplies, for example, has been to turn vast amounts of the mid-West

---

[6]'Deutsche Bank Head Calls for Government Help', *Spiegel Online International*, 18 March 2008.

over to growing corn for the production of ethanol. By the end of 2008, it is predicted that United States ethanol production capacity will reach 11.4 billion gallons per year. But this comes at a high price – the direct cost of corn subsidies to US farmers equaled $8.9 billion in 2005.[7] And it has knock-on effects for other countries, pushing up the price of food all around the world, including America. You can't isolate yourself from global economics.

In the past it's been relatively easy for powerful forces to protect their interests by exhausting all the resources in one area and then moving on. Take the extreme case of shrimp farming. For decades, companies have been establishing this multi-billion dollar industry on tropical coastlines. Shrimp ponds are built on newly cleared mangrove swamp – an environment that will support a diverse ecosystem of plants and animals on its own. But producing a monoculture of shrimp in commercial quantities destroys everything else. A typical shrimp farmer in Indonesia will spend over half of production costs on shrimp feed and antibiotics, but much of this feed is not consumed by the shrimp and settles on the bottom of the pond. Within 5 years the water in the shrimp pool becomes too polluted to raise new stock, and production moves further down the coast, leaving barren land in its wake.

Destroying and moving on can work as a policy if there's enough virgin territory to move into and insufficient resistance to your plans. In an open system you can do this (if you're prepared to make enemies and ignore the consequences to other people). But in today's interconnected world we're rapidly reaching the boundaries of the system. And while isolationism of the less rapacious kind may look like a good strategy, it too only works if you have secure access to all the resources you need, and there is no need to worry about the impact you have on others. In the long term, it's rarely sustainable.

It would be comforting to think that leaders could extend the boundaries of their tribe to cover all of humanity and work for the common good, but in our belief, that's simply not realistic. As human beings we're not wired that way. Future collaborative leaders have to live with the dilemma of working for local and global good at the same time. In business terms they need to work for the good of the organisation they lead, while at the same time protecting the wider environment in which they operate. The future of successful collaborative leadership is not about altruism, but sustainable self-interest.

THE CHALLENGES FOR LEADERS: INNOVATION, SUSTAINABILITY AND RESILIENCE

In our view, great collaborative leaders of the future will have to do three things for the organisations and systems that they work in: foster innovation, ensure sustainability and build resilience.

---

[7] 'How Biofuels Could Starve the Poor', C. Ford Runge and Benjamin Senauer, *Foreign Affairs* (published by the Council on Foreign Relations), May/June 2007, Vol. 86, No. 3.

Fostering Innovation: Collaboration as a Chance to Experiment

In a world of ever-increasing complexity and change, companies have to innovate or die – and collaboration may well be the answer. Not only do partnerships allow you to create things together that you couldn't alone, but they can also help you innovate more along the way. Joining forces can give you greater diversity, increased flexibility and nimbleness and far more connection to the outside world – all essential in encouraging new ideas.

What's more, collaboration is relatively safe: although the costs of partnership are high, they're not nearly so high as mergers and acquisitions. In fact partnership can provide an ideal testing ground to see how effective your collaboration is before moving on to a full-blown merger. The story of Disney and Pixar is perhaps the best example of this. In the early days of the relationship, both operations were kept as separate entities to ensure that the different talents of the two organisations were preserved and respected. But over time, people were encouraged to work within each other's organisation to see how their different perspectives on animation could spark off new creative ideas. 'There is an assumption in the corporate world that you need to integrate swiftly', Disney CEO Robert Iger has been quoted as saying. 'My philosophy is exactly the opposite. You need to be respectful and patient'.

The more people you collaborate with, the greater the possibility of breakthrough thinking. Companies are now beginning to see the results of mass collaboration – with customers, with external experts and with the public at large. 'Winning companies today have open and porous boundaries and compete by reaching outside their walls to harness external knowledge, resources and capabilities', write Don Tapscott and Anthony D Williams in *Wikinomics*. 'They're like a hub for innovation and a magnet for uniquely qualified minds. They focus their internal staff on value integration and orchestration, and treat the world as their R&D department'.[8]

The final take on the creative potential of collaborative working is best illustrated through a game we use in workshops at the formation state of new partnerships. The room is divided into teams of four or five people around a table, each with a set of shuffled playing cards. Each team has to race against the clock to lay the cards out in rows of spades, diamonds, clubs and hearts, placing each suit in a set pattern. We repeat the process several times for teams to see how quickly they can learn and improve their times.

At first, teams tend to divide up the roles, allocating each of the four suits to a different member. After a few attempts, you can get quite fast doing it this

---

[8]*Wikinomics: How Mass Collaboration Changes Everything*, Don Tapscott and Anthony D Williams, Atlantic Books, 2006, 2008 [first published in the United States in 2006 by Portfolio, a member of Penguin Group (USA) Inc.].

way, completing the task in around a minute. However, there's a much faster way – we've seen it done in 29 s. And for that, the team has to create a life-sized template on the tabletop of the pattern they have to reproduce, and then everyone in the group takes a pile of cards at random and lays them out in one big free-for-all.

The traditional method – breaking down the task and giving each person specific responsibilities for one suit – is not nearly as effective as making all the information visible to everyone, and collaborating on everything. Freeform collaboration seems counter-intuitive – and yet in this exercise it turns out to be twice as good. So although collaborative working can carry a big overhead, it can work out considerably more effective than conventional methods.

As a collaborative leader, then, you need to ask yourself what you are doing to foster a culture of innovation within your organisation and that of your partners, and to think hard about how you can use the different skills and experience of your partners to challenge you to work in new and more creative ways.

Ensuring sustainability: Learning from others

Successful organisations in the twenty-first century need to be increasingly aware of the sustainability of their operations in terms of energy, raw materials, waste products and also in terms of the network of relationships they rely on to deliver service to their customers.

In many industry sectors, collaborative ventures are still seen as a relatively new phenomenon. But one study suggests that the ability to collaborate may be a factor in corporate longevity.

In his book *The Living Company*,[9] Dutch business thinker Arie de Geus describes a study he commissioned for Royal Dutch/Shell Group when he was co-ordinator for worldwide planning there in 1983. In a world where the average lifespan of a multinational company is between 40 and 50 years, Shell wanted to know what allowed some companies to weather fundamental change and survive for well over a century with their corporate identity intact. Shell's own origins were in the 1890s, and the study examined 30 of the 40 companies that they found of comparable size, importance and lifespan.[10]

---

[9]*The Living Company*, Arie de Geus, first published by Nicholas Brealey Publishing Limited, 1997.

[10]Royal Dutch/Shell Group Planning PL/1, *Corporate Change: A Look at How Long-Established Companies Change*, September 1983. The study covered 30 companies, for 27 of which case histories were prepared. The companies were Anglo American Corporation, Booker McConnell, British American Tobacco, Daimaru, DuPont, East India Companies, Anthony Gibbs, W R Grace, Hudson's Bay Company, IBM, Kennecott, Kodak, Kounike, 3M, Mitsubishi, Mitsui, Pilkington, Rolls-Royce, Rubber Culture, SKF, Siemens, Société Générale, Suez Canal Company, Sumitomo, Suzuki, Unilever and Vestey.

De Geus outlines four key factors that the study team found were common to all these companies:

1. Long-lived companies were sensitive to their environment.
2. Long-lived companies were cohesive, with a strong sense of identity.
3. Long-lived companies were tolerant (in the Shell report the authors called this point 'decentralization'.
4. Long-lived companies were conservative in financing.

We believe all of these are relevant to the future of collaborative leadership, but the third point has particular resonance for us. De Geus describes tolerance and decentralization as 'the company's awareness of ecology: its ability to build constructive relationships with other entities, within and outside itself'. In other words, these are companies that know how to collaborate.

De Geus describes a number of traits that help companies build these constructive relationships, but we'll focus here on just one, which he calls 'flocking'. Blue tits, he notes, have adapted remarkably over the twentieth century to tap the new food source of bottled milk delivered to our doorsteps. Not only did they learn to siphon off the cream from the early topless bottles, but by the 1950s the entire blue tit population had also learned to pierce the aluminum caps of new bottles introduced between the wars. Robins also learned the first step – but failed at the second. Although individual robins learned how to pierce the aluminum caps, the skill wasn't passed on to the species as a whole. What was causing the difference?

The answer is that blue tits flock for 2 or 3 months in the summer. Robins, meanwhile, are highly territorial, with fixed boundaries they won't allow others to cross. And the ability to flock is the determining factor that allows learning to be spread throughout the population. Birds that flock increase their chances of surviving – and De Geus believes the same is true of organisations.

Collaborative leaders need to build their own and their organisation's awareness of sustainability. Understanding what relationships will be vital for long-term survival is essential – and part of that is joining wider networks and learning from people outside your immediate organisation. That way you can scan the knowledge of a larger 'flock' to explore different ways of ensuring long-term sustainable success.

Building resilience – collaboration in difficult times

Since the tail end of the twentieth century we've seen a massive outburst of collaborative working. Partnerships of all shapes and sizes – outsourcing, joint ventures, alliances, consortia, public–private partnerships, coalitions – have flourished in the rich soil of economic prosperity. But now that the world faces an economic downturn that may become a full-blown recession, what impact will that have on collaboration and partnership?

Though the drivers of collaboration we examined in Chapter 1 – atomization, technology and size and complexity – look set to continue, the rise in partnerships has also coincided with a period of economic prosperity, optimism and confidence. In less prosperous times, will collaborative working come to be regarded as an optional extra, easily dispensed with if recession begins to bite? David Sterry, chief executive of highly collaborative construction services firm May Gurney recalls how tentative gains in collaborative partnerships within his industry all rolled back when the last recession hit. 'Everyone went back to confrontation', he remembers.

'The natural tendency when there's less money to go round is for things to get more adversarial, as each side tries to wring more cash out of the contract', says John Yard, former leader of the Inland Revenue's IT outsourcing project. 'But that's a short-sighted approach. The reality for many public–private partnerships is that they commit to long term deliverables, where the detailed requirements actually change over time, despite the fact that funds are fixed. Both sides therefore need to be able to discuss changing circumstances and to work together to find innovative solutions to difficult funding problems. And that requires a trusting relationship on both sides'.

Think back to the slime mold example from Chapter 1 – the arch-collaborator when times are tough. Normally functioning as single-celled amoeba-like creatures, slime mold cells get together when faced with hostile conditions (such as a lack of moisture) to form a single organism. For a long time, scientists believed that slime mold aggregated at the command of specific 'pacemaker' cells. But, as Steven Johnson relates in *Emergence*, it turns out that this just isn't true.[11] With slime mold, there's no central control of any kind. Instead, any individual slime mold cell that detects changes to its environment can trigger aggregation by pumping out enough of a substance called acrasin. Other cells encountering the same change do the same, and clusters of cells form around these single cells. As more cells join the clusters, they join up to become a single organism.

It's an object lesson in self-organizing collaboration. Slime mold is able to be highly adaptive to its environment because each cell effectively works for the greater good by sharing its information with those around it. And from those groups of small-scale collaboration a greater level of 'intelligence' emerges that benefits all.

It's a challenging but potent image for the collaborative leader in tough times. You may feel you need to be the 'controlling mind' that is responsible for seeing the way forward and leading your organisations through a financial crisis. But the lesson of slime mold shows there is another way. It may be more effective to take on a twofold role: creating the conditions whereby people throughout the organisation can share information and respond locally, and

---

[11] *Emergence: The Connected Lives of Ants, Brains, Cities and Software*, Steven Johnson, Penguin, 2002 [first published in the US by Scribner 2001 and in UK by Allen Lane The Penguin Press, 2001].

then encouraging the aggregation of all that information so that new insights can emerge. By doing those things you can help to create a highly resilient organisation that can collaborate effectively both internally and externally.

THE COLLABORATIVE LEADER 20 YEARS AHEAD

What does all this mean for the development of a collaborative leader in the foreseeable future? While nothing is certain, we can make some educated guesses about the likely scenarios you may face. The five types of partnership we listed in Chapter 1 will still exist, and the development of public infrastructure will still require public–private partnerships. The world will continue to need collaborative leaders. But if we project ahead 20 years, what might the leadership landscape look like?

Let's start by making some assumptions.

- The growth of Asian economies has continued and China is the dominant world economic power. In every sector, collaborating with (or being owned by) organisations based in the Far East and with an Asian culture will be the norm, and leaders will need to be able to manage those differences.
- The workforce is changing. In much of Europe and North America, increasing life expectancy forces those who can to have a longer working life. A large mobile population from Africa and Eastern Europe is prepared to travel to follow job opportunities. Many more people are self-employed, and even those starting out on their careers see a job as a short-term deal rather than a long-term commitment, moving on as it suits them. All of this means that as a leader your relationship with your workforce has to change. You have to collaborate with your people rather than employ and deploy them.
- Globalization and technology combine to produce the conditions for very big and very small companies to trade and work together on a daily basis as vital components in a common supply chain. The challenge for the collaborative leader is to help your organisation build relationships with multiple partners you will never meet face to face, who have business models and ways of working that are very different from your own.
- Countries and international institutions are struggling to cope with climate change and shortages of natural resources, leading to terribly destructive small-scale wars in poorer parts of the world. It's an unpredictable political environment. This means leaders have to be prepared for unpredictable change – so you need to foster flexible relationships that can cope with new realities on a regular basis. Tight inflexible contracts won't help – resilient trusting relationships will.
- In the business world, too, resources are tight in every area – access to investment, materials and specialist skills. The days of abundance are long gone. Collaborative leaders need to sustain creative relationships and

encourage innovative solutions in order to deliver joint results in new and profitable ways.

WHAT DOES THIS MEAN TO YOU?

And what will make you an effective leader?

Our belief is that collaborative working will become even more important. More than ever before, you will need the attributes we identified in the successful collaborative leaders (Chapter 7). In particular you will need the following qualities.

Tenacity

The world we describe is a less stable one. Governments come and go; dramatic events happen. In this world you cannot produce a detailed plan of action and expect to be able to see it through step-by-step. The successful collaborative leader needs to be tenacious in the pursuit of results that deliver the overall purpose of the partnership.

Patience

The terrain will change, but you can't afford to get too frustrated by this. Collaborative leaders need to be patient with their partners and with themselves. Your direction may be clear, but you will need a flexible approach to get there. Accept that this will take time.

Self-Awareness and Empathy

Know yourself, know how you react to pressure and stress and understand how others behave when operating in difficult circumstances. Are you aware of your own emotional triggers and do you know those of your partners? The skill is to be able to lead in ways that maintain relationships even under extreme stress.

The Ability to Network and Build Relationships

Find future partners, identify sponsors, make new alliances – and be prepared to do this in unexpected places. Successful collaborative leaders will be those who invest the energy in doing this sort of networking activity ahead of time, so they can call on these relationships when the pressure is on.

Courage and Quick Thinking

You need to be able to see both opportunities and risks before others do, and act in response to them. This requires a quick intellect and the confidence and courage to implement these ideas in the face of opposition and before you have perfect information.

And Finally

Looking ahead 20 years is a useful exercise for any leader to do – and for us it has confirmed many of the themes that have emerged as we have been writing this book. But just leaving you with a list of attributes seemed rather cold, so instead we want to end with an individual leader – someone who encapsulates and embodies many of the themes of collaborative leadership that we have been discussing in this book. Finding the right example isn't easy. Collaborative leaders (by definition) don't exist in isolation – they succeed by building successful relationships, and to do that they need other collaborative leaders to build relationships with. So one name never really stands out in a given situation.

If we take the Northern Ireland peace process, for example, a great many people were involved in coalition building over the years. So who would you choose as the great collaborative leader? Among the politicians, Tony Blair, David Trimble, Gerry Adams and Bertie Ahern all took a direct leadership role. But what about the role of independent outsiders such as the Special Envoy to Northern Ireland, Senator Mitchell? And of course there are thousands of officials, community leaders, religious leaders, mothers and fathers of victims, and ordinary people, all of whom added their leadership skills to push the whole complex system toward a lasting peace settlement. As we read and reflect on the successes of major complex collaborations, it's the stories of these sorts of people, working behind the scenes for lasting change, that we want to leave you with.

One thing we've noticed over the years is that great collaborative leaders are often quiet people doing most of their work out of the public eye. They needn't be the CEO or the figurehead leader – we've seen examples of great collaborative leadership at all levels in organisations – people who are doing it out of self-interest but also working for a greater good.

Succeeding in an Interconnected World

So we want to end with a true story – a description of a leader you won't have heard of, but whose work has left enduring results. We hope this example inspires you in your own development as a collaborative leader.

Danny Feeley was a physicist who, after a spell of working in a biscuit factory (he worked out how to manufacture biscuits with chocolate on *both* sides), entered the education sector. In time he became the design and technology advisor for a North London local education authority. Unusually for someone in this role, he was intimately involved with a number of schools, helping staff and head teachers to improve the standards of education in his chosen area.

One small school drew his attention – a special school for students with emotional and behavioural difficulties. It had failed its Ofsted inspection and lost its head teacher in the process. The school was leaderless and under 'special measures', the term used to describe schools where improvements are mandated by the inspectors. The staff were demoralized and felt isolated. They saw critics everywhere and felt unsupported, even by the groups and organisations that should have been able to offer them help.

Danny was already involved in the school as an advisor and saw an opportunity to make a difference. The local education authority knew him and was aware of his leadership skills and competence. A deal was struck where Danny built a business case to deliver a successful school. The LEA gave him the job even though he'd never been a head teacher before. The 'contract' was signed and the challenge clear.

Leading a school is a huge collaborative challenge. Head teachers have to manage their own staff, inspire their pupils and work closely with the LEA, with parents and with government inspectors. Danny was pitched into this new role without having led anything on this scale before.

But Danny passionately believed in the power of education to enable pupils to improve their own behaviour. Swiftly he made clear his new vision for the school. He gained agreement to this ethos, and to his expectations and the implications these had for resources from all parties – staff, the LEA and the students. But he knew that he couldn't deliver this vision on his own. He had a number of relationships to build, and the most important was with the staff. He knew that the confidence of the staff was at the core of turning the school around. He also knew that it would be a long journey.

Danny set about clarifying and simplifying the policies that the school really needed. He built trust with staff, listening to them, clarifying their roles, setting out what was required and then giving them space to deliver. He didn't shirk from taking personal risks, ditching some of his initial plans, supporting the ideas of staff and building partnerships wherever necessary.

One essential partnership was with the LEA. Danny engaged them to review progress, and to give the staff reassurance as they started to make improvements. He also used his relationship with HM Inspectors of Schools to actively support what he and his staff were doing. Confidence built confidence as the ripples spread throughout the school. But it was Danny's leadership style that made the collaboration really work.

If you ask people about Danny's approach to leadership, you get an interesting list of attributes – clever, kind, funny, determined, a risk-taker. In his time as a head teacher, he achieved great things. In its last inspection, the school had moved away from being on special measures and was now judged as outstanding in every area, the highest assessment possible from Ofsted. But perhaps more important than these results was the confidence and positive attitude of staff, parents and pupils in a challenging special school environment. It's hard to imagine a more effective organisation – anywhere!

As with all collaborations, these results took time to deliver. This last inspection took place after Danny had retired, but his staff carried forward and built on the work he started. He understood about succession.

Danny hasn't given up on creating successful collaborations to deliver amazing results. He now works in Uganda as a volunteer at a teacher training college where, besides developing the quality of teaching skills, he is helping groups prepare bids to donors to fund future developments. Working across cultures is Danny's current collaboration challenge.

Back in North London his staff are still not really clear how he did it. One thing they point to was that Danny came in early each morning to drink tea and have a chat. Yet it must have been more than that. One member of staff once asked him, 'What exactly do you do, Danny'? He answered by telling the following story.

A whisky distillery was having problems with its production process and they called in an expert to help. After some time the expert hit one of the valves with a wrench and immediately the problem was solved. He charged the distillery £1000 for his time. When the distillery complained about the bill, the expert said that it only cost £1 to fix the valve, but £999 to know which valve to hit and which to leave alone.

That was Danny's philosophy of collaborative leadership – to take time to listen, to think and to act with courage and conviction in a very complex environment. Like all good collaborative leaders, he recognized that he couldn't achieve success on his own. He instinctively knew that he needed to build strong relationships – he knew what to do and what to leave alone. As we look at the challenges for business in an interconnected world, we are sure that Danny's instincts are right. And the world needs more collaborative leaders like Danny.

AN AFTERWORD: *LAGOM*

Throughout this book, we've talked about the need for collaborative leaders to help their organisations thrive within an ecosystem of suppliers, stakeholders and customers. Organisations that see themselves as part of a network of mutuality have to learn to live in balance with their partners. Push too hard in one direction and you risk breaking a relationship that you may need to rely on in future.

By chance, many years ago in a bar in Stockholm we found that the Swedes have a phrase and a word for this – *lagom*. It has no direct English translation, but if you ever hear the word while having a drink in a Swedish bar and you ask for definition of *lagom*, you will be sure to be told a story. It's an old Norse myth – one that many Swedes say defines their country's character.

In Viking times a group of warriors would stand in a circle passing around a horn full of mead. When your turn came to take a sip, the question was how much to drink. If you took too much, someone else in the circle might not get their fair share (and you'd be facing an angry and sober Viking with an axe). If you took too little, you wouldn't be joining in the fun and having your fill. So you should drink *lagom* – not too much but not too little.

It's a concept that guides much of Scandinavian political, cultural and business life. People talk about getting a *lagom* deal. Great differences in salaries between grades are frowned upon – and the same goes for relationships between business partners. The philosophy of *lagom* also sums up an attitude of building a sustainable relationship with the natural environment.

So the traditional reply when asked how much you want to drink in a Swedish bar is also a good motto for a collaborative leader – in all your dealings.

Lagom är bäst – enough is best.

Index